MARYLAND HSA Coach™

America's Best for Student Success®

HIGH SCHOOL

Algebra / Data Analysis

Maryland HSA Coach, Algebra/Data Analysis, High School
112MD
ISBN-10: 1-59823-695-4
ISBN-13: 978-1-59823-695-8

Author: Molly Wetterschneider
Cover Image: Drum Point Lighthouse, Calvert Marine Museum, Solomons, Maryland. ©SuperStock

Triumph Learning® 136 Madison Avenue, 7th Floor, New York, NY 10016
A Haights Cross Communications, Inc. company

Printed in the United States of America.

10 9 8 7 6 5 4 3 2

Table of Contents

Letter to the Student

Dear Student,

Welcome to the ***Maryland HSA Coach, Algebra/Data Analysis, High School***. This book will help you to strengthen your Mathematics skills this year. *Coach* also provides practice with the kinds of questions you will have to answer on tests, including the state test.

The *Coach* book is divided into chapters and lessons. Before you begin the first chapter, you may want to take the Pretest at the beginning of the book. The Pretest will show you your strengths and weaknesses in the skills and strategies you will need this year. This way, you will be aware of what you need to concentrate on to be successful. At the end of the *Coach* book is a Posttest that will allow you and your teacher to evaluate how much you have learned. We have tried to match the style of the state test in the Pretest and Posttest for better test practice.

The lessons in this book will help you review and practice your skills and get you ready to take tests. Some of the practice will be in the style of the state test. In general, you will be answering multiple-choice, response-grid, brief constructed-response, and extended constructed-response questions. Questions like these will appear on your state test. Practicing with these types of questions will give you a good idea of what you need to review to triumph.

Here are some **tips** that will help you as you work through this book. Remembering these tips will also help you do well on the state test.

- Listen closely to your teacher's directions.
- When answering multiple-choice questions, read each choice carefully before choosing the BEST answer.
- When answering response-grid questions, be sure to mark your answer carefully and completely in the grid provided.
- When answering brief and extended constructed-response questions, think about how you will answer the question before you begin to write.
- Time yourself so that you have time at the end of a test to check your answers.

We hope you will enjoy using *Coach* and that you will have a fun and rewarding year!

Letter to the Family

Dear Parents and Families,

The *Coach* series of workbooks is designed to prepare your child to master grade-appropriate skills in mathematics and to take the High School Assessment Algebra/Data Analysis (HSA) test which is administered each year in the state of Maryland. In your state, the grade-appropriate skills are called Core Learning Goals. These are the skills the state has chosen as the building blocks of your child's education in mathematics, and these are the skills that will be tested on the HSA. Your child's success will be measured by how well he or she masters these skills.

You are an important factor in your child's ability to learn and succeed. Get involved! We want to be your partner in making learning a priority in your child's life. To help ensure success, we suggest that you review the lessons in this book with your child. While teachers will guide your child through the book in class, your support at home is also vital to your child's comprehension.

Please encourage your child to read and study this book at home, and take the time to go over the sample questions and homework together. The more students practice, the better they do on the actual exam and on all the tests they will take in school. Try talking about what your child has learned in school. Perhaps you can show your children real-life applications of what they have learned. For example, you could discuss why math skills are important in life and how they apply to everyday situations.

You will also want to foster good study habits. Students should set aside quiet time every day to do their homework and study for tests. Children need to learn to pace themselves to avoid cramming, or last-minute preparation, for the challenges they will face in school. These are behaviors that young students carry with them for life.

We ask you to work with us this year to help your child triumph. Together, we can make a difference!

Maryland Indicators Correlation to *Coach* Lessons

Maryland Indicator	Expectation and Indicator Descriptions	*Coach* Lesson(s)
Goal 1 Functions and Algebra The student will demonstrate the ability to investigate, interpret, and communicate solutions to mathematical and real-world problems using patterns, functions, and algebra.		
Expectation 1.1 **The student will analyze a wide variety of patterns and functional relationships using the language of mathematics and appropriate technology.**		
1.1.1	The student will recognize, describe, and/or extend patterns and functional relationships that are expressed numerically, algebraically, and/or geometrically.	1, 2, 5
1.1.2	The student will represent patterns and/or functional relationships in a table, as a graph, and/or by mathematical expression.	3, 4
1.1.3	The student will apply addition, subtraction, multiplication, and/or division of algebraic expressions to mathematical and real-world problems.	6
1.1.4	The student will describe the graph of a non-linear function and discuss its appearance in terms of the basic concepts of maxima and minima, zeros (roots), rate of change, domain and range, and continuity.	7
Expectation 1.2 **The student will model and interpret real-world situations using the language of mathematics and appropriate technology.**		
1.2.1	The student will determine the equation for a line, solve linear equations, and/or describe the solutions using numbers, symbols, and/or graphs.	8, 10, 11
1.2.2	The student will solve linear inequalities and describe the solutions using numbers, symbols, and/or graphs.	14
1.2.3	The student will solve and describe using numbers, symbols, and/or graphs if and where two straight lines intersect.	9, 12
1.2.4	The student will describe how the graphical model of a non-linear function represents a given problem and will estimate the solution.	13
1.2.5	The student will apply formulas and/or use matrices (arrays of numbers) to solve real-world problems.	15, 16
Goal 3 Data Analysis and Probability The student will demonstrate the ability to apply probability and statistical methods for representing and interpreting data and communicating results, using technology when needed.		
Expectation 3.1 **The student will collect, organize, analyze, and present data.**		
3.1.1	The student will design and/or conduct an investigation that uses statistical methods to analyze data and communicate results.	20
3.1.2	The student will use the measures of central tendency and/or variability to make informed conclusions.	17, 18, 19
3.1.3	The student will calculate theoretical probability or use simulations or statistical inference from data to estimate the probability of an event.	21

Maryland Indicator	Expectation and Indicator Descriptions	*Coach* Lesson(s)
Expectation 3.2 **The student will apply the basic concepts of statistics and probability to predict possible outcomes of real-world situations.**		
3.2.1	The student will make informed decisions and predictions based upon the results of simulations and data from research.	22
3.2.2	The student will interpret data and/or make predictions by finding and using a line of best fit and by using a given curve of best fit.	23, 24
3.2.3	The student will communicate the use and misuse of statistics.	25

Maryland HSA Coach,
Algebra/Data Analysis, High School

PRETEST

Name: ______________________________

Session 1

PRETEST

1 The table below shows a relationship between f and g.

f	g
1	4
2	13
3	28
4	49

Which of these equations represents this relationship?

A $g = f^2 + 1$

B $g = f^2 + 3$

C $g = 3f^2 + 1$

D $g = 3f^2 + 3$

2 Antonio set up a savings plan with his father. He puts $200 in a savings account, and his father agrees to give him $2.50 every month he leaves the money in the bank and doesn't spend it. Which of these graphs shows the relationship between the number of months he leaves the money in the bank and the total amount of money that Antonio has when he combines his savings and the money his father gives him?

F

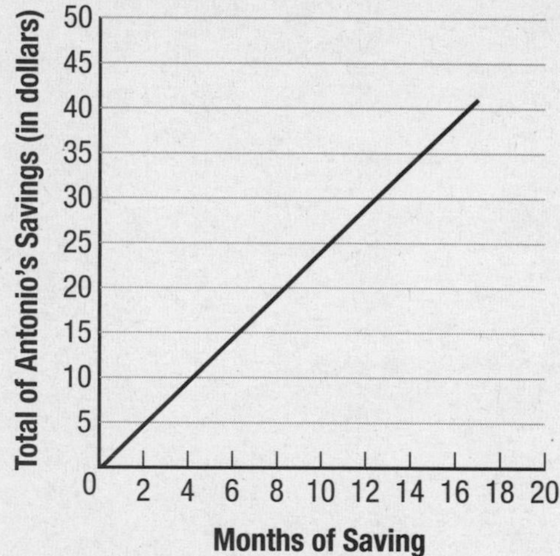

H

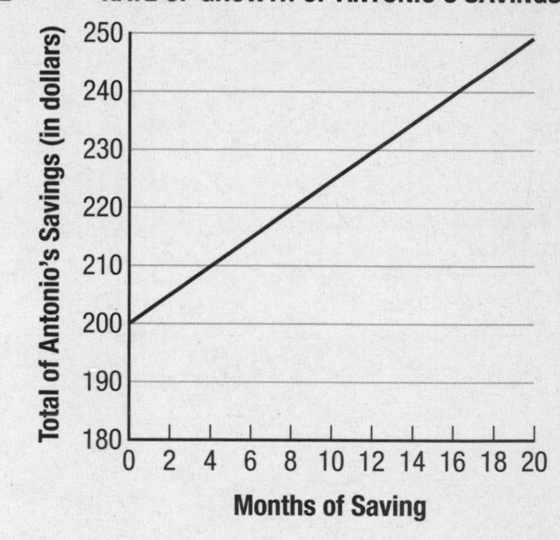

G

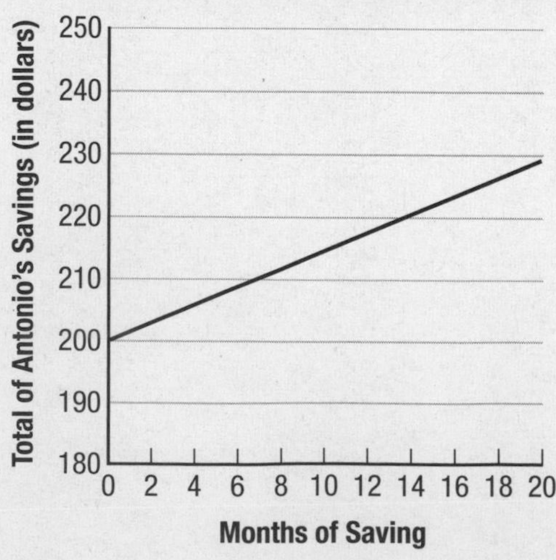

J

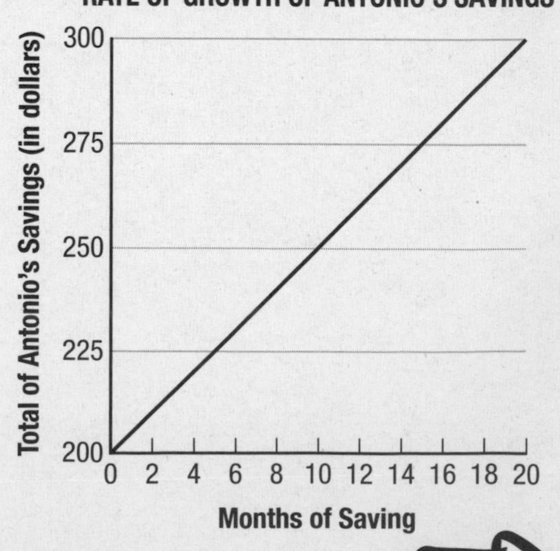

GO ON

3 **The spinner shown below is spun 20 times.**

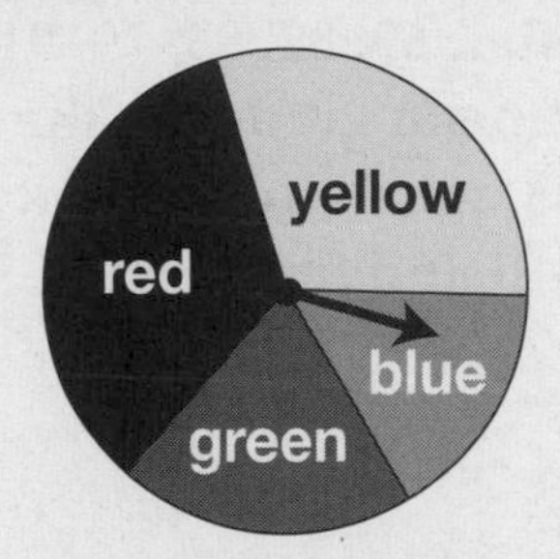

The results of the spins are shown below.

red	yellow	green	red
green	red	red	yellow
blue	yellow	blue	red
yellow	red	yellow	red
red	yellow	yellow	yellow

Based on these results, how many times would "red" be expected to appear in 50 spins?

A 4

B 5

C 8

D 20

4 **Tom wants to conduct a survey to find out where the film society wants to hold their meeting next month. Which of these methods provides Tom with the most representative sample of society members?**

F Survey non-society members who are thinking of joining.

G Survey the first 100 society members that arrive at the next meeting.

H Survey society members who live near the location of the next meeting.

J Survey a group of society members selected from a list by a random number generator.

5 **Karen is x years old. Wayne is 3 years older than Karen. Nicolas is one-third Karen's age. Which expression represents how much older Wayne is than Nicolas?**

A $\frac{x}{3}$

B $(x + 3) - \frac{x}{3}$

C $\frac{(x + 3)}{3}$

D $\frac{(x + 3) - x}{3}$

GO ON

PRETEST

6 The rectangular box below has a volume of 480.5 cubic inches, a width of 6.2 inches, and a length of 15.5 inches.

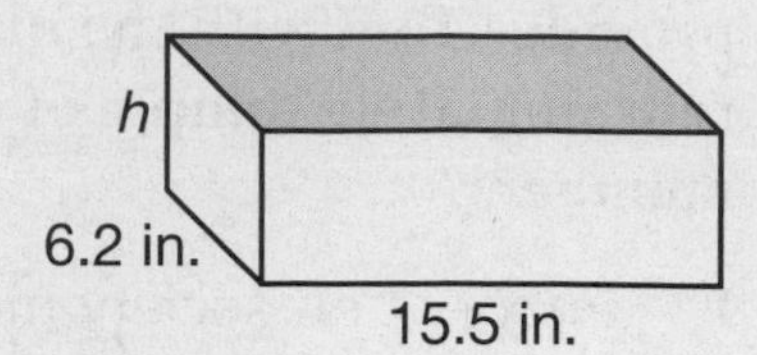

What is the height (*h*) of the rectangular box?

F 5.0 inches

G 6.2 inches

H 24.8 inches

J 458.8 inches

7 The box-and-whisker plots below show the points scored by four different soccer teams last season.

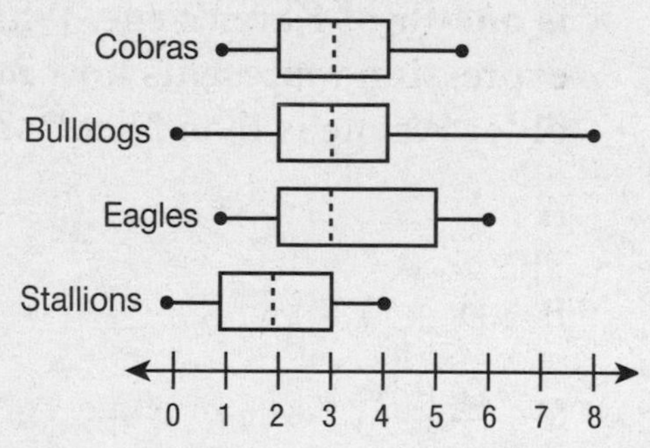

Which team's scores have the largest interquartile range?

A Cobras

B Bulldogs

C Eagles

D Stallions

8 Hank made the following grades on the first six math tests for the semester: 69, 82, 83, 79, 91, and 88. If his mean grade for the semester was 83, what did he make on the seventh and final test?

F 82

G 83

H 89

J 93

9 The first four designs in a pattern are shown below.

 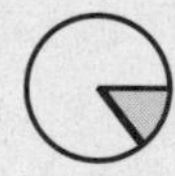 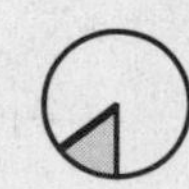 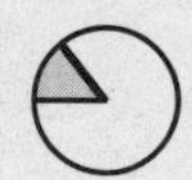

If the pattern continues, what will be the eleventh design in the pattern?

A

B

C

D

GO ON

PRETEST

Use the Response Grids to complete Numbers 10 through 12.

10 Pablo is renting a cabin for a vacation. He pays a flat fee of $75.00 plus $43.95 per day. Pablo has $450 to spend on the cabin rental. What is the maximum number of days he can rent the cabin?

11 Anton surveys students about their favorite planet. The survey results are shown in the table below.

SURVEY RESULTS

Planet	Number of Students
Mars	25
Saturn	18
Jupiter	10
Earth	7

Based on the survey results, what is the probability, expressed as a fraction, that a randomly selected student's favorite planet is Jupiter?

GO ON

PRETEST

12 The table below shows the number of sales of magazine subscriptions made by students in the French club last week.

MAGAZINE SUBSCRIPTIONS SOLD

Club Member	Subscriptions Sold
Monique	12
Pierre	13
Madeleine	10
Adele	25
Jacques	20
Bernard	16
Bernadette	19
Francoise	22

What is the third quartile for this data set?

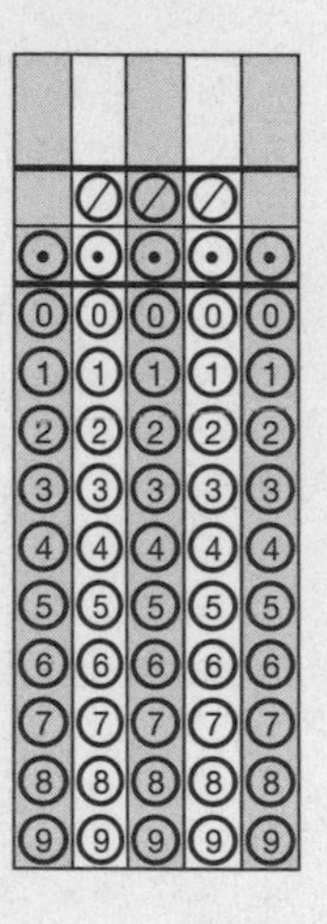

13 Look at the graph below.

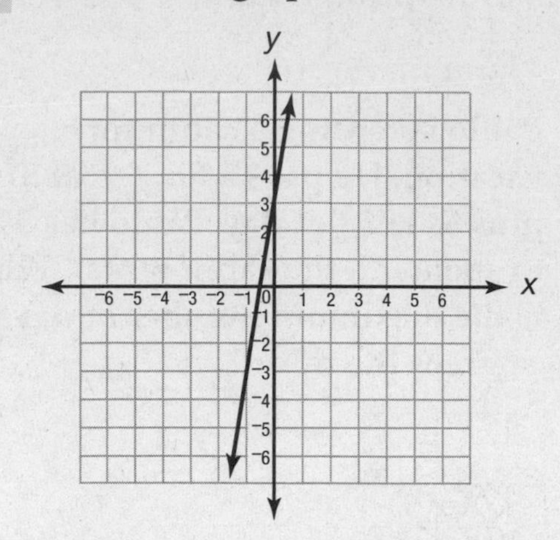

What is the slope of the line?

A 0.5

B 2

C 3

D 6

14 The drawing below shows the plans for a doghouse with a door.

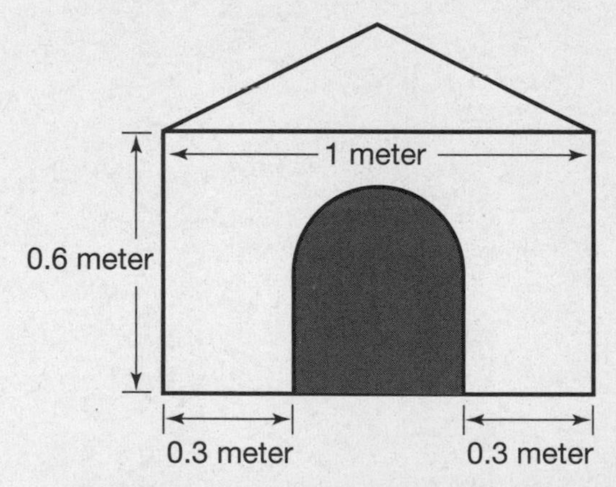

Which of the following expressions represents the width of the base of the door, in meters?

F $1 + 0.3 + 0.3$

G $1 - 0.3 - 0.3$

H $0.6 - 0.3$

J $1 - 0.6 - 0.3$

15
BCR

The graphs below show the number of bottles collected by two members of the Recycle Club each day last week. The Recycle Club president uses the graphs to claim that Anna is a more effective collector than Arnold.

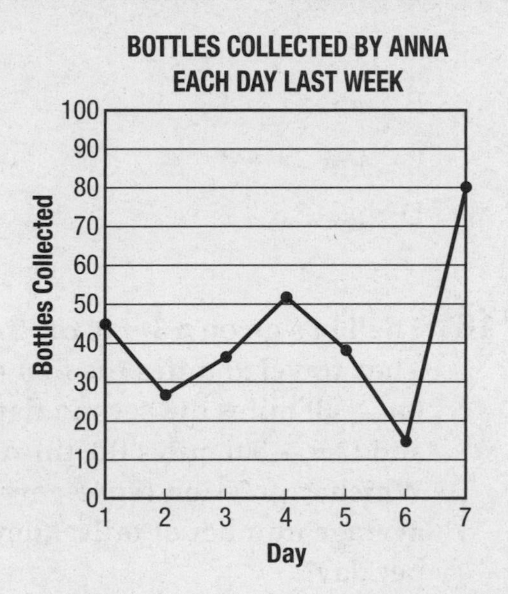

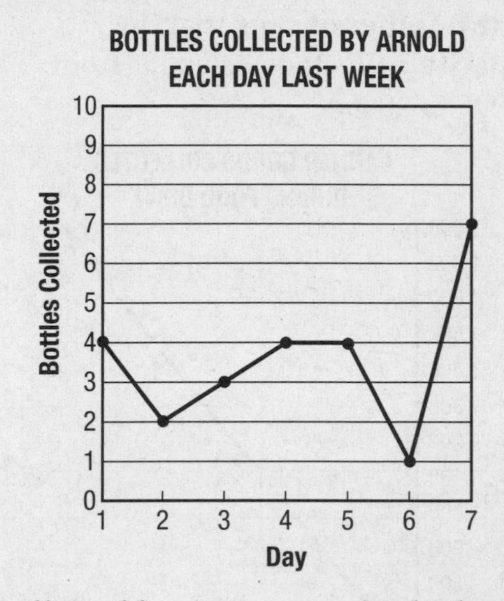

- **What is the greatest number of bottles collected by Anna on a single day? What is the greatest number of bottles collected by Arnold on a single day?**

- **According to the information given, why might these graphs be considered misleading? Use mathematics to explain how you determined your answer. Use words, symbols, or both in your explanation.**

16 Each year a charity group collects cans of food during a food drive. The graph below models the number of cans that the charity collected each year from 1996 to 2006.

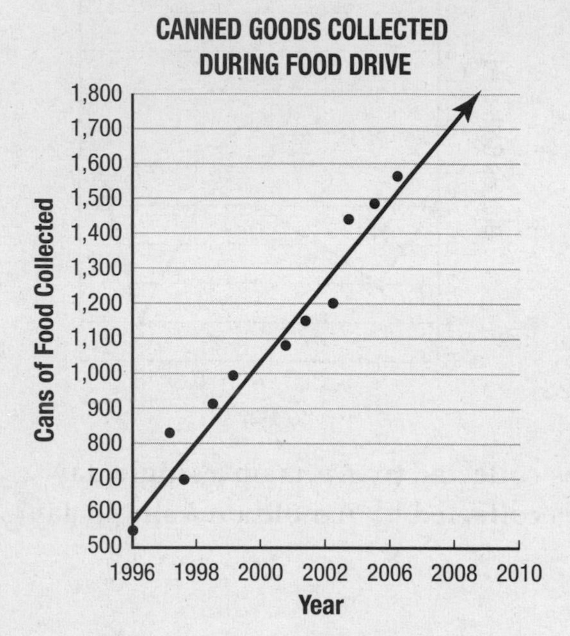

According to the line of best fit, how many cans would the charity group expect to collect in 2008?

F 1,600

G 1,700

H 1,800

J 1,900

17 Which of these equations represents a line with an x-intercept of 2 and a y-intercept of 3?

A $y = -\frac{3}{2}x + 3$

B $y = \frac{3}{2}x + 3$

C $y = 2x + 3$

D $y = 3x + 2$

18 The Liu's go on a 3-day car trip. They travel m miles the first day, $(m - 30)$ miles the second day, and $(2m - 50)$ miles the third day. Which expression represents the average number of miles they travel per day?

F $m + (m - 30) + (2m - 50)$

G $\frac{m + (m - 30) + (2m - 50)}{3}$

H $\sqrt{m + (m - 30) + (2m - 50)}$

J $(m + (m - 30) + (2m - 50))^3$

GO ON

PRETEST

19
ECR

Lucille and Juanita babysit on weekends to earn money. Lucille charges a base fee of $10 plus an additional $4 per hour. Juanita changes $6 per hour with no base fee.

TABLE I

Number of hours (h)	Total Fee (f)
2	$12
4	$24
6	$36
8	$48

TABLE II

Number of hours (h)	Total Fee (f)
2	$18
4	$26
6	$34
8	$42

- **Which table represents how much Lucille charges her babysitting customers? Use mathematics to explain how you determined your answer. Use words, symbols, or both in your explanation.**

- **What equation represents the total fee (f) charged by Lucille for a customer who requires she babysit for h hours?**

- **What equation represents the total fee (f) charged by Juanita for a customer who requires she babysit for h hours?**

- **If the Jackson's need a babysitter for 10 hours, how much would Lucille charge them for her services?**

PRETEST

20 **Look at the pattern below.**

12.4, 8.3, 4.2, 0.1, $^{-}4$,…

If the pattern continues, what will be the seventh term?

F $^{-}8.1$

G $^{-}8.3$

H $^{-}12.2$

J $^{-}12.4$

21 **The table below lists the types of pets most frequently owned by students at Tina's school.**

TYPES OF PETS MOST FREQUENTLY OWNED BY STUDENTS

Rank	Pet Type	Number
1	Cat	250
2	Dog	229
3	Fish	175
4	Hamster	96

Tina concludes that one third of the students at her school own a cat. Why is Tina's conclusion incorrect?

A Tina did not consider the breed of each pet.

B Tina did not consider students who used to have a pet.

C Tina did not consider what the students in other schools own.

D Tina did not consider that there were some students who do not own a pet.

22 **BCR** **The table below gives values for x and y.**

x	1	2	3	4	5
y	21	27			

Difference in y values	6	6	6	6

- **If the difference in adjacent values for y is always 6, fill in the boxes for the values of y.**

- **What is the value of y for $x = 10$?**

- **What is the difference between the values of y when $x = 99$ and $x = 100$? Use mathematics to explain how you determined your answer. Use words, symbols, or both in your explanation.**

PRETEST

PRETEST

23 Evan makes a graph of the total amount of money he makes mowing lawns each week. The graph is shown at the right.

Approximately how much more did Evan make in Week 7 than he made in Week 5?

A $135

B $215

C $260

D $385

WEEKLY INCOME FROM MOWING LAWNS

Total Income (in dollars): 0, 25, 50, 75, 100, 125, 150, 175, 200, 225, 250, 275, 300, 325, 350

Week: 1, 2, 3, 4, 5, 6, 7, 8, 9, 10, 11, 12

24 Look at the graph below.

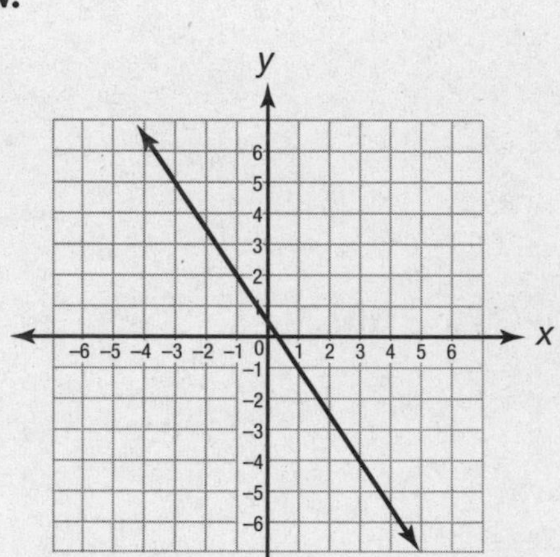

Which of these tables corresponds to the line that is graphed?

F

x	y
−3	−5
−1	−2
1	1
3	4

H

x	y
−3	3
−1	1
1	−1
3	−3

G

x	y
−3	5
−1	2
1	−1
3	−4

J

x	y
−3	−3
−1	−1
1	1
3	3

At the garden store Chris bought 4 house plants and one small cactus plant for a total of $10.35. Nina bought 3 small cactus plants and 2 house plants for a total of $11.55.

- Let h be the number of house plants and c be the number of cactus plants. Write an equation that represents Chris's total cost. Write an equation that represents Nina's total cost.

- Use mathematics to justify your answers for the cost of one house plant and the cost of one small cactus plant.

PRETEST

Session 2

26 **Look at the system of equations below.**

$$y = \frac{3}{5}x + 1$$
$$y = \frac{3}{5}x - 1$$

Which of these <u>best</u> describes the relationship between the two lines?

F They have no points in common.

G They have one point in common.

H They have two points in common.

J They have infinite points in common.

27 **Look at the graph below.**

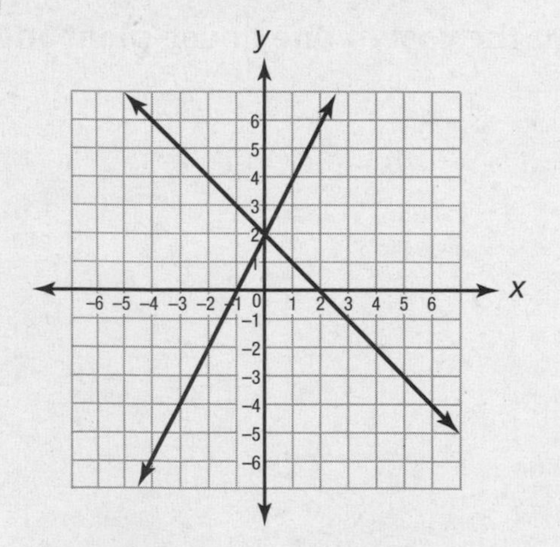

Which of these statements describes the relationship between the two lines?

A The lines never intersect.

B They intersect at the point (0, 2).

C They intersect at the point (0, $^-2$).

D They intersect at the point (2, 0).

28 **A store owner wants to find out how many of her customers came to the store because of a television advertisement. Which of the following methods gives a sample that is most representative of the customers who come to the store?**

F Choose the first 300 customers who come into the store.

G Choose the last 300 customers who come into the store.

H Randomly choose 30 customers who come into the store throughout the day.

J Randomly choose 300 customers who come into the store throughout the day.

29 **Look at the graph below.**

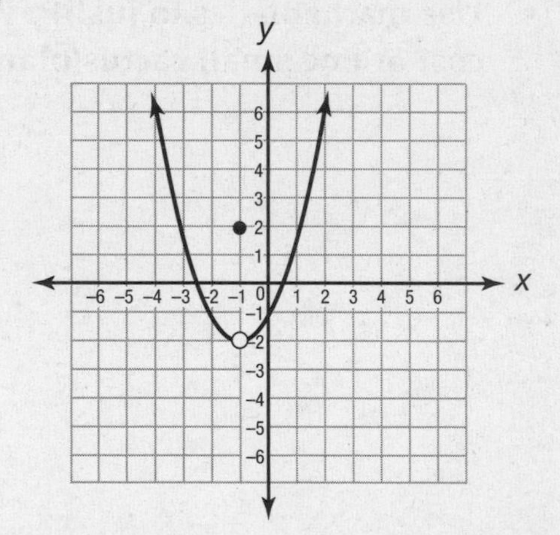

What is the x-value of the point where the graph is not continuous?

A $^-2$

B $^-1$

C 2

D 4

GO ON

30 Barry and Nikil buy fish at the pet shop. Barry buys 6 guppies and 4 goldfish for $5.10. Nikil buys 10 guppies and 2 goldfish for $5.00. What is the cost, in dollars, of each guppy?

F 0.35

G 0.42

H 0.51

J 0.75

31 The table below shows a relationship between x and y.

x	1	2	3	4	5	6
y	2	$^{-}1$	$^{-}4$	$^{-}7$	$^{-}10$	$^{-}13$

Which of these equations represents this relationship?

A $y = 3 - 5x$

B $y = 5 - 3x$

C $y = 5 + 3x$

D $y = 3 + 5x$

32 Look at the function that is graphed below.

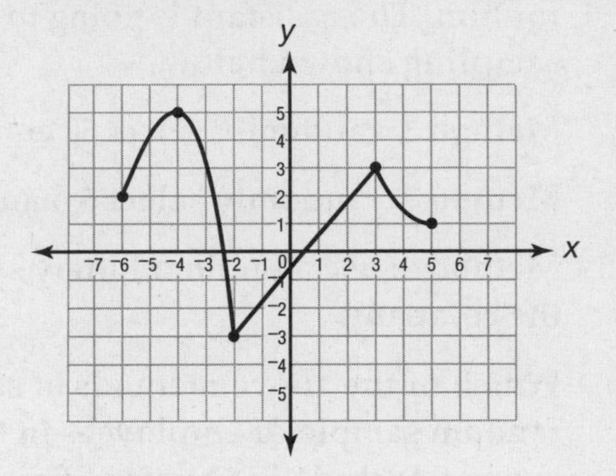

What is the range of this function?

F $^{-}6 \le y \le 5$

G $^{-}6 \le y \le 3$

H $^{-}4 \le y \le {}^{-}3$

J $^{-}3 \le y \le 5$

PRETEST

GO ON

PRETEST

33
BCR

The owner of a company wants to find out whether his employees need training in dealing with customers over the phone. He asks one of his assistants to gather data for him. The assistant is going to survey 50 employees. Consider the methods of sampling shown below.

Method 1: randomly select 50 employees from the sales department.

Method 2: randomly select 5 managers and ask them each to select 10 employees.

Method 3: use a random lottery system to choose 50 employees from all over the company.

Which of the above methods of sampling would give the most representative random sample of employees in the company? Use mathematics to justify your answer. Include in your justification why you chose that method and why you did not choose each of the other two methods.

34 **Angela is emptying her family's swimming pool using a pump. The graph below shows a linear model of the number of gallons of water that are still remaining in the swimming pool each hour.**

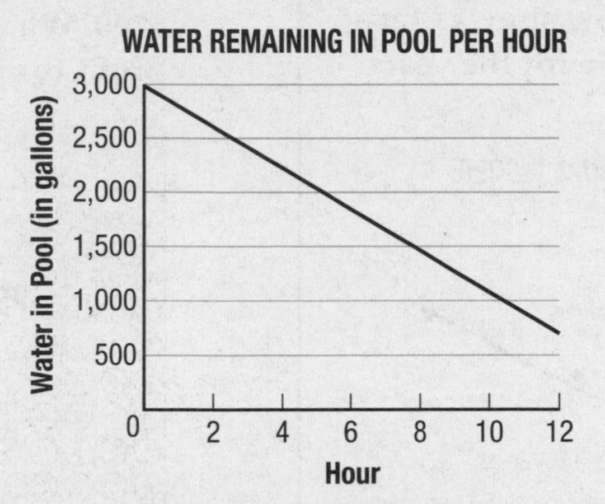

What is the slope, in gallons per hour, of this linear model?

F $^{-}200$

G $^{-}100$

H 100

J 200

35 **The graph below shows the cost of riding public transportation for discount-card holders and for non-card holders.**

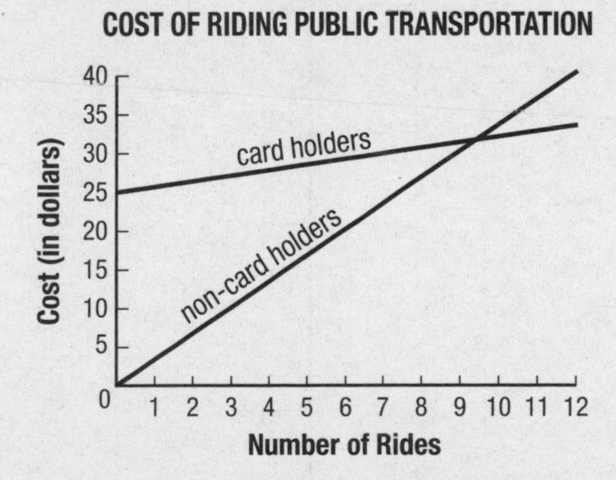

According to the graph, which of these statements is true?

A Non-card holders pay less for 11 rides.

B Card holders pay less for 9 rides.

C Card holders and non-card holders pay the same for 7 rides.

D Non-card holders pay less for 8 rides.

Use the Response Grids to complete Numbers 36 through 40.

36 **The scatter plot below shows Mary Beth's annual income for the years 1999 to 2007.**

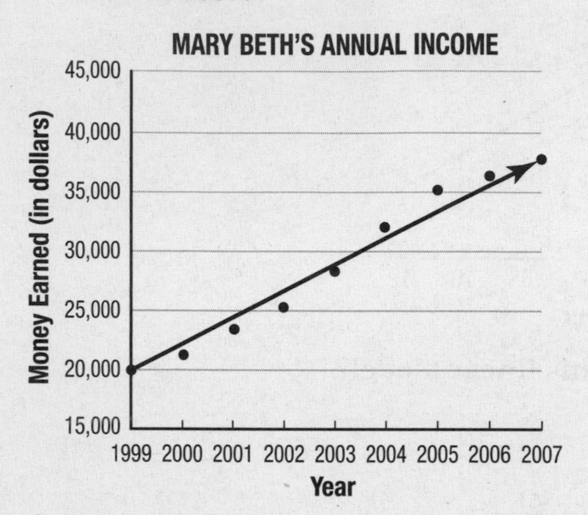

Mary Beth earned $20,000 in 1999 and $38,000 in 2007. What is the slope of the line of best fit in dollars per year?

37 **Melanie recorded the following weekly profits from last month's fundraiser: $366, $494, $556, and $760. What is the mean weekly profit for last month in dollars?**

GO ON

Remove Pretest Here

38 The table below lists the prices of items at a garage sale and the frequency of those prices. What is the range, in dollars, of the prices at the garage sale?

Price (in dollars)	Frequency
0.25	135
0.50	75
0.75	56
1.00	45
1.50	10
2.00	12
3.00	5

39 A scientist looks at the average number of baby mice born in a litter to a mother who has a limited supply of food during her pregnancy. The graph below models the relationship between average litter size and the number of grams of food per day.

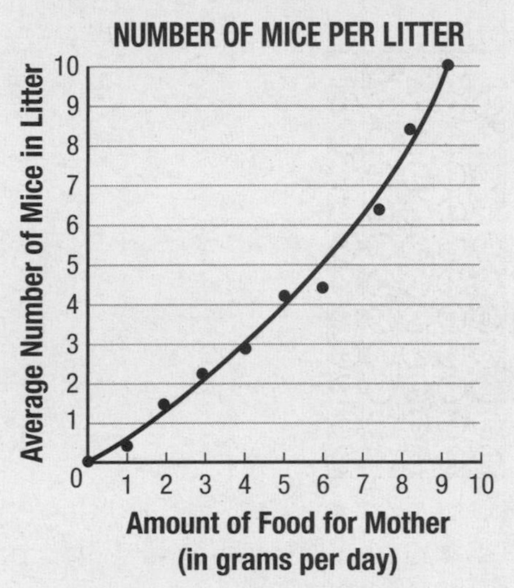

According to the line of best fit, how many mice would the scientist expect to be born to a mother who ate 6 grams of food per day?

GO ON

40 May has a sack with 100 marbles. Twenty-five of the marbles are white and 35 are red. The rest of the marbles are blue. If May randomly chooses a marble from the bag, what is the probability that the marble is not red or white?

	⊘	⊘	⊘	
⊙	⊙	⊙	⊙	⊙
0	0	0	0	0
1	1	1	1	1
2	2	2	2	2
3	3	3	3	3
4	4	4	4	4
5	5	5	5	5
6	6	6	6	6
7	7	7	7	7
8	8	8	8	8
9	9	9	9	9

41 The expression $(r^2 + 3r - 1)$ represents the length of one side of a square. Which of these expressions represents the perimeter of the square?

A $\dfrac{(r^2 + 3r - 1)}{4}$

B $(r^2 + 3r - 1) \times 4$

C $\sqrt{r^2 + 3r - 1}$

D $(r^2 + 3r - 1)^2$

GO ON

42 **ECR** **Brie held a contest to determine which of her classmates could collect the most signatures on a petition. She recorded her data in the following table.**

Student	Number of Signatures
Daniel	86
Zach	45
Latrice	90
Ernesto	66
Brie	125
Mary	90
Laura	82
Zelda	100

- **What are the range, interquartile range, and quartiles?**

- **Draw a box-and-whisker plot for this data.**

- **Brie decided not to include her own number in the data. How does dropping her number of signatures affect the range of this data? Use mathematics to justify your answer.**

PRETEST

43 **Over the weekend, Juan worked x hours at the ticket booth. Dennis worked $(x + 11)$ hours at the booth. Philippa worked $(2x - 4)$ hours. Which of these expressions represents the combined number of hours that all three students worked at the ticket booth over the weekend?**

A $x + (x + 11) + (2x - 4)$

B $x \times (x + 11) \times (2x + 4)$

C $\frac{x + (x + 11) + (2x - 4)}{3}$

D $3 \times (x + (x + 11) + (2x + 4))$

44 **BCR** **Constance surveyed the 40 students in her gym class about which color streamers she should use to decorate the school gym for the dance. Jonas surveyed 40 students chosen at random from the entire school about the same issue. The results of both surveys are shown in the tables below.**

CONSTANCE'S SURVEY RESULTS

Color	Number of Students
Red	9
Blue	6
Pink	15
Purple	10

JONAS'S SURVEY RESULTS

Color	Number of Students
Red	18
Blue	10
Pink	4
Purple	8

- **Use principles of simple random sampling to justify why Constance and Jonas should have more confidence in the results of Jonas's survey.**

- **According to the data collected from Jonas's survey, of the 1,200 total students in the school, how many students should Constance and Jonas expect to prefer the ribbon be purple? Use mathematics to explain how you determined your answer. Use words, symbols, or both in your explanation.**

45
ECR

The matrix below shows the budgets for two theatrical productions.

BUDGETS FOR PRODUCING TWO PLAYS

	Set	Props	Costumes	Advertising
Cinderella	$1,350	$250	$850	$600
Snow White	$1,400	$200	$650	$500

- **What is the total amount of money budgeted to spend on sets for both plays?**

- **What is the total amount that the play *Cinderella* will cost to produce?**

- **The plays' producer was able to get more money and wants to increase the budget for each part of each play by 4%. Make a matrix that represents the new budgets for producing these two plays.**

46 **Liz counts the number of eggs in each of 18 nests. She looks at each nest and marks how many eggs are in each nest on the following line plot. What is the median number of eggs in each nest?**

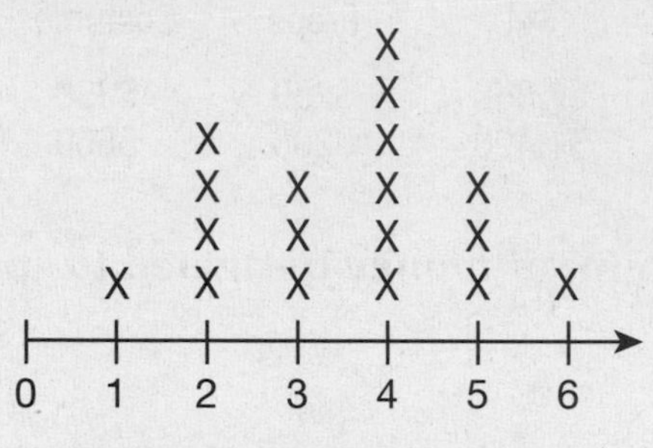

NUMBER OF EGGS IN EACH NEST

X = 1 nest

F 2

G 3

H 4

J 5

47 **Kenny is ordering T-shirts for his family reunion. He has a record of the numbers and sizes of the T-shirts ordered last year for the three different branches of the family.**

T-SHIRTS ORDERED LAST YEAR

	S	M	L
Browns	12	5	4
Wallaces	10	7	2
Petersons	8	8	6

Which of these matrices represents the total number of T-shirts ordered for each branch of the family?

A

	TOTAL
Browns	4
Wallaces	2
Petersons	6

B

	TOTAL
Browns	12
Wallaces	10
Petersons	8

C

	TOTAL
Browns	21
Wallaces	19
Petersons	22

D

	TOTAL
Browns	62
Wallaces	62
Petersons	62

PRETEST

48 At a school bake sale, the math team sells cupcakes (c) and pies (p). The math team makes \$1.50 for each cupcake sold and \$5.00 for each pie sold. The captain of the math team wants to earn at least \$250 from the bake sale. Which of these inequalities represents this situation?

F $1.5c + 5p \leq 250$

G $1.5c + 5p \geq 250$

H $5c + 1.5p \leq 250$

J $5c + 1.5p \geq 250$

49 Look at the pattern below.

$$1, \frac{1}{8}, \frac{1}{27}, \frac{1}{64}, \frac{1}{125}, \ldots$$

If the pattern continues, what will be the next term?

A $\frac{1}{144}$

B $\frac{1}{216}$

C $\frac{1}{250}$

D $\frac{1}{1{,}000}$

50 The spinner below is divided into 6 equal sections.

If the arrow lands on a shape, what is the probability that it will land on a triangle?

F $\frac{1}{6}$

G $\frac{1}{4}$

H $\frac{1}{3}$

J $\frac{1}{2}$

STOP

CHAPTER

Goal 1, Expectation 1.1

Patterns and Functional Relationships

Lesson

Recognizing Patterns

A **pattern** is a series of shapes or numbers in which each shape or number depends on the one before it. The following tips can help you solve problems involving patterns:

- Circle or highlight the part of the pattern that changes from one figure to the next.
- Make drawings of the next figures in the pattern.
- Assign values to each figure in the pattern and examine how those values change.

EXAMPLE 1

The first four tiles in a pattern are shown below.

If the pattern continues, what will be the next tile in the pattern?

STRATEGY **Identify the part that changes from one figure to the next.**

STEP 1 In the first square the top side is gray, while in the second square the left side is gray.

STEP 2 To change the first square so that it looks like the second square, you would have to rotate the first square 90° counterclockwise.

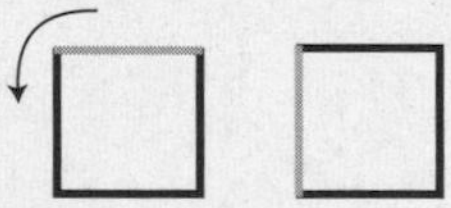

STEP 3 Check that performing the same movement to the second square will give you the third square.

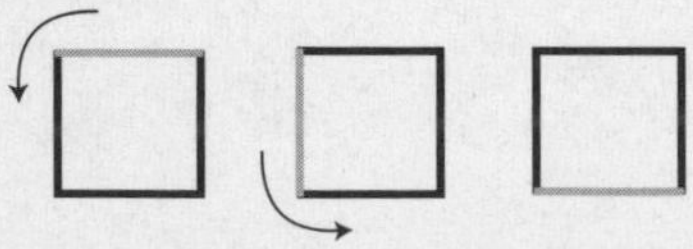

STEP 4 Perform that same movement on the fourth square to get the next tile in the pattern.

SOLUTION **The next tile in the pattern is .**

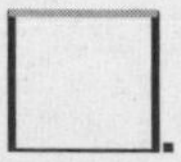

EXAMPLE 2

Celine drew the following pattern of four figures.

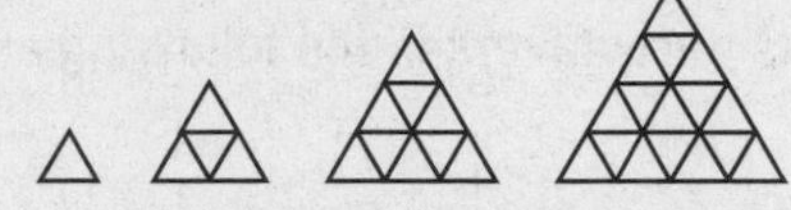

If the pattern continues, how many triangles will there be in the sixth figure?

STRATEGY **Assign values to each figure.**

STEP 1 Count the number of triangles in each figure.

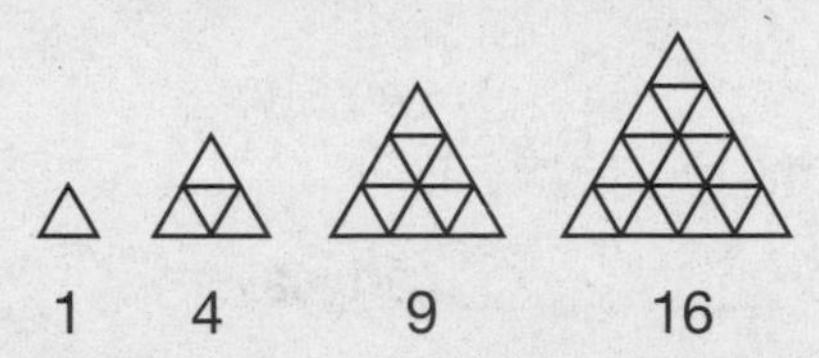

STEP 2 Find a pattern in the values for each figure by subtracting each value from the previous value.

1		4		9		16	← values for each figure
	3		5		7		← difference of adjacent values
		2		2			← difference of differences

STEP 3 Use the pattern in the numbers to determine the values for the next two figures.

1		4		9		16		25		36
	3		5		7		9		11	
		2		2		2		2		

SOLUTION **The sixth figure will have 36 triangles.**

COACHED EXAMPLE

To prepare for a party, Dario stacks party favors in the following arrangement.

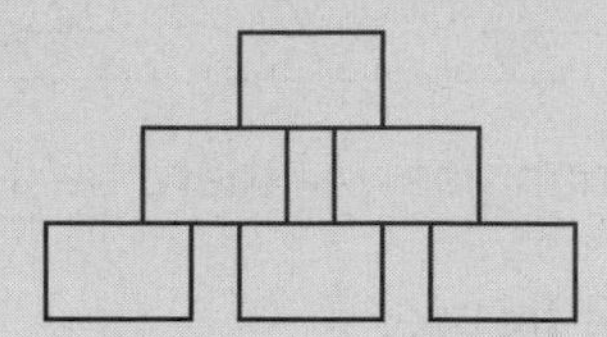

If he follows this pattern and makes a stack that is five rows high, how many party favors will he use?

THINKING IT THROUGH

Each row has __________ fewer party favors than the row below it.

In a stack that is five rows high, the top row will have __________ party favor.

In a stack that is five rows high, the second highest row will have __________ party favors.

In a stack that is five rows high, the third highest row will have __________ party favors.

In a stack that is five rows high, the fourth highest row will have __________ party favors.

In a stack that is five rows high, the bottom row will have __________ party favors.

The total number of party favors will be __________.

Lesson Practice

Choose the correct answer.

1. The first three figures in a pattern are shown below.

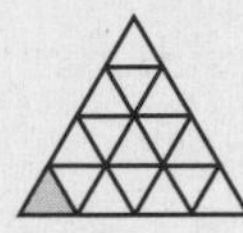 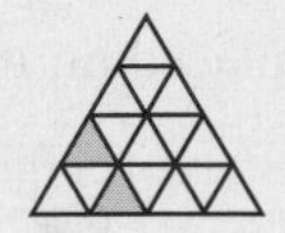 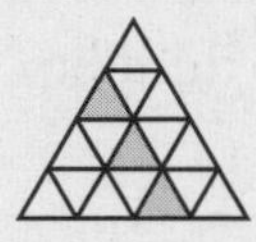

If the pattern continues, what will be the next figure in the pattern?

A. 

B. 

C. 

D. 

2. Look at the pattern below.

  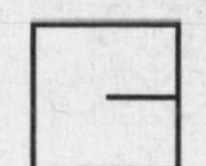 

If this pattern continues, what will be the sixth figure?

F. 

H. 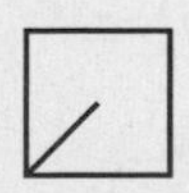

G. 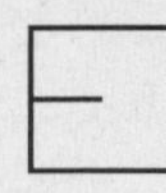

J. 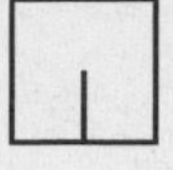

3. The diagram below shows a serving platter that is moved in different positions.

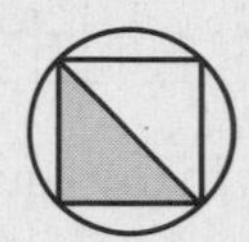 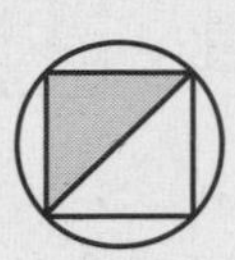 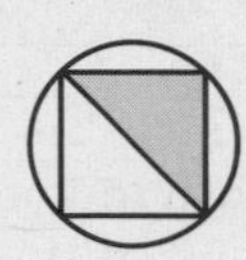 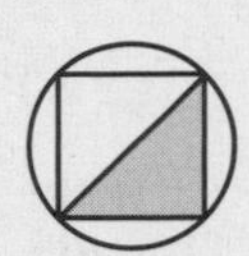

Which of these describes the movement of the serving platter at each step?

A. turned clockwise 90°

B. turned clockwise 180°

C. turned counterclockwise 90°

D. turned counterclockwise 180°

4. Look at the pattern in the table below.

Figure				
Fraction shaded	$\frac{1}{1}$	$\frac{1}{2}$	$\frac{1}{4}$	$\frac{1}{8}$

If the pattern continues, what fraction will represent the next figure?

F. $\frac{1}{5}$

G. $\frac{1}{9}$

H. $\frac{1}{10}$

J. $\frac{1}{16}$

5. Min made the five figures below with colored squares arranged in a pattern.

If the pattern continues, how many squares will he use in the seventh figure?

A. 14

B. 21

C. 28

D. 49

6. Charlotte is sewing triangular patches of fabric together to make a quilt. She adds triangular patches in the pattern shown in the following four figures.

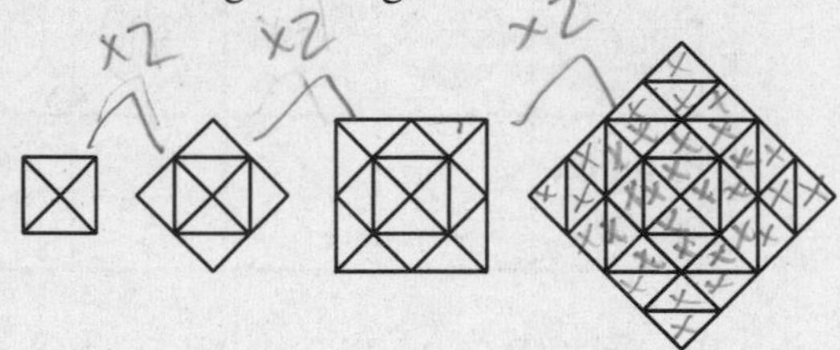

If the pattern continues, how many triangles will she have to add to make the figure in the next pattern?

F. 5

G. 16

H. 32

J. 40

Use the Response Grid to complete Number 7.

7. Janet built a store display using boxes of soda cans. She made the three-story tower shown below by placing the boxes of soda so that every two boxes placed on end support a third box placed on its side.

If she uses the same pattern, how many boxes will she need for a tower with six stories?

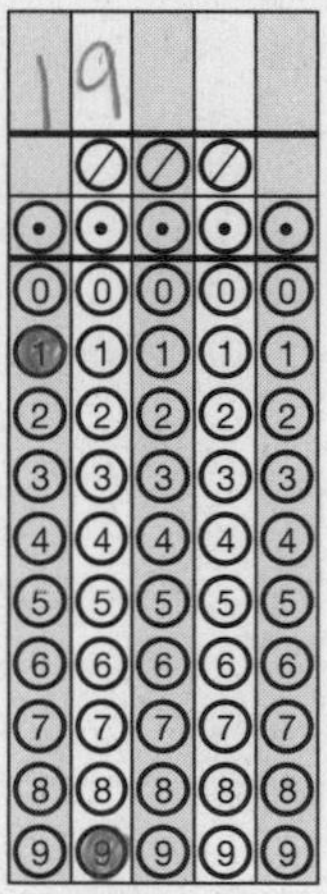

8. **BCR** Keenan is laying decorative tiles in his family's bathroom. He lays the square tiles so that each set of white or gray tiles forms a square around the previous set. The figures below show how he arranged the first three sets of tiles.

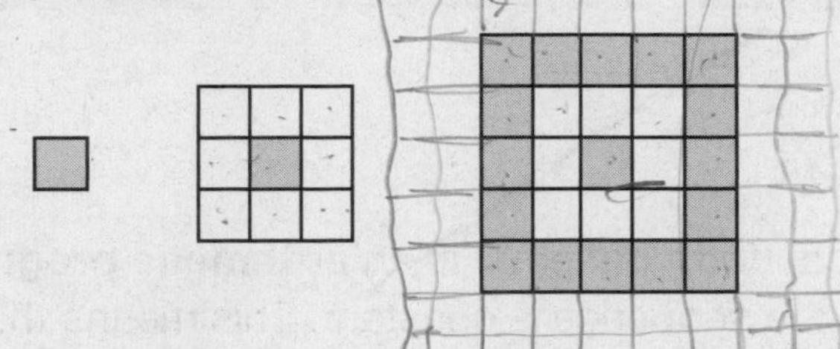

- Draw the tile arrangement as it appears after Keenan has added the fourth set of tiles.

- How many tiles will be in the pattern after he has added the sixth set of tiles?

49

- What color will the eleventh set of tiles be?

Dark

Lesson

Numerical Patterns

1.1.1

Numbers in a sequence can form patterns. In an **arithmetic progression,** the difference between two numbers in the sequence is constant. This means that the difference is the same for any two consecutive numbers in the sequence. In a **geometric progression,** any two consecutive numbers in the sequence will have the same quotient. Other sequences use a combination of addition, subtraction, multiplication, and division to form a pattern.

EXAMPLE 1

Look at the pattern below.

109.12, 140.17, 171.22, 202.27, . . .

If this pattern continues, what will be the sixth term?

STRATEGY **Find the difference between pairs of numbers.**

STEP 1 Subtract the first term from the second term.

$140.17 - 109.12 = 31.05$

STEP 2 Subtract the second term from the third term.

$171.22 - 140.17 = 31.05$

STEP 3 Compare these differences. Are they alike?

Yes, both differences have the same value, 31.05.

To get the next term in the pattern, you must add 31.05.

STEP 4 If they are alike, keep adding that value to the last known term until you have the term you want to find.

For the fifth term: $202.27 + 31.05 = 233.32$

For the sixth term: $233.32 + 31.05 = 264.37$

STEP 5 To check your answer, multiply the difference by 1 less than the place value of the term you want to find and add that number to the first term.

For the sixth term: $31.05 \times (6 - 1) + 109.12 = 264.37$

SOLUTION **The sixth term in the pattern is 264.37.**

EXAMPLE 2

Look at the pattern below.

$\frac{1}{2}, \frac{1}{4}, \frac{1}{8}, \frac{1}{16}, \frac{1}{32}, \ldots$

If this pattern continues, what will be the eighth term?

STRATEGY **Divide pairs of numbers.**

STEP 1 Divide the second term by the first term.

$\frac{1}{4} \div \frac{1}{2} = \frac{1}{2}$

STEP 2 Divide the third term by the second term.

$\frac{1}{8} \div \frac{1}{4} = \frac{1}{2}$

STEP 3 Compare these quotients. Are they alike?

Yes, both quotients have the same value, $\frac{1}{2}$.

To get the next term in the pattern, you must multiply by $\frac{1}{2}$.

STEP 4 If they are alike, keep multiplying each term by that value until you get the term that you want to find.

For the sixth term: $\frac{1}{32} \times \frac{1}{2} = \frac{1}{64}$

For the seventh term: $\frac{1}{64} \times \frac{1}{2} = \frac{1}{128}$

For the eighth term: $\frac{1}{128} \times \frac{1}{2} = \frac{1}{256}$

SOLUTION **The eighth term in the pattern is $\frac{1}{256}$.**

EXAMPLE 3

Ken collects tomatoes from his family's garden. The table below shows how many tomatoes he has harvested so far this year, as of each week of the growing season.

Week	Number of Tomatoes
1	45
2	75
3	105
4	135

If the tomatoes continue to grow at this rate, how many will Ken have harvested by the tenth week?

STRATEGY **Make a formula.**

STEP 1 Assign variables to the different parts of the question.

The week number is w and the number of tomatoes is t.

STEP 2 Try a formula that multiplies one variable by a given value.

For $w = 1$, what number do you multiply w by to get 45?

$45w = t$

$45(1) = 45$

STEP 3 Plug another value from the chart into the formula and see if it gives the correct value for the second variable.

$45w = t$

$45(2) = 90 \neq 75$

This formula does not work.

STEP 4 Try a formula that adds a given value to one variable.

$44 + w = t$

$44 + (1) = 45$

$44 + (2) = 46 \neq 75$

This formula does not work.

STEP 5 Try a formula that uses both addition and multiplication to relate the two values.

The difference between each value for t is 30.

The value for Week 1 is $30 + 15$.

$30w + 15 = t$

For $w = 1$, $30(1) + 15 = 45$

STEP 6 Plug other values from the chart into the formula and see if it gives the correct values for the second variable.

$30w + 15 = t$

For $w = 2$, $30(2) + 15 = 75$

For $w = 3$, $30(3) + 15 = 105$

STEP 7 Use this formula to find the requested value.

For $w = 10$, $30(10) + 15 = 315$

SOLUTION **By the tenth week, Ken expects to have collected 315 tomatoes.**

COACHED EXAMPLE

The table below shows a relationship between *m* and *n*.

m	0	1	2	3	4
n	2	5	8	11	?

What is the next value for *n*?

THINKING IT THROUGH

What do you add to $m = 0$ to get 2? 2________

Does the sum $m + 2 = n$ for $m = 0$? yes________

Does the sum $m + 2 = n$ for $m = 1$? No________

This means that you must also multiply m by a number x for the sum to equal n. The equation would be $xm + 2 = n$.

For $m = 1$ and $n = 5$, the equation $xm + 2 = n$ can be rewritten as x(1)+2=________.

For $m = 1$ and $n = 5$, the value of x must be __________.

Plugging in this value of x gives a new equation, __________ $m + 2 = n$.

For $m = 4$ in this new equation, $n =$ __________.

Lesson Practice

Choose the correct answer.

1. Look at the pattern below.

   36, 37.7, 39.4, 41.1, 42.8,…

   If this pattern continues, what will be the ninth term?

   A. 49.6
   B. 44.5
   C. 15.3
   D. 10.7

2. Look at the pattern below.

   $45, 15, 5, \frac{5}{3}, \frac{5}{9}, \ldots$

   If this pattern continues, what will be the seventh term?

   F. $\frac{5}{81}$
   G. $\frac{1}{3}$
   H. $\frac{5}{7}$
   J. $\frac{45}{7}$

3. The table below shows a relationship between x and y.

x	2	4	6	8	10	12
y	5	?	9	11	13	?

   What are the missing two values for y?

   A. 3 and 11
   B. 6 and 14
   C. 7 and 15
   D. 15 and 17

4. Look at the pattern below.

   $3n + 9, 3n + 2, 3n - 5, \ldots$

   If the pattern continues, what will be the sixth term?

   F. $3n + 8$
   G. $2n - 6$
   H. $3n - 12$
   J. $3n - 26$

5. The table below shows the cost of ordering replacement ink cartridges based on the number of cartridges purchased.

Number of Cartridges Purchased	Cost of Order (in dollars)
1	15.30
5	54.50
10	103.50
15	152.50

   If the manager of an office purchases 20 replacement ink cartridges, what is the total cost of the order?

   A. \$201.50
   B. \$305.00
   C. \$305.50
   D. \$306.00

6. The table below shows the number of cups of flour needed for a given number of eggs in a pancake recipe.

Number of Eggs	Number of Cups of Flour
2	$1\frac{1}{2}$
3	$2\frac{1}{4}$
4	3
8	6

If Hatim wants to use a dozen eggs to make pancakes, how many cups of flour will he need?

F. $7\frac{1}{2}$

G. 9

H. 12

J. 24

Use the Response Grid to complete Number 7.

7. Look at the pattern below.

5,175; 1,035; 207; 41.4;...

If the pattern continues, what will be the next term?

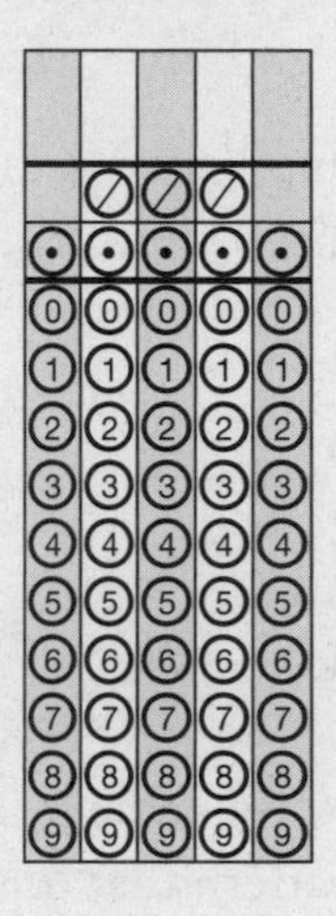

8. The table below shows values of p and q.

ECR

p	1	2	3	4	5
q	0	3	8	15	24

Difference in q values				

- What is the relationship between the values for p and the values for q? Use mathematics to explain the relationship. Use words, symbols, or both in your explanation.

- Fill in the boxes below the table by finding the difference between the values for q in adjacent boxes. Describe the pattern that exists between the differences in q values.

- What is the difference between the values of q for $p = 8$ and for $p = 9$? Use mathematics to explain how you determined your answer. Use words, symbols, or both in your explanation.

- What are the values of q for $p = 8$ and for $p = 9$?

Lesson

Linear Equations

A **linear equation** is an equation that relates two variables that are each to the first power. For example, the equation $y = x + 3$ is a linear equation. The graphs of linear equations are straight lines. The graph of $y = x + 3$ is shown below.

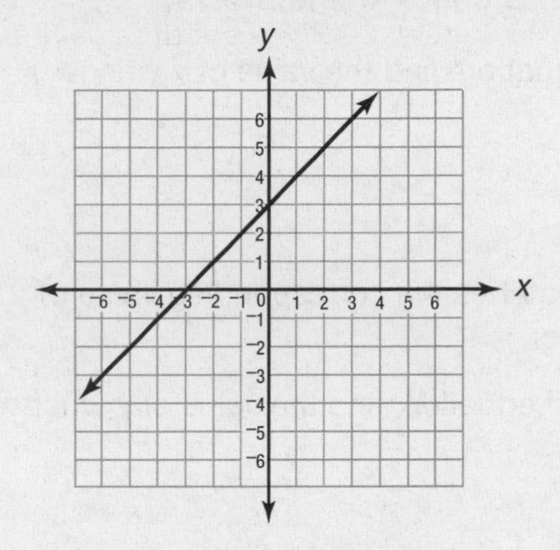

You can find points on the line $y = x + 3$ in the graph above by using the coordinates shown in the table below.

x	y
$^-3$	0
$^-2$	1
$^-1$	2
0	3
1	4
2	5

Linear equations can also represent relationships in word problems. A word problem that describes a linear relationship has two quantities that depend on one another.

EXAMPLE 1

The table below shows a relationship between x and y.

x	1	2	3	4	5
y	7	9	11	13	15

Which of these equations represents this relationship?

$y = 2x + 5$ or $y = 2x - 5$

STRATEGY **Plug in values and check the answers.**

STEP 1 Using the first equation, find the value of y when $x = 1$.

$y = 2x + 5$

$y = 2(1) + 5$

$y = 2 + 5 = 7$

This value of y matches the corresponding value of y when $x = 1$ in the table, so this equation is correct.

STEP 2 Using the second equation, find the value of y when $x = 1$.

$y = 2x - 5$

$y = 2(1) - 5$

$y = 2 - 5 = {}^{-}3$

This value of y does not match the corresponding value of y when $x = 1$ in the table, so this is not the correct equation.

STEP 3 Check your answer by trying other values in the table.

$y = 2(2) + 5 = 4 + 5 = 9$

$y = 2(3) + 5 = 6 + 5 = 11$

$y = 2(4) + 5 = 8 + 5 = 13$

$y = 2(5) + 5 = 10 + 5 = 15$

SOLUTION **The equation $y = 2x + 5$ represents the relationship in the table.**

EXAMPLE 2

Look at the graph below.

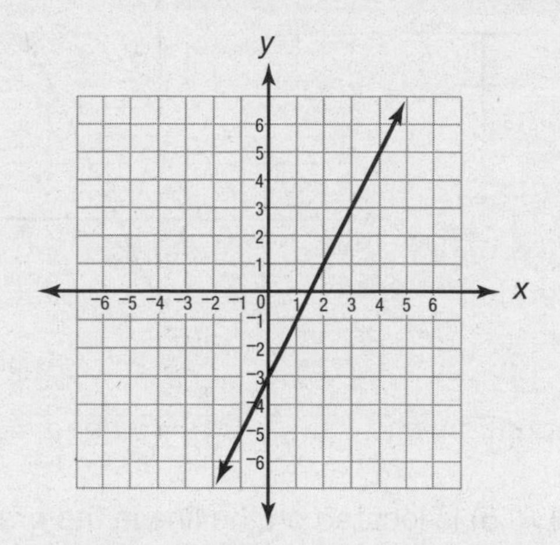

Which of these tables corresponds to the line that is graphed?

x	y
⁻1	5
0	3
1	1
2	⁻1
3	⁻3

x	y
⁻1	⁻5
0	⁻3
1	⁻1
2	1
3	3

STRATEGY **Check coordinates on the graph.**

STEP 1 Using the first table, find a set of coordinates on the graph.

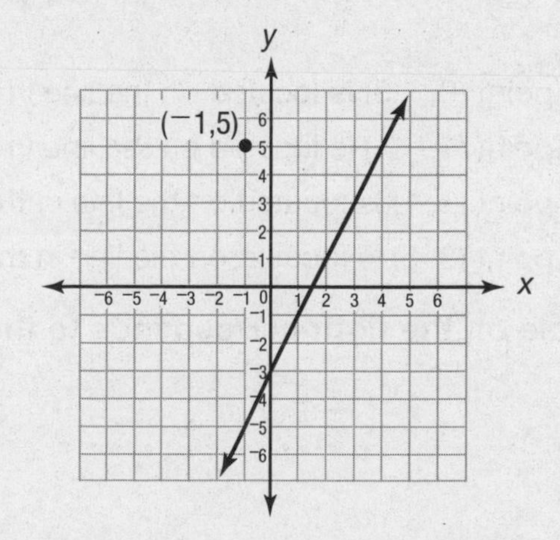

The point (⁻1, 5) is not located on the line in the graph.

Thus, the line does not include this set of coordinates.

STEP 2 Using the second table, find a set of coordinates on the graph.

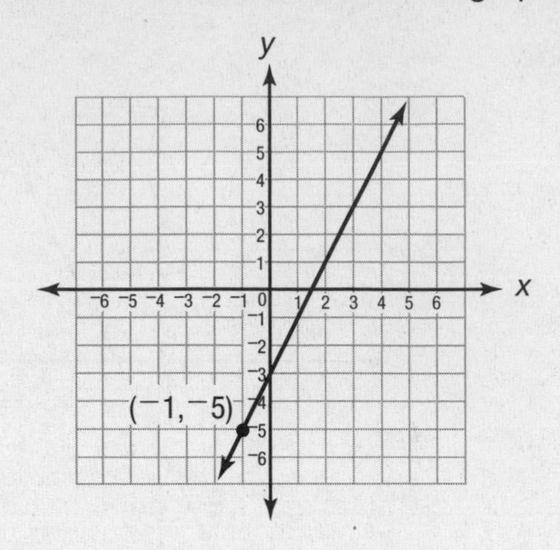

The point (⁻1, ⁻5) is located on the line in the graph.

This table could correspond to the line that is graphed.

STEP 3 Check your answer by trying other coordinates in the table.

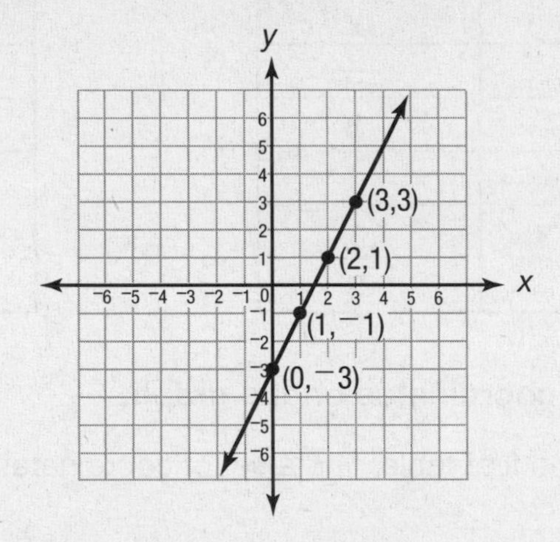

The point (0, ⁻3) is located on the line in the graph.

The point (1, ⁻1) is located on the line in the graph.

The point (2, 1) is located on the line in the graph.

The point (3, 3) is located on the line in the graph.

SOLUTION **The table on the right corresponds to the line that is graphed.**

COACHED EXAMPLE

Robert is using a hose to fill his parents' swimming pool with water. The hose delivers 120 gallons of water each hour. Which of these tables shows the number of gallons delivered (*g*) after *h* hours?

Hours (*h*)	Gallons delivered (*g*)
1	120
2	240
3	360
4	480

Hours (*h*)	Gallons delivered (*g*)
1	120
2	240
3	480
4	960

THINKING IT THROUGH

The two variables given in the table are ____________.

The equation that represents the relationship between these two variables is $g =$ ____________ $\times h$.

How many gallons are delivered when $h = 2$? ____________

How many gallons are delivered when $h = 3$? ____________

These answers correspond to the table on the ____________.

Lesson Practice

Choose the correct answer.

1. Look at the graph below.

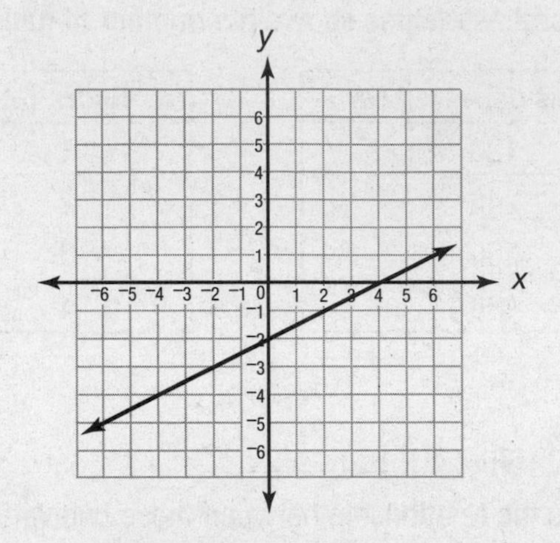

Which of these tables corresponds to the line that is graphed?

A.

x	*y*
−4	−4
−3	−2
−2	0
−1	2
0	4

C.

x	*y*
−4	4
−2	3
0	2
2	1
4	0

B.

x	*y*
−4	−4
−2	−3
0	−2
2	−1
4	0

D.

x	*y*
4	−4
3	−2
2	0
1	2
0	4

2. Jeremy always gives a 15% tip. Which of these tables shows the amount of tip (t) in dollars that Jeremy would give for a meal that costs m dollars?

F.

Cost of meal (m)	6	7	8	9	10
Amount of tip (t)	0.90	1.05	1.20	1.35	1.50

H.

Cost of meal (m)	6	7	8	9	10
Amount of tip (t)	6.90	8.05	9.20	10.35	11.50

G.

Cost of meal (m)	6	7	8	9	10
Amount of tip (t)	1.20	1.40	1.60	1.80	2.00

J.

Cost of meal (m)	6	7	8	9	10
Amount of tip (t)	6.15	7.15	8.15	9.15	10.15

3. Maria is preheating her oven in order to roast a chicken. The room temperature in her kitchen is 75 degrees Fahrenheit. Her oven temperature increases 50 degrees every minute. Which of these graphs shows the relationship between the number of minutes of preheating and the temperature of her oven in degrees Fahrenheit?

A.

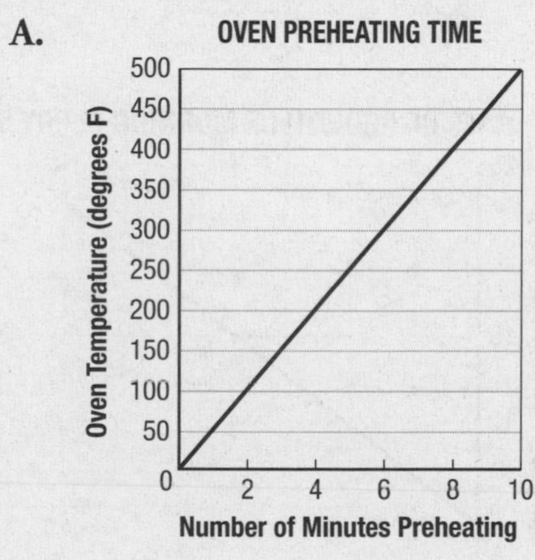

C.

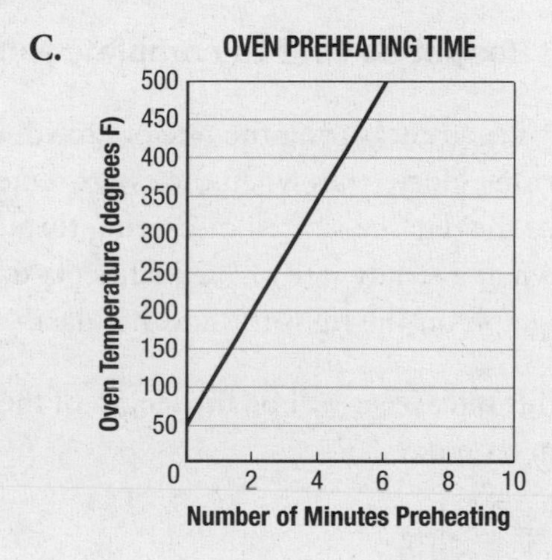

B.

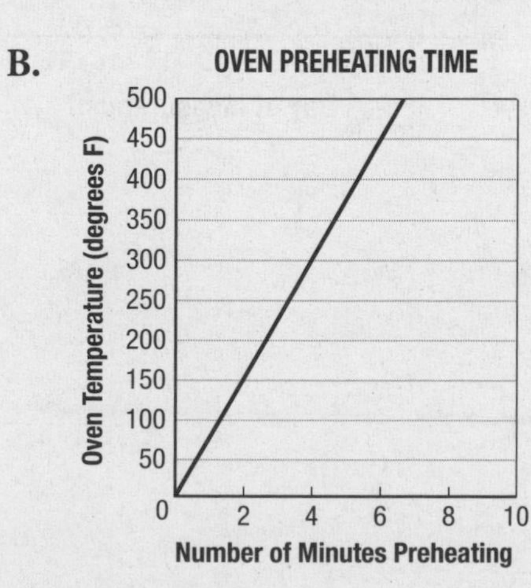

D.

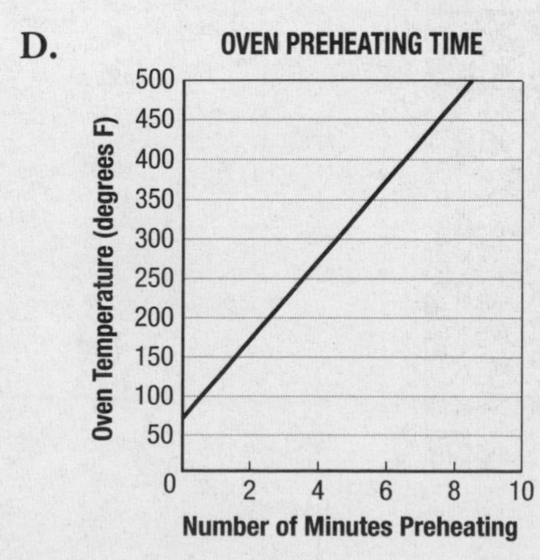

4. Ricky and his brother run a snow-cone stand. For four weeks, Ricky tallied the number of snow cones they sold each week. In the first week, they sold 450 snow cones. Ricky noticed that each week they sold 50 more cones than the previous week. Which of these tables shows the number of snow cones sold (s) for each of four given weeks of the summer (w)?

F.

Week (w)	Snow cones sold (s)
1	50
2	100
3	150
4	200

H.

Week (w)	Snow cones sold (s)
1	500
2	550
3	600
4	650

G.

Week (w)	Snow cones sold (s)
1	450
2	500
3	550
4	600

J.

Week (w)	Snow cones sold (s)
1	450
2	900
3	1350
4	1800

Use the Response Grid to complete Number 5.

5. Tilly began measuring the rate of growth of her morning glory vines when they were 4 inches long. Since the day she started measuring them, they have grown at a steady rate of 1.2 inches per day. She made the graph on the right to show her data.

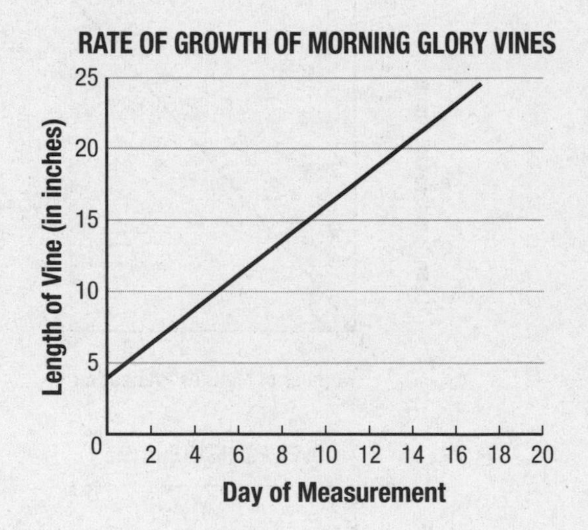

At this rate, what will be the length of the vines, in inches, on day 16?

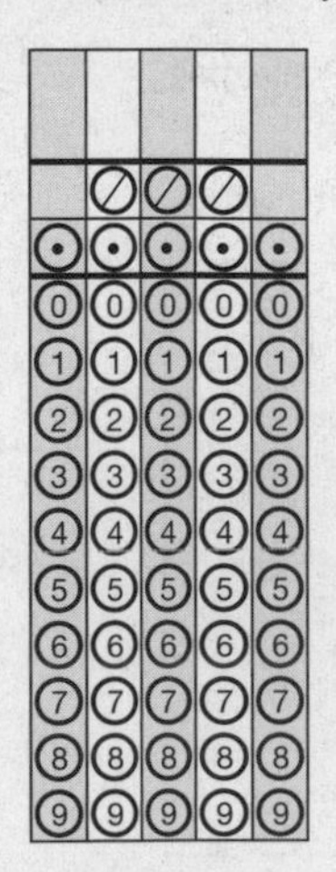

6. Elton's Lawn Care charges customers a service fee of \$50 plus a dollar for each square foot of grass when installing a new lawn. Their competitor, Milto's Lawn and Tree Service, charges \$1.50 for each square foot of grass.
ECR

TABLE I

Lawn Area in Square Feet (a)	Total Charge (t)
100	150
200	300
300	450
400	600

TABLE II

Lawn Area in Square Feet (a)	Total Charge (t)
100	150
200	250
300	350
400	450

- Which table represents the rates that Elton's Lawn Care charges its customers? Use mathematics to explain how you determined your answer. Use words, symbols, or both in your explanation.

- What equation represents the total amount (t) charged by Elton's Lawn Care for a customer with a new lawn that is a square feet?

- What equation represents total amount (t) charged by Milto's Lawn and Tree Service for a customer with a new lawn that is a square feet?

- If Mrs. Green wants a 250-square-foot lawn, how much would Elton's Lawn Care charge to plant it?

Lesson

4 Simple Quadratic Equations

A **quadratic equation** is a polynomial equation that has a term with a variable to the second power. A **square number**, or a perfect square, results when a number is multiplied by itself. For example, the square of x is $x \times x$, or x^2. To find patterns that result from simple quadratic equations, look for square numbers such as the following:

$$1 = 1^2$$
$$4 = 2^2$$
$$9 = 3^2$$
$$16 = 4^2$$
$$25 = 5^2$$

EXAMPLE

The table below shows a relationship between a and b.

a	b
$^-4$	27
$^-1$	$^-3$
0	$^-5$
1	$^-3$
4	27

Which of these equations represents this relationship?

$b = 2a^2 + 5$ or $b = 2a^2 - 5$

STRATEGY **Plug in values and check the answer.**

STEP 1 Using the first equation, find the value of b when $a = {}^-4$.

$$b = 2a^2 + 5$$
$$b = 2(^-4)^2 + 5$$
$$b = 2(16) + 5$$
$$b = 32 + 5 = 37$$

This value of b does not match the corresponding value of a in the table.

STEP 2 Using the second equation, find the value of b when $a = {}^{-}4$.

$b = 2a^2 - 5$

$b = 2({}^{-}4)^2 - 5$

$b = 2(16) - 5$

$b = 32 - 5 = 27$

This value of b matches the corresponding value of a in the table, so this equation must be correct.

STEP 3 Check your answer by trying other values in the table.

$b = 2({}^{-}1)^2 - 5 = 2 - 5 = {}^{-}3$

$b = 2(0)^2 - 5 = 0 - 5 = {}^{-}5$

$b = 2(1)^2 - 5 = 2 - 5 = {}^{-}3$

$b = 2(4)^2 - 5 = 32 - 5 = 27$

SOLUTION The equation $b = 2a^2 - 5$ represents the relationship in the table.

COACHED EXAMPLE

Renata wants to build a square garden with a wooden border. Within the garden's border, she will place a small bench that takes up 3 square feet. She calculates the amount of garden space she has by squaring the length of one side of wooden border and subtracting the square footage of the bench. Which of these tables shows the square footage of garden space (*s*) for a given length of wooden border (*b*)?

length of one side of wooden border (*b*)	square footage of garden (*s*)
3	6
4	13
5	22
6	33

length of one side of wooden border (*b*)	square footage of garden (*s*)
3	12
4	19
5	28
6	39

THINKING IT THROUGH

The two variables given in the table are ______________.

The equation that represents the relationship between these two variables is $s =$ ______________ ${}^{-}3$.

What is the square footage of the garden for $b = 3$? ______________

What is the square footage of the garden for $b = 4$? ______________

These answers correspond to the table on the ______________.

Lesson Practice

Choose the correct answer.

1. The table below shows a relationship between r and s.

r	1	2	3	4	5
s	1	$^-5$	$^-15$	$^-29$	$^-47$

Which of these equations represents the relationship?

A. $s = {}^-2r^2 + 3$

B. $s = {}^-r^2 + 2$

C. $s = r^2 - 3$

D. $s = 2r^2 + 3$

2. The table below shows a relationship between g and h.

g	h
$^-1$	3
0	2
$\frac{1}{2}$	$\frac{9}{4}$
1	3
2	6

Which of these equations represents the relationship?

F. $h = 1 - \left(\frac{1}{4}\right)g^2$

G. $h = \frac{1}{4} + g^2$

H. $h = 4 - g^2$

J. $h = 2 + g^2$

3. The table below shows a relationship between p and q.

p	q
$^-3$	3
$^-2$	0.5
$^-1$	$^-1$
0	$^-1.5$
1	$^-1$

Which of these equations represents the relationship?

A. $q = \frac{p^2 - 3}{2}$

B. $q = \frac{2p^2 - 3}{2}$

C. $q = {}^-\left(\frac{1}{2}\right)p^2 - 3$

D. $q = {}^-2p^2 - 3$

4. Mika is buying bags of grass seed to spread on her lawn. The bags say to use 1 pound of grass seed for every 400 square feet of lawn. She wants to buy enough grass seed to cover the lawn and have 2 pounds left over to store for later use. Which of these tables shows how many pounds of grass seed (g) she should buy if she has a square lawn with sides that are each x feet long?

F.

length of each side of lawn (x)	pounds of grass seed (g)
20	1
40	2
60	3
80	4

H.

length of each side of lawn (x)	pounds of grass seed (g)
20	3
40	6
60	9
80	12

G.

length of each side of lawn (x)	pounds of grass seed (g)
20	3
40	4
60	5
80	6

J.

length of each side of lawn (x)	pounds of grass seed (g)
20	3
40	6
60	11
80	18

5. Mrs. Berg is getting carpet put into a square room. The carpeting service suggests she buy enough carpet to cover the floor plus an additional 30 square meters for future repairs. Which of these tables shows how many square meters of carpet (c) she should buy if her front room has sides that are each l meters long?

A.

length of one side of square room, in meters (l)	square meters of carpet to buy (c)
10	40
12	42
14	44
16	46

B.

length of one side of square room, in meters (l)	square meters of carpet to buy (c)
10	70
12	114
14	166
16	226

C.

length of one side of square room, in meters (l)	square meters of carpet to buy (c)
10	100
12	144
14	196
16	256

D.

length of one side of square room, in meters (l)	square meters of carpet to buy (c)
10	130
12	174
14	226
16	286

6. The graph below represents the function $y = {}^{-}2x^2 + 3$.

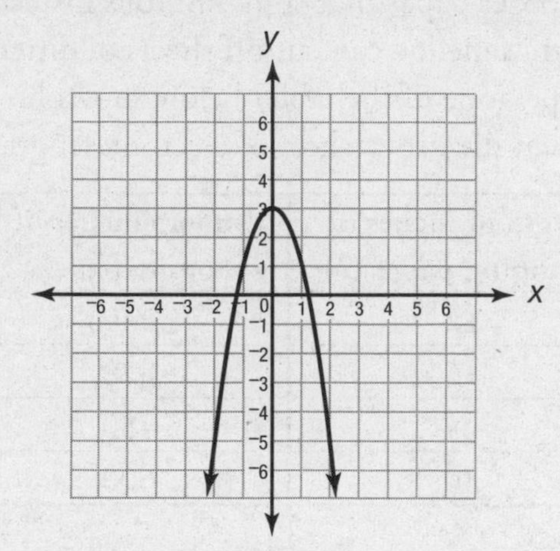

What will be the value of y when $x = 0$?

F. $^{-}1$

G. 0

H. 1

J. 3

Use the Response Grid to complete Number 7.

7. The graph below represents the function $y = x^2 - 4$.

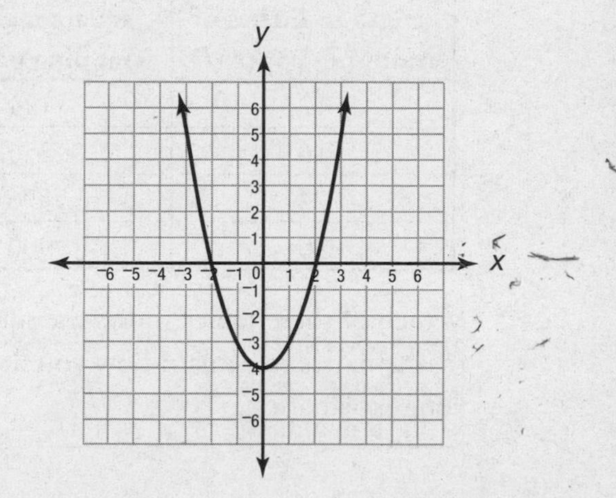

What will be the value of y when $x = {}^{-}3$?

8.
ECR

Madeline works at a bookstore in the gift-wrapping department. She wraps the books in paper that comes in square sheets. Her supervisor decides to order paper that comes in rolls instead of loose sheets. Each roll of paper is 20 inches wide and Madeline can cut off sheets of different lengths. For each of the different types of wrapping paper, one of the tables below shows how many square inches of wrapping paper (a) there are when she uses a sheet of a certain length (l).

length in inches of wrapping paper (l)	square inches of wrapping paper (a)
12	144
16	256
24	576
30	900

length in inches of wrapping paper (l)	square inches of wrapping paper (a)
12	240
16	320
24	480
30	600

- Which of these tables shows the square inches of wrapping paper for the loose sheets? Use mathematics to explain how you determined your answer. Use words, symbols, or both in your explanation.

12×20=240
16×20=320

The table on the right.

- What equation represents the number of square inches of wrapping paper (a) there are when Madeline uses a loose sheet of wrapping paper with sides of length l?

a×20=L

- What equation represents the number of square inches of wrapping paper (a) there are when Madeline cuts off a certain length of wrapping paper (l) from a roll of wrapping paper?

?

a÷20=L

- How many square inches of wrapping paper will Madeline get if she cuts off a length of 36 inches from the roll?

36×20=720

Lesson

5 Simple Cubic Equations

A **cubic equation** is a polynomial equation that has a term with a variable to the third power. A **cubed number,** or a perfect cube, results when a number is multiplied by itself three times. For example, the cube of x is $x \times x \times x$, or x^3. To find patterns that result from simple cubic equations, look for cubed numbers such as the following:

$$1 = 1^3$$
$$8 = 2^3$$
$$27 = 3^3$$
$$64 = 4^3$$
$$125 = 5^3$$

EXAMPLE

Look at the pattern below.

$m, 8m, 27m, 64m, 125m, \ldots$

If the pattern continues, what will be the sixth term?

STRATEGY **Look for cubed numbers.**

STEP 1 Compare each term in the pattern and find out what quantity they have in common.

Each term has the variable m.

STEP 2 Subtract or divide each term by the quantity that each term has in common.

$(m, 8m, 27m, 64m, 125m, \ldots) \div m$

1, 8, 27, 64, 125,...

STEP 3 Look for cubed numbers in the terms.

$1 = 1^3$

$8 = 2^3$

$27 = 3^3$

... and so on.

STEP 4 Write an expression that represents each term in the pattern.

The nth term is $n^3 \times m$.

STEP 5 Use the expression to determine the sixth term.

$6^3 \times m = 216m$

SOLUTION **The sixth term is 216*m*.**

COACHED EXAMPLE

The table below shows a relationship between s and t.

s	t
1	3
2	24
3	81
4	192

Which of these equations represents this relationship?

A. $t = 2s^2$

B. $t = 2s^3$

C. $t = 3s^2$

D. $t = 3s^3$

THINKING IT THROUGH

Are all the values for t even? ____________

This means that you can eliminate answers ____________ and ____________, which would always result in values of t that are divisible by 2.

When you divide each value for t by 3, you get ____________.

Are the values that result squares or cubes? ____________

This means that equation ____________ represents the relationship.

To check the answer, plug into the equation a value for s and see if you get the corresponding value for t. ____________

Lesson Practice

Choose the correct answer.

1. Look at the pattern below.

$^{-}1, ^{-}8, ^{-}27, ^{-}64, ^{-}125, \ldots$

If the pattern continues, what will be the seventh term?

A. 216

B. $^{-}147$

C. $^{-}216$

D. $^{-}343$

2. Look at the pattern below.

$2y, 16y, 54y, 128y, 250y, \ldots$

If the pattern continues, what will be the eighth term?

F. $192y$

G. $432y$

H. $512y$

J. $1{,}024y$

3. Look at the pattern below.

$x^3, 8x^3, 27x^3, 64x^3, \ldots$

If the pattern continues, what will be the next term?

A. $128x$

B. $72x^3$

C. $125x^3$

D. $128x^3$

4. Look at the pattern below.

$3x^3 - 6, 6x^3 - 12, 9x^3 - 18, \ldots$

If the pattern continues, what will be the sixth term?

F. $6x^3 - 216$

G. $12x^3 - 24$

H. $12x^3 - 216$

J. $18x^3 - 36$

5. The table below shows a relationship between x and y.

x	y
$^{-}2$	16
$^{-}1$	2
0	0
1	$^{-}2$

Which of these equations represents this relationship?

A. $y = 4x^2$

B. $y = 2x^3$

C. $y = x^3$

D. $y = {^{-}2}x^3$

6. The volume of a cube is the cube of the length of its sides. If the diagram below represents one side of a cube-shaped box, what is the volume of the box?

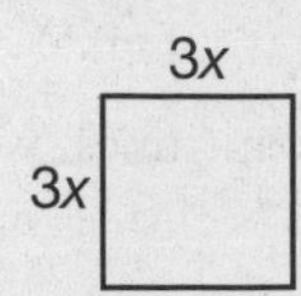

F. $27x$

G. $9x^2$

H. $3x^3$

J. $27x^3$

Use the Response Grid to complete Number 7.

7. The pattern in the table below results from the equation $q = 5p^3 - 300$.

p	2	4	6	8	10
q	$^{-}260$	20	780	2,260	4,700

What will be the value of q when $p = 16$?

8.
ECR

Sherry wants to ship an item in a cube-shaped container. The volume of the item is 20 cubic units. She can choose from four sizes of shipping containers, each with sides of 1 unit, 2 units, 3 units, or 4 units. Once she has placed the item in the container, she will fill up the rest of the container with foam packing peanuts.

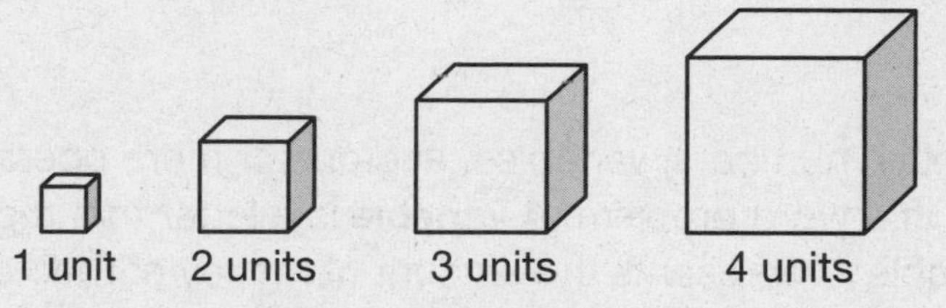

- What is the volume of each shipping container?

- If she ships the item in the container with sides that are each 3 units long, what volume of foam packing peanuts will she use?

- Imagine that u represents the length in units of each side of the container that Sherry chooses and p represents the volume of foam packing peanuts. What equation represents the volume of foam packing peanuts she will use with that container? Use mathematics to explain how you determined your answer. Use words, symbols, or both in your explanation.

- What volume of foam packing peanuts would Sherry need to ship the item in a container that has sides that are each 10 units long?

Lesson

Writing Expressions

An **expression** may contain numbers, variables, and one or more operations. It may be used to represent a situation in a word problem. A **variable** is a letter that represents a number. For example, if the variable x represents the amount of money earned each day, then the expression $7x$ represents the amount of money earned in 7 days.

EXAMPLE

Sadaf has n stamps in her collection. Her older brother Farhad has $(3n - 8)$ stamps in his collection. If they combined their stamps into a single collection, what expression represents the total number of stamps they would have?

STRATEGY **Make a word equation.**

STEP 1 Identify which operation the problem requires.

The problem uses the word "total," which means it requires addition.

STEP 2 Make a simple equation of the amounts to be added together.

total number of stamps = (Sadaf's stamps) + (Farhad's stamps)

STEP 3 Replace the words in the word equation with their equivalent expressions.

total number of stamps = $(n) + (3n - 8)$

SOLUTION **The total number of stamps would be $n + (3n - 8)$.**

COACHED EXAMPLE

The expression $(12 + x^2)$ represents the perimeter of a regular hexagon. What expression represents the length of one side?

THINKING IT THROUGH

A regular hexagon has how many sides of equal length? ________________

Perimeter is the sum of the lengths of all the sides.

What expression represents the perimeter of the given hexagon? ________________

Dividing that perimeter by ________________ gives the length of one side.

The expression ________________ represents the length of one side.

Lesson Practice

#1-7 HW

Choose the correct answer.

1. Mona spent a total of \$52.46 last night going out to dinner and to a concert. If x represents the cost of the concert, which of these expressions represents the cost of dinner?

   A. $\$52.46 + x$

   B. $\$52.46 - x$

   C. $\$52.46 \times x$

   D. $\$52.46 \div x$

2. Some friends go to a restaurant. The cost of food comes to \$119.79. If d represents the cost of the drinks, which of these expressions represents the total cost of drinks and food?

   F. $\$119.79 + d$

   G. $\$119.79 - d$

   H. $\$119.79 \times d$

   J. $\$119.79 \div d$

3. Anita is y years old. Her younger sister Manuela is $(y - 4)$ years old. The oldest, Renaldo, is $(2y - 1)$ years old. Which of these expressions represents the difference in age between Manuela and Renaldo?

   A. $(2y - 1) + (y - 4)$

   B. $(2y - 1) - (y - 4)$

   C. $(y - 4) \div (2y - 1)$

   D. $(2y - 1) - y - (y - 4)$

4. The expression $(m^2 - 11m)$ represents the perimeter of an equilateral triangle. Which of these expressions represents the combined length of two sides of the triangle?

   F. $2(m^2 - 11m)$

   G. $\frac{(m^2 - 11m)}{3}$

   H. $\frac{2(m^2 - 11m)}{3}$

   J. $\sqrt{(m^2 - 11m)}$

5. For one week, a bakery offers cookies for 30% off the usual price of c dollars. During that week, they sell 375 cookies at the discounted price. Which of these expressions represents the total amount, in dollars, that the bakery earned in cookie sales that week?

   A. $0.3(c - 375)$

   B. $375(0.3c)$

   C. $375(c - 0.3)$

   D. $375(c - 0.3c)$

6. In one month, David works h hours one week, $2h$ hours the second week, $(3h - 8)$ hours the third week, and $(h - 2)$ hours the fourth week. Which of the following expressions represents the average number of hours he worked each week that month?

   F. $h + 2h + (3h - 8) + (h - 2)$

   G. $(h + 2h + (3h - 8) + (h - 2)) - 4$

   H. $4 \times (h + 2h + (3h - 8) + (h - 2))$

   J. $\frac{h + 2h + (3h - 8) + (h - 2)}{4}$

7. The drawing below shows the dimensions of a wall and a window in Gerardo's house.

ECR

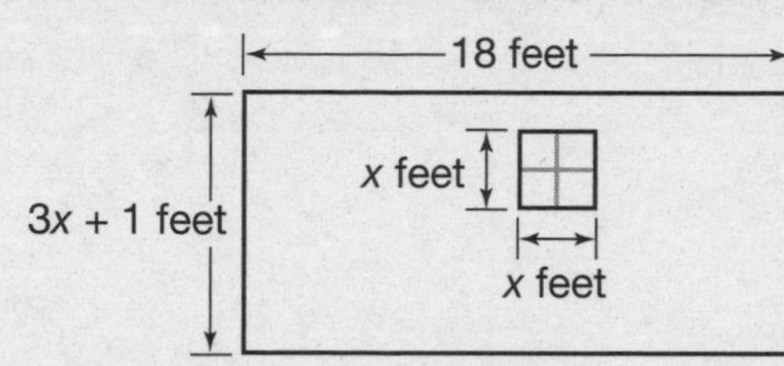

- Gerardo plans to paint the wall and not the window. What expression represents the area of the wall less the area of the window in square feet? Use mathematics to explain how you determined your answer. Use words, symbols, or both in your explanation.

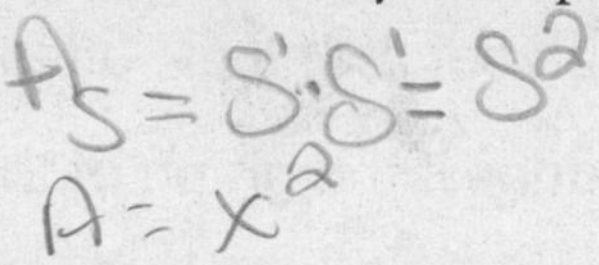

- If one can of paint covers 57 square feet of wall, what expression represents the number of cans of paint Gerardo needs to paint this wall? Use mathematics to explain how you determined your answer. Use words, symbols, or both in your explanation.

- If x is 3, what is the area of the wall less the area of the window in square feet?

- If x is 3, how many cans of paint does Gerardo need to paint the wall?

Lesson

7 Functional Relationships

- A **function** is a mathematical correspondence between two sets of values. In a function, each value of the first set pairs with only one value of the second set.
- The **domain** of a function is the first set of values, often represented by x. The **range** of a function is the second set of values, often represented by $f(x)$ or y.
- A function is **continuous** if the graph of the line that represents the function is not broken.
- The **maximum value** is a peak (high point) in the graph of the line that represents the function, while the **minimum value** is a valley (low point) in the graph.
- The **zeros** of a function are the values for x such that $f(x) = 0$. These are the values in which the function crosses the x-axis in the graph of the line that represents the function.

EXAMPLE

Look at the function that is graphed below.

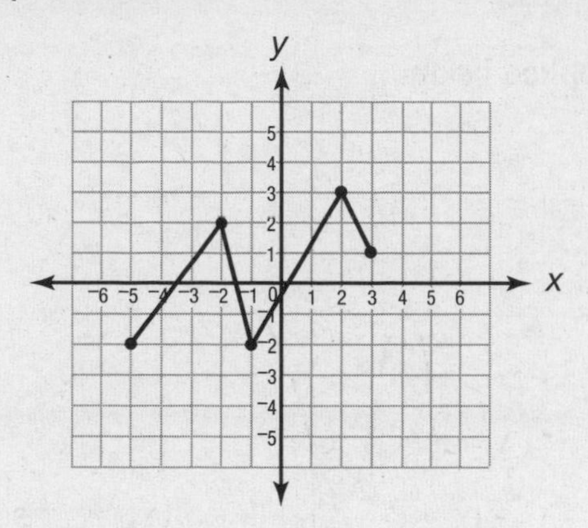

What is the range of this function?

STRATEGY **Find the lowest and highest *y*-values.**

STEP 1 Find the lowest *y*-value, the *y*-value for the lowest point in the graph of the function.

The lowest points in the graph are ($^-5$, $^-2$) and ($^-1$, $^-2$). The *y*-value for both of these points is $^-2$.

STEP 2 Find the greatest *y*-value, the *y*-value for the highest point in the graph of the function.

The highest point in the graph is (2, 3). The *y*-value for this point is 3.

STEP 3 Write the range as the set of points between and including these *y*-values, expressed using 'less than or equal to' signs.

$^-2 \leq y \leq 3$

SOLUTION **The range is $^-2 \leq y \leq 3$.**

COACHED EXAMPLE

Look at the function that is graphed below.

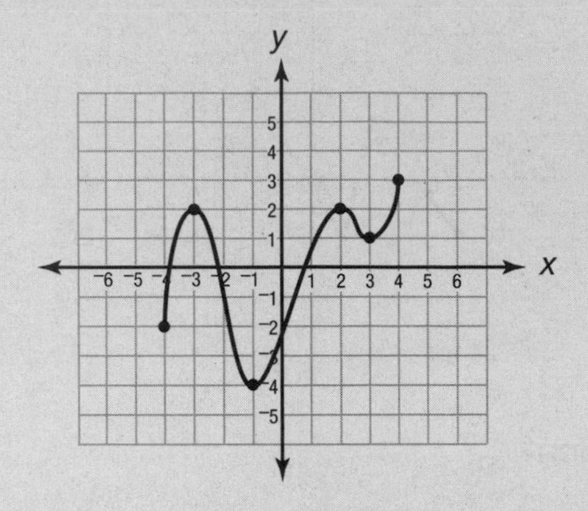

What is the domain of this function?

THINKING IT THROUGH

The point that is farthest left is ___________.

The x-value for that point is ___________.

The point that is farthest right is ___________.

The x-value for that point is ___________.

The domain of this function is ___________ $\leq x \leq$ ___________.

Lesson Practice

Choose the correct answer.

1. Look at the graph below.

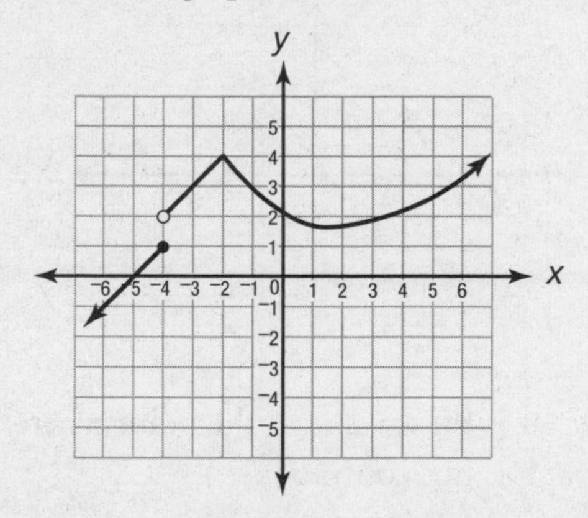

What is the x-value of the point where the graph is not continuous?

A. $^-4$

B. $^-2$

C. 1

D. 4

2. Look at the function that is graphed below.

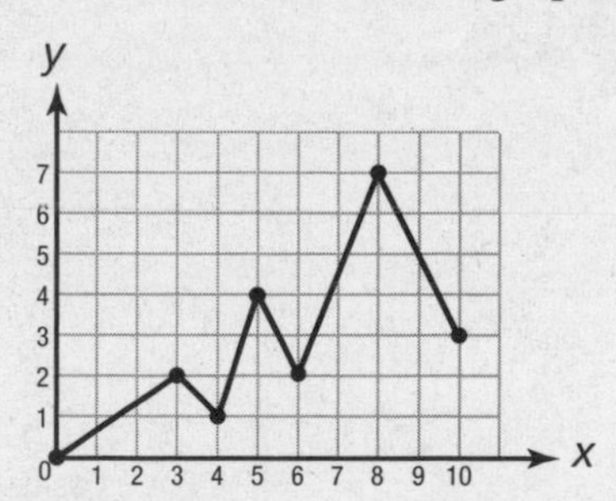

What is the range of this function?

F. $0 \le y \le 7$

G. $0 \le y \le 8$

H. $1 \le y \le 10$

J. $1 \le y \le 7$

3. Look at the function that is graphed below.

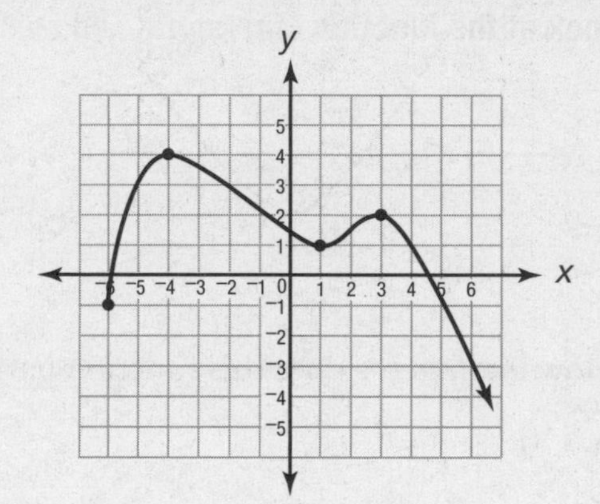

What is the maximum value of this function?

A. 2

B. 4

C. 6

D. 7

4. Look at the function that is graphed below.

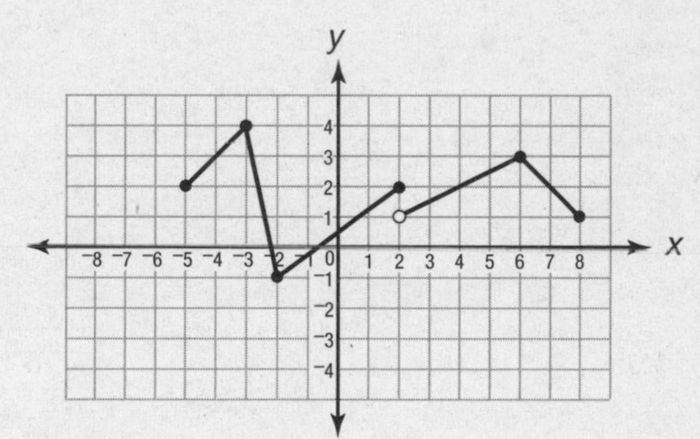

What is the domain of this function?

F. $^-5 \le x \le 8$

G. $^-3 \le x \le 4$

H. $^-1 \le x \le 4$

J. $1 \le x \le 2$

5. Look at the function that is graphed below.

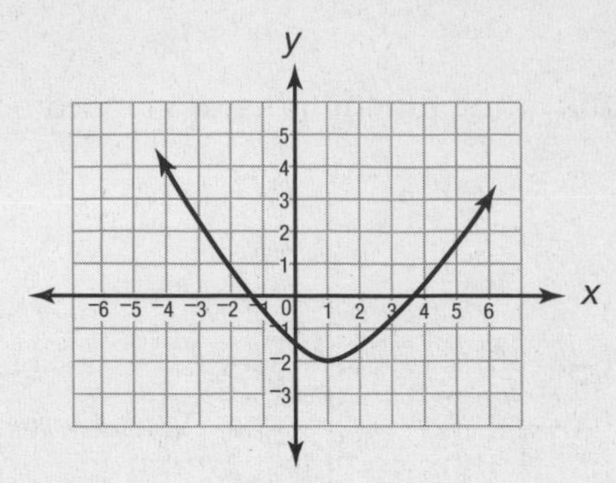

How many zeros does this function have?

A. 0

B. 1

C. 2

D. 3

Use the Response Grid to complete Number 6.

6. Look at the graph below.

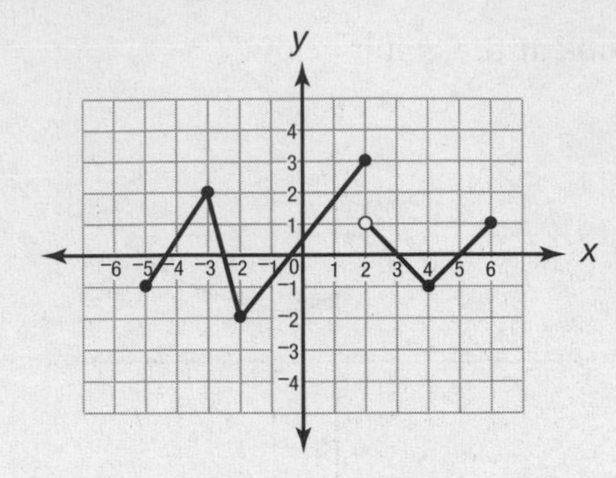

What is the x-value of the point where the graph is <u>not</u> continuous?

7.
BCR

Look at the function that is graphed below.

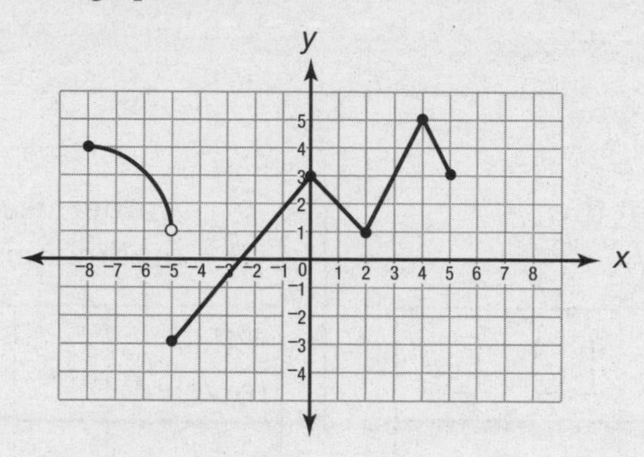

- What is the domain of this function? •

- What is the range of this function?

- What are the maximum and minimum values of this function?

- How many zeros does this function have?

HSA Review

1 **Look at the pattern in the table below.**

Figure	◻	◫	◫	◫
Number of Sections	1	2	3	4

If the pattern continues, how many sections will there be in the eighth figure?

A 5

B 8

C 16

D 32

2 **Look at the pattern below.**

$$\frac{2}{5}, 1, \frac{5}{2}, \frac{25}{4}, \ldots$$

If the pattern continues, what will be the next term?

F $\frac{4}{25}$

G $\frac{5}{2}$

H 5

J $\frac{125}{8}$

3 **Amber uses the following table to predict her gas mileage.**

miles traveled	10	20	30	40	50	95
gas (gallons)	0.30	0.60	0.90	1.20	1.50	?

If she plans to take a 95-mile road trip, how many gallons of gas will she use?

A 1.80

B 2.85

C 8.30

D 9.50

4 **Look at the graph below.**

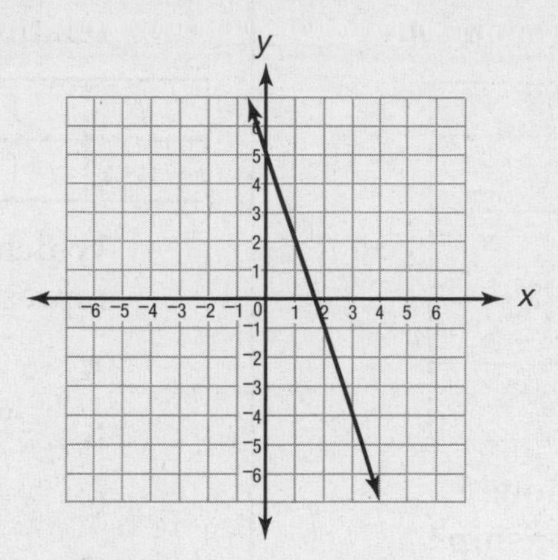

Which of these tables corresponds to the line that is graphed?

F

x	y
0	5
1	2
2	−1
3	−4
4	−7

G

x	y
0	3
1	2
2	1
3	0
4	−1

H

x	y
0	−2
1	0
2	2
3	4
4	10

J

x	y
0	5
1	8
2	11
3	14
4	17

5 **The table below shows a relationship between *m* and *n*.**

m	n
0	1
1	$\frac{4}{3}$
2	$\frac{7}{3}$
3	4

Which of these equations represents this relationship?

A $n = 3m^2 + \frac{1}{3}$

B $n = 3\left(m^2 + \frac{1}{3}\right)$

C $n = \frac{m^2 + 1}{3}$

D $n = \frac{m^2 + 3}{3}$

6 **Look at the pattern below.**

$^{-}2, {}^{-}16, {}^{-}54, {}^{-}128, {}^{-}250, \ldots$

If the pattern continues, what will be the eighth term?

F $^{-}216$

G $^{-}432$

H $^{-}512$

J $^{-}1{,}024$

7 **The table below shows a relationship between *y* and *z*.**

y	1	2	3	4	5
z	41	13	$^{-}63$	$^{-}211$	$^{-}455$

Which of these equations represents this relationship?

A $z = {}^{-}4y + 45$

B $z = 41y$

C $z = {}^{-}y^3 + 21$

D $z = {}^{-}4y^3 + 45$

8 **The expression $(3x^2 + 7)$ represents the perimeter of a regular pentagon. Which of these expressions represents the length of one side?**

F $\frac{(3x^2 + 7)}{5}$

G $(3x^2 + 7) \times 5$

H $\sqrt{3x^2 + 7}$

J $(3x^2 + 7)^5$

9 **The total cost of going skiing for one day is $79.15, which includes renting the skis and the cost of a one-day pass. If *s* represents the cost of renting the skis, which of these expressions represents the cost of a one-day pass?**

A $\$79.15 + s$

B $\$79.15 - s$

C $\$79.15 \times s$

D $\$79.15 \div s$

Use the Response Grid to complete Number 10.

10 **Look at the function that is graphed below.**

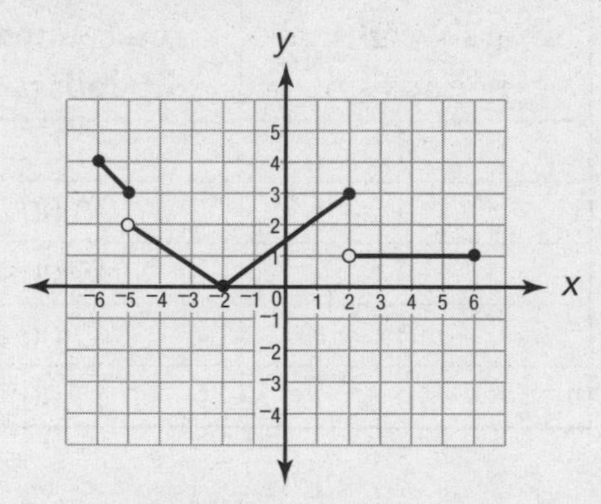

How many zeros does this function have?

11 **ECR** **Groovy Groomers charge customers a base fee of $20 plus $0.50 per pound for dog grooming. Their competitor, Posh Pets, charges $1.25 per pound to groom a dog.**

TABLE I

Dog's Weight, in pounds (p)	Total Amount, in dollars (t)
10	25.00
20	30.00
30	35.00
40	40.00
50	45.00

TABLE II

Dog's Weight, in pounds (p)	Total Amount, in dollars (t)
10	12.50
20	25.00
30	37.50
40	50.00
50	62.50

- **Which table represents the rates that Groovy Groomers charges its customers? Use mathematics to explain how you determined your answer. Use words, symbols, or both in your explanation.**

- **What equation represents the total amount (t) charged by Groovy Groomers for a customer with a dog that weighs p pounds?**

- **What equation represents the total amount (t) charged by Posh Pets for a customer with a dog that weighs p pounds?**

- **Which grooming service is less expensive for larger dogs?**

CHAPTER

Goal 1, Expectation 1.2

Modeling and Interpreting Real-World Situations

Lesson

8 Solving Word Problems Using Variables and Equations

To solve a word problem, assign variables to unknown quantities. Then look for the following common words to help you choose the operations needed to set up an equation:

- Addition: a sum of, a total of, plus, and, increase
- Subtraction: a difference of, less than, minus, take away, decrease, less
- Multiplication: a product of, multiplied by, times, in groups of
- Division: a quotient of, an average of, a ratio of, divided by, per, over

EXAMPLE

Ernesto went to an amusement park. It costs \$5 to enter the amusement park and \$0.50 for a ride ticket. If Ernesto spent a total of \$12.50, how many ride tickets did he buy?

STRATEGY **Write a word equation.**

STEP 1 Identify the known and unknown quantities.

Known: cost to enter park, cost for a ride ticket, total spent

Unknown: amount spent on tickets, how many ride tickets Ernesto bought

STEP 2 Write a word equation.

Total spent = cost to enter park + amount spent on tickets

Amount spent on tickets = cost for a ride ticket × number of ride tickets Ernesto bought

Total spent = cost to enter park + cost for a ride ticket × number of ride tickets Ernesto bought

STEP 3 Assign a variable to the unknown quantity in the word equation.

\$5 = cost to enter park

\$0.50 = cost for a ride ticket

\$12.50 = total spent

t = number of ride tickets Ernesto bought

STEP 4 Plug the variable and the known quantities into the word equation.

Total spent = cost to enter park + cost for a ride ticket × number of ride tickets Ernesto bought

$12.50 = 5 + 0.50 \times t$

STEP 5 Solve for the unknown.

$$12.50 = 5 + 0.50 \times t$$

$$12.50 - 5 = 5 - 5 + 0.50 \times t$$

$$7.5 = 0.50 \times t$$

$$\frac{7.5}{0.50} = \frac{(0.50 \times t)}{0.50}$$

$$15 = t$$

SOLUTION **Ernesto bought 15 tickets.**

COACHED EXAMPLE

Nellie collects special-edition coins. So far, she has 6 of the coins. A new special-edition coin comes out every 4 months. In how many months will she have all 50 special edition coins in her collection?

THINKING IT THROUGH

How many special edition coins are there in all to collect? ____________

How many coins does Nellie have now? ____________

How many coins does she still have left to collect? ____________

How often does a new coin come out? ____________

It will take her ____________ months to collect the coins she still has left to collect.

Lesson Practice

Choose the correct answer.

1. A row of turnstiles allows people to exit an auditorium at a steady rate of 3 people per second. There are 800 people in the auditorium. Which of these equations represents the number of people (p) remaining in the auditorium after s seconds?

A. $p = 800 - 3s$

B. $p = 800 + 3s$

C. $p = \frac{3s}{800}$

D. $p = \frac{800}{3s}$

2. At the bowling alley, the rental cost for bowling shoes is $5 plus an additional $0.80 per hour. Rita bowled for 4.5 hours. What is the total amount Rita paid to rent the bowling shoes?

F. $3.60

G. $8.60

H. $23.30

J. $26.10

3. The Browns go on a road trip. They begin with 12.5 gallons of gas in their car. The car uses 29.5 miles per gallon. Which of these equations could Mrs. Brown use to find the total number of gallons (g) left in the gas tank after m miles of driving?

A. $g = 12.5 - 29.5m$

B. $g = 12.5 - \frac{m}{29.5}$

C. $g = 12.5 + 29.5m$

D. $g = 12.5 + \frac{m}{29.5}$

4. Henrietta is buying gear for her volleyball team. She orders one volleyball for $17. Uniforms cost $13.99 each. She spends a total of $226.85. How many uniforms did she buy?

F. 7

G. 13

H. 15

J. 16

5. Marigold works at a bakery. She opens a bag of flour that holds 40 cups. The muffin recipe she uses calls for 3 cups of flour for each batch of muffins. She makes muffins until there are only 4 cups of flour left. How many batches of muffins did she make?

A. 5

B. 10

C. 12

D. 13

Use the Response Grid to complete Number 6.

6. Bruno has a stamp collection that has 42 stamps. He gets an additional pack of 12 stamps each week. In how many weeks will he have a total of 210 stamps in his collection?

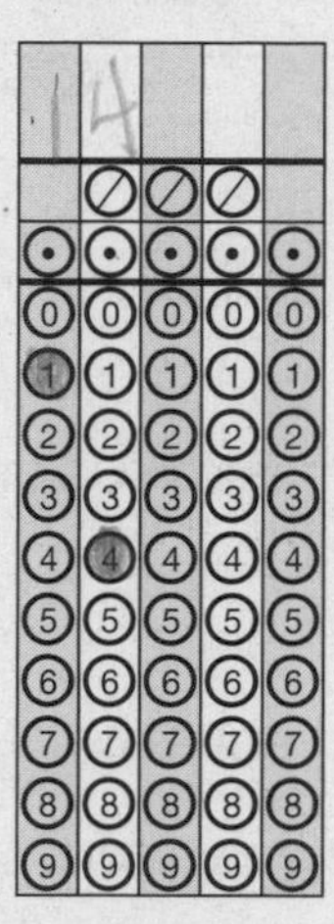

7. BCR — Sun is making beaded jewelry to sell at the craft fair. She has 650 beads. She uses half of those to make necklaces. The bracelets that she makes require 24 beads each.

- Write an equation that represents the number of beads (n) Sun has left if she makes b bracelets.

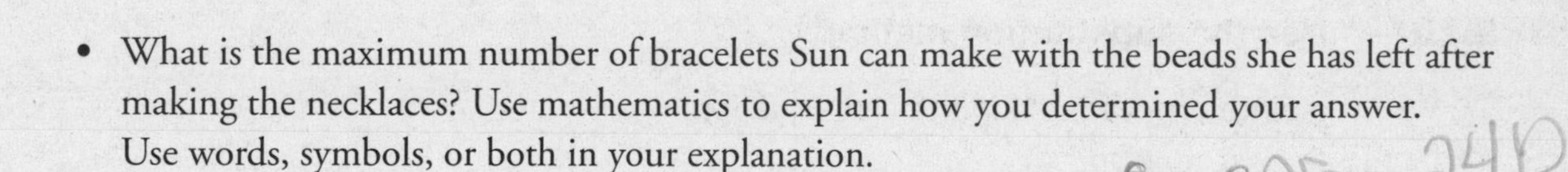

- What is the maximum number of bracelets Sun can make with the beads she has left after making the necklaces? Use mathematics to explain how you determined your answer. Use words, symbols, or both in your explanation.

- How many beads would Sun have left if she made only 4 bracelets?

Lesson

Solving Problems Using More Than One Equation

Sometimes problems will have two equations that are related by the same two variables. You can use the **substitution method** to solve these problems:

1. Isolate one variable on one side of the equal sign in the first equation. The expression on the other side of the equal sign can be substituted for that variable in the second equation.
2. Substitute that equivalent expression for the same variable in the second equation.
3. You now have an equation that has only one type of variable, so you can solve for that variable.
4. To solve for the first variable, substitute the known value of the second variable into your first equation and solve for the first variable.

EXAMPLE

Solve the following equations.

$z + 3 = 2y$

$3z = y - 6$

STRATEGY **Use the substitution method.**

STEP 1 Isolate one variable in the first equation.

$z + 3 = 2y$

$z + 3 - 3 = 2y - 3$

$z = 2y - 3$

STEP 2 Substitute that expression into the second equation.

$3z = y - 6$

$3(2y - 3) = y - 6$

STEP 3 Solve for y.

$3(2y - 3) = y - 6$

$6y - 9 = y - 6$

$6y - 9 + 9 = y - 6 + 9$

$6y - y = y + 3 - y$

$5y = 3$

$y = \frac{3}{5}$

STEP 4 Substitute the known value of y into your first equation and solve for z.

$z + 3 = 2y$

$z + 3 = 2\left(\frac{3}{5}\right)$

$z + 3 = \frac{6}{5}$

$z + 3 - 3 = \frac{6}{5} - 3$

$z = \frac{6}{5} - \frac{15}{5}$

$z = -\frac{9}{5}$

SOLUTION **The solution is $y = \frac{3}{5}$ and $z = -\frac{9}{5}$**

COACHED EXAMPLE

Frida and Guy buy CDs and DVDs at a yard sale. Frida buys 2 CDs and 4 DVDs for $11.50. Guy buys 3 CDs and 2 DVDs for $10.25. What is the cost, in dollars, of each DVD?

THINKING IT THROUGH

Assign a variable to the cost of a CD. ____________

Assign a variable to the cost of a DVD. ____________

Using those variables, what equation represents Frida's purchase? ____________

What equation represents Guy's purchase? ____________

Solve the equation for Frida's purchase for the cost of a CD. ____________

Rewrite the equation for Guy's purchase using the equivalent expression for the cost of a CD. ____________

The cost of a DVD is ____________.

Lesson Practice

Choose the correct answer.

1. What are the solutions for x and y in the following equations?

   $y = 4x - 1$

   $2y = 3x - 22$

   A. $x = {}^{-}17, y = {}^{-}4$
   B. $x = {}^{-}4, y = {}^{-}17$
   C. $x = 4, y = 15$
   D. $x = 15, y = 4$

2. What are the solutions for m and n in the following equations?

   $n = 6m - 4$

   $4n = 12m - 8$

   F. $m = \frac{1}{3}, n = {}^{-}2$
   G. $m = \frac{2}{3}, n = 0$
   H. $m = \frac{3}{2}, n = 5$
   J. $m = 3, n = 14$

3. There are 36 students in the chess club. The number of boys in the chess club is six more than half the number of girls. How many girls are in the chess club?

   A. 12
   B. 16
   C. 20
   D. 24

4. Tammy spent \$140.95 to buy pairs of socks and shoes. She bought a total of 5 pairs of items. Each pair of shoes cost \$44.99 and each pair of socks cost \$2.99. How many pairs of each clothing item did Tammy buy?

   F. 1 pair of socks and 4 pairs of shoes
   G. 2 pairs of socks and 3 pairs of shoes
   H. 17 pairs of socks and 2 pairs of shoes
   J. 32 pairs of socks and 1 pair of shoes

5. Chris and Amy are buying lunch at a taco stand. Chris buys 3 tacos and 5 jalapeno poppers for \$4.22. Amy buys 4 tacos and 2 jalapeno poppers for \$4.46. What is the cost, in dollars, of each taco?

   A. \$0.25
   B. \$0.99
   C. \$1.73
   D. \$2.97

6. Tim has 3 more than half as many baseball cards as Curtis. Together, the boys have 42 baseball cards. How many baseball cards does Tim have?

   F. 26
   G. 24
   H. 18
   J. 16

Use the Response Grid to complete Number 7.

7. The table below shows the fee plans for two online video-rental services.

	Sign-up Fee	**Monthly Fee**
Dee's DVDs Online	$10	$30
Millie's Mail-In Movies	$25	$25

For what number of months is the total cost the same for both online video-rental services?

8. At Mickey's Rent-a-Van, there are two fee plans for renting a van. The table below outlines both plans.

ECR

Fee Plan	Base Fee	Cost per Mile
A	\$45	\$0.50
B	\$35	\$1.00

- Write an equation for the total cost (t) to a customer for renting under Fee Plan A. Write an equation for the total cost (t) for Fee Plan B. Let m represent the number of miles the customer will drive the van.

- How many miles would the customer have to drive for the total cost of renting under plans A and B to be equal? Use mathematics to explain how you determined your answer. Use words, symbols, or both in your explanation.

- A customer plans to drive 40 miles. To pay the lowest cost of renting a van, which fee plan should he choose? Use mathematics to justify your answer.

Lesson 10 Interpreting Graphs of Linear Functions

- A **linear equation** is an equation that relates two variables that are each to the first power. Linear equations form lines when graphed.
- The **slope** of a line is the change in y over the change in x.
- The **x-intercept** is the x-value of the point at which the line intersects the x-axis, where $y = 0$.
- The **y-intercept** is the y-value of the point at which the line intersects the y-axis, where $x = 0$.

When a linear equation is in the form $y = mx + b$, the letter m stands for the slope of the line and the letter b stands for the y-intercept. For example, the graph of the equation $y = 2x + 3$ is shown below. The slope, m, is 2. The y-intercept, b, is 3.

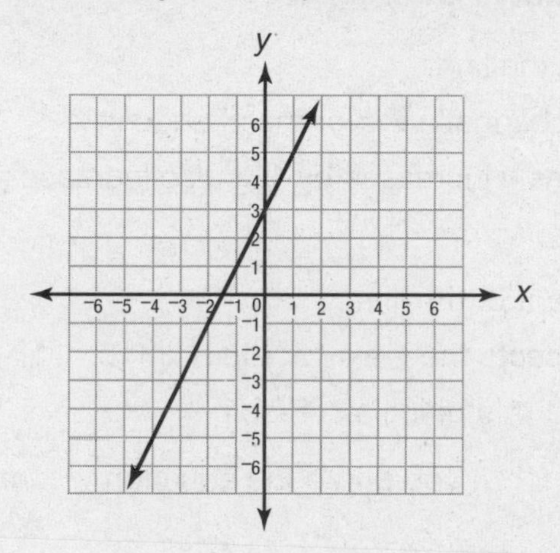

EXAMPLE 1

Look at the line that is graphed below.

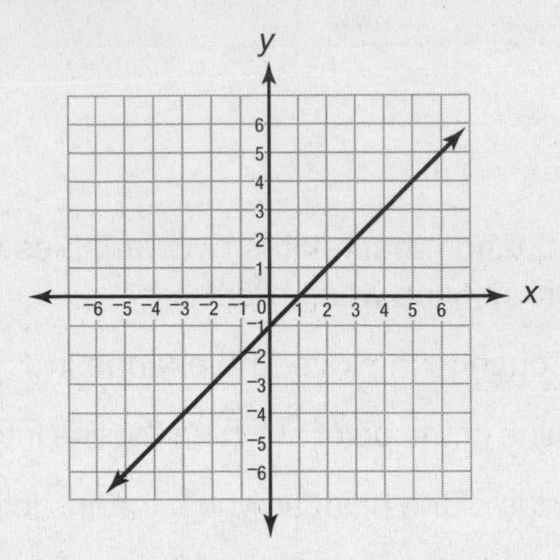

What equation describes this line?

STRATEGY **Find the slope and *y*-intercept.**

STEP 1 Find the slope of the line.

Slope is the change in *y* over the change in *x*.

For this line, as *y* increases by 1, *x* also increases by 1.

The slope is $\frac{1}{1}$, so $m = 1$.

STEP 2 Find the *y*-intercept of the line.

The line intersects the *y*-axis at the point $(0, {}^{-}1)$.

The *y*-value at this point is $^{-}1$, so $b = {}^{-}1$.

STEP 3 Plug your values for *m* and *b* into the equation $y = mx + b$.

$y = mx + b$

$y = (1)x + ({}^{-}1)$

$y = x - 1$

SOLUTION **The equation for the line is $y = x - 1$.**

EXAMPLE 2

What is the x-intercept of the line $y = -\frac{1}{2}x + 2$?

STRATEGY **Set $y = 0$ in the equation.**

STEP 1 Substitute $y = 0$.

$$y = -\frac{1}{2}x + 2$$
$$0 = -\frac{1}{2}x + 2$$

STEP 2 Solve the equation for x.

$$0 = -\frac{1}{2}x + 2$$
$$0 - 2 = -\frac{1}{2}x + 2 - 2$$
$$^-2 = -\frac{1}{2}x$$
$$(^-2)(^-2) = (^-2)\left(-\frac{1}{2}\right)x$$
$$4 = x$$

SOLUTION **The x-intercept is $x = 4$.**

COACHED EXAMPLE

What equation represents a line with a slope of -3 and a y-intercept of 5?

THINKING IT THROUGH

The slope of the line is $m =$ ____________.

The y-intercept of the line is $b =$ ____________.

What general form for a linear equation uses the letters m and b? ____________.

The equation for the line in this form is $y =$ ____________.

Lesson Practice

Choose the correct answer.

1. Look at the line that is graphed below.

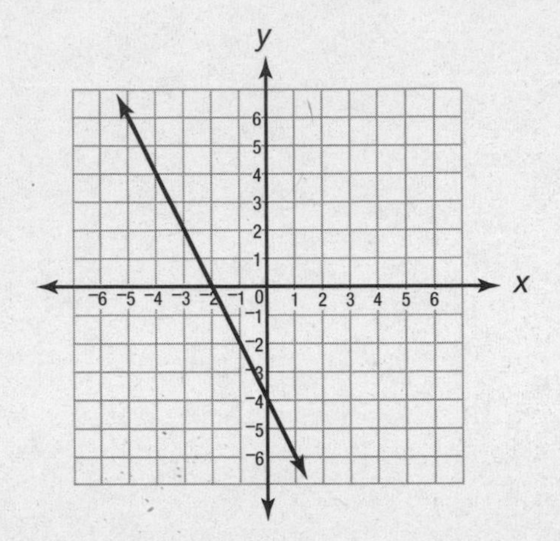

Which of these equations describes this line?

A. $y = {}^{-}2x - 4$

B. $y = {}^{-}4x - 2$

C. $y = {}^{-}4x + 2$

D. $y = {}^{-}2x + 4$

2. Look at the line that is graphed below.

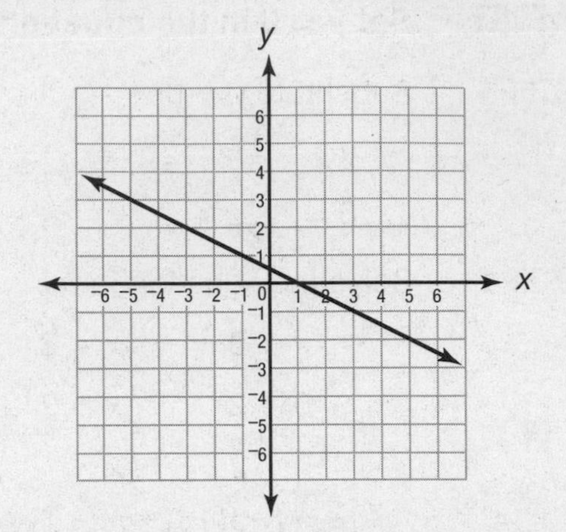

Which of these equations describes this line?

F. $y = {}^{-}\frac{1}{2x} - \frac{1}{2}$

G. $y = {}^{-}\frac{1}{2}x - 1$

H. $y = {}^{-}\frac{1}{2}x + \frac{1}{2}$

J. $y = {}^{-}\frac{1}{2}x + 1$

3. Which of these equations represents a line with a slope of 16 and a *y*-intercept of 7?

A. $y = 7x - 16$

B. $y = 7x + 16$

C. $y = 16x - 7$

D. $y = 16x + 7$

4. Which of these equations represents a line with an *x*-intercept of 2 and a *y*-intercept of $^{-}5$?

F. $y = {}^{-}5x - 2$

G. $y = {}^{-}\frac{5}{2}x - 5$

H. $y = \frac{5}{2}x - 5$

J. $y = 2x - \frac{5}{2}$

5. The formula below converts Fahrenheit temperatures (F) into approximate Celsius temperatures (C).

$$C = \frac{5}{9}F - 18$$

Which of these graphs represents this formula?

A.

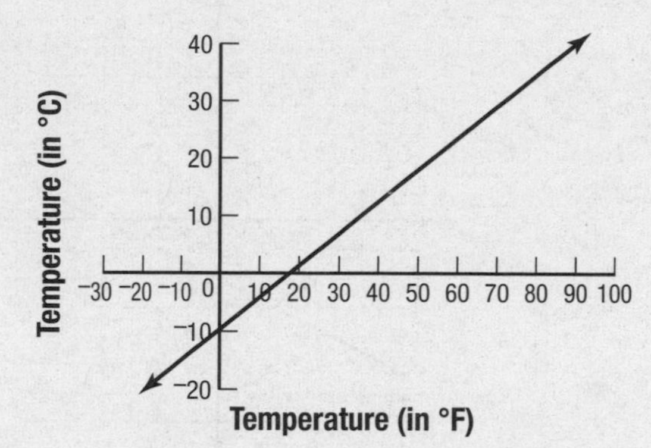

B.

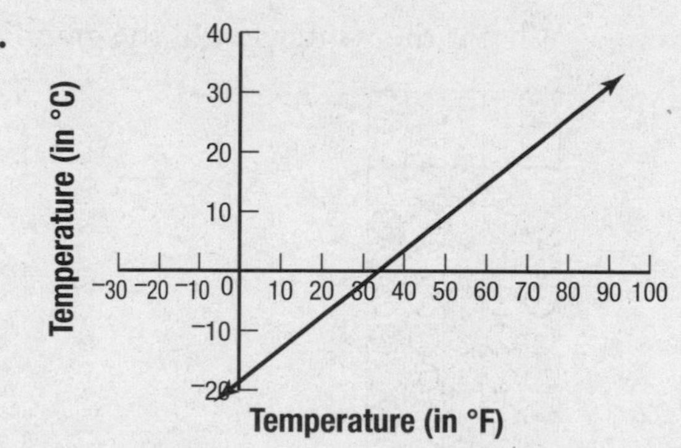

C.

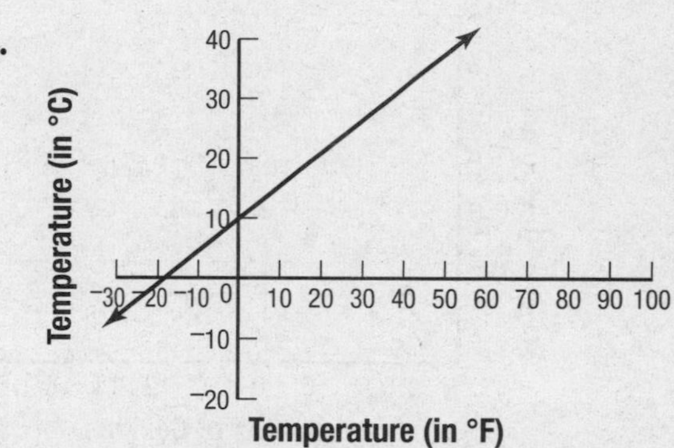

D.

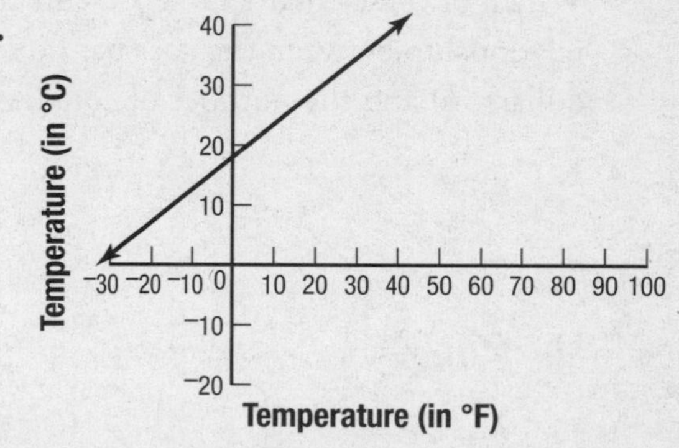

6. Yummy Gifts sells boxes of fancy cookies. The graph below represents the total cost per box based on the number of cookies in the box.

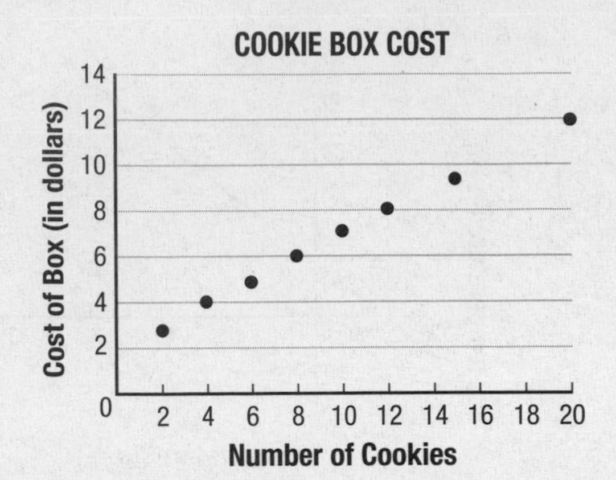

Which of these equations represents the relationship between the cost per box in dollars (b) and the number of cookies (c)?

F. $b = -\frac{1}{2}c + 2$

G. $b = \frac{1}{2}c + 2$

H. $b = 2c + \frac{1}{2}$

J. $b = 2c - \frac{1}{2}$

Use the Response Grid to complete Number 7.

7. Look at the line that is graphed below.

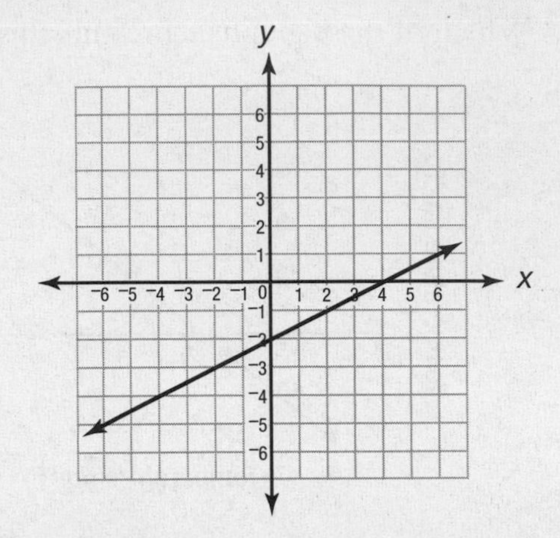

What is the x-intercept of the graph?

8. **ECR** Frankie's family sells balloons at the carnival. Frankie keeps track of how many balloons they have left every hour. The graph below represents the relationship between the number of hours that have passed since the carnival opened and the number of balloons they have left.

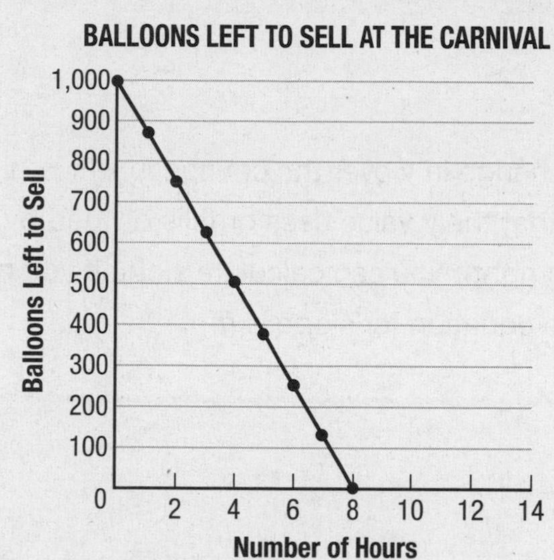

- What does the y-intercept of the graph represent?

- What does the x-intercept of the graph represent?

- If the slope of the line shown in the graph above is $^{-}125$, what equation represents the relationship between the number of hours that have passed since the carnival opened (h) and the number of balloons they have left (b)?

- If the carnival opens at 9:00 A.M., at what hour does Frankie's family run out of balloons to sell?

Finding Slope

The **slope** of a line is the change in *y* over the change in *x*. It is also called the "rise over run," which means the amount that the *y* value rises or falls divided by the amount that the *x*-value increases (runs from left to right). You can calculate slope if you have two coordinates for a line, (x_1, y_1) and (x_2, y_2). The equation for slope is $m = \frac{y_2 - y_1}{x_2 - x_1}$.

EXAMPLE 1

Look at the graph below.

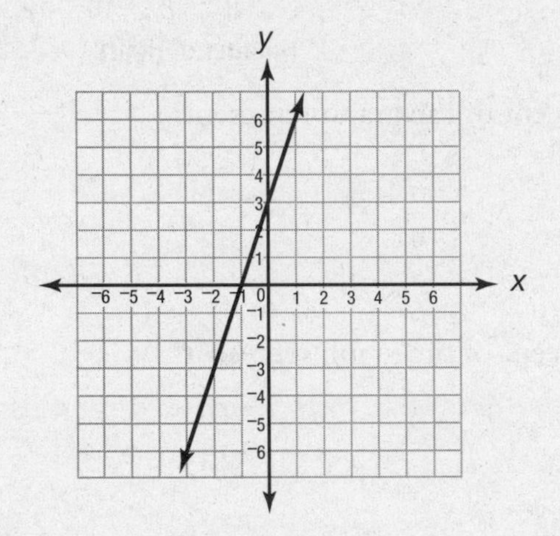

What is the slope of the line?

STRATEGY **Calculate rise over run.**

STEP 1 Identify two coordinates on the graph.

The x-intercept is at point ($^-1$, 0).

The y-intercept is at point (0, 3).

STEP 2 Plug the *x* and *y* values into the equation for slope.

$$m = \frac{y_2 - y_1}{x_2 - x_1}$$

$$m = \frac{3 - 0}{0 - (^-1)}$$

$$m = \frac{3}{1}$$

$$m = 3$$

SOLUTION **The slope of the line is 3.**

EXAMPLE 2

What is the slope of the line described by the equation $x = 2y - 4$?

Strategy **Write the equation in the form $y = mx + b$.**

STEP 1 Write the equation in the form $y = mx + b$.

$$x = 2y - 4$$
$$x + 4 = 2y - 4 + 4$$
$$x + 4 = 2y$$
$$\frac{1}{2}(x + 4) = \frac{1}{2}(2y)$$
$$\frac{1}{2}x + 2 = y$$
$$y = \frac{1}{2}x + 2$$

STEP 2 Identify the slope as the coefficient of x.

$$y = mx + b$$
$$y = \frac{1}{2}x + 2$$
$$m = \frac{1}{2}$$

SOLUTION **The slope of the line is $\frac{1}{2}$.**

COACHED EXAMPLE

An animal shelter houses 200 cats. The number of these cats (c) that are adopted over a week depends on the cost of the adoption fee (f), in dollars. This relationship is represented by the equation shown below.

$$c = {}^{-}10f + 200$$

What does the slope of this equation represent?

THINKING IT THROUGH

The slope is multiplied by the fee, which determines how many cats are adopted.

How many cats are adopted if the cats are free, $f = 0$? ____________

How many cats are adopted if the adoption fee is \$1, $f = 1$? ____________

How many cats are adopted if $f = 2$? ____________

____________ fewer cats are adopted for every dollar the adoption fee increases.

Lesson Practice

Choose the correct answer.

1. Look at the graph below.

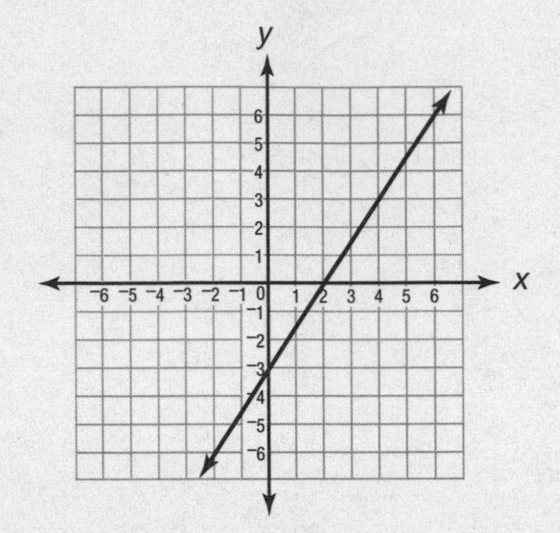

What is the slope of the line?

A. $-\frac{3}{2}$

B. $^{-}1$

C. 1

D. $\frac{3}{2}$

2. Look at the graph below.

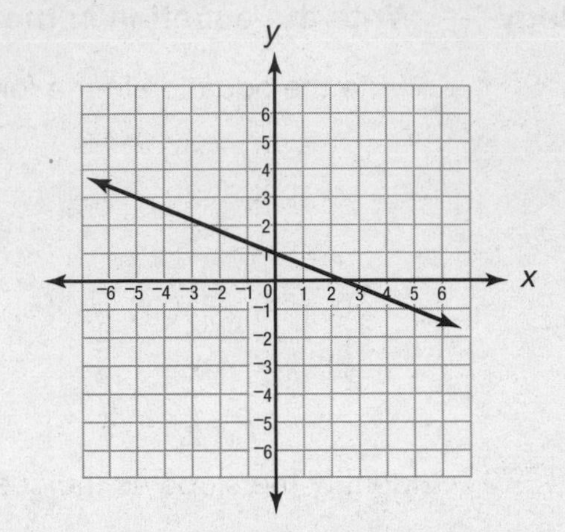

What is the slope of the line?

F. $-\frac{5}{2}$

G. $-\frac{2}{5}$

H. $^{-}1$

J. $\frac{5}{2}$

3. A line is defined by points at (250, 10) and ($^{-}150$, 14). What is the slope of the line?

A. $-\frac{1}{100}$

B. $\frac{1}{100}$

C. $\frac{3}{50}$

D. $\frac{25}{6}$

4. Felisha has a part-time job after school. The graph below shows a linear model of the amount of money that Felisha puts into her savings account from her job earnings each month.

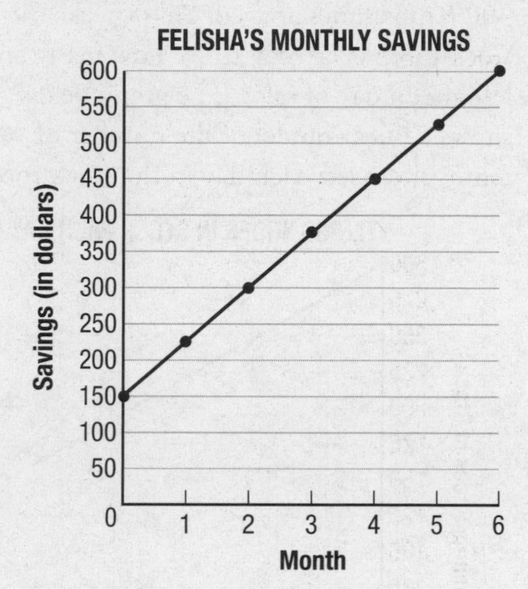

What is the slope, in dollars per month, of this linear model?

F. 25

G. 50

H. 75

J. 150

5. Sean's father owns a chocolate factory. One of the vats in his factory empties chocolate slowly onto a conveyor belt to form candies. The graph below shows a linear model of the relationship between the amount of chocolate in the vat and the hour of the day.

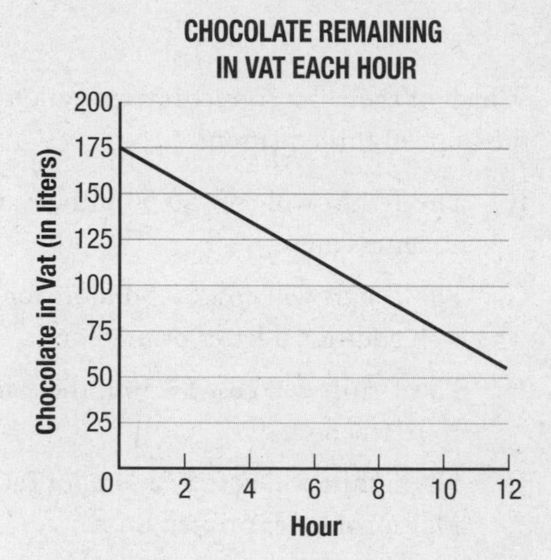

Which of these is a correct interpretation of the slope of this graph?

A. The slope describes the rate at which the chocolate is added to the vat.

B. The slope describes the rate at which the chocolate empties from the vat.

C. The slope describes the amount of chocolate in the vat at the end of the day.

D. The slope describes the amount of chocolate in the vat at the beginning of the day.

6. Lena is ordering T-shirts for the pep squad. She wants the T-shirts to have a word or phrase on them. The price of each T-shirt (p), in dollars, depends on the number of letters (l) printed on it. This relationship is represented by the equation shown below.

$$p = 7 + \frac{1}{2}l$$

Which of these is a correct interpretation of the slope of this equation?

F. The T-shirt will cost \$0.50 if there are no letters on it.

G. The T-shirt will cost \$0.50 more for each additional letter printed on it.

H. The T-shirt will cost \$3.50 if there are no letters on it.

J. The T-shirt will cost \$7 more for each additional letter printed on it.

Use the Response Grid to complete Number 7.

7. Yuki sells shoes at the local sports store. At the beginning of the month, a shipment of 300 tennis shoes arrived. Yuki checks the stock room every day to see how many are left after a day of sales. The graph below shows a linear model of the number of tennis shoes left each day in the stock room.

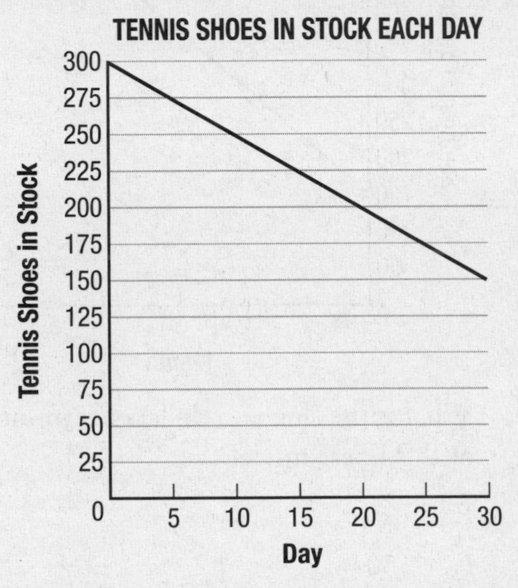

What is the number of tennis shoes sold per day according to this linear model?

8. Tito opens a savings account with money he has received for his birthday. He adds money from
ECR a part-time job every week. The amount of money that Tito has in his savings account (s), in dollars, depends on how many weeks he has been saving (w). This relationship is represented by the equation shown below.

$$s = 200 + 40w$$

- What is the slope of the line described by the equation?

- What does this slope represent?

- According to the equation, how much money did Tito receive for his birthday and place in the savings account?

Intersecting Lines

Two or more equations represent a **system.** For linear equations, if the lines represented by the equations intersect, the point at which they intersect is called the **solution** of that system of equations. In a system of lines that do not intersect (lines that are parallel), there is no solution. To find the solution of a system of equations, you can graph the lines and find the point at which they intersect.

Another way to find the solution of a system is to use substitution. Substitute the equivalent expression of one variable in the first equation for the same variable in the second equation and solve.

EXAMPLE 1

Look at the graph below.

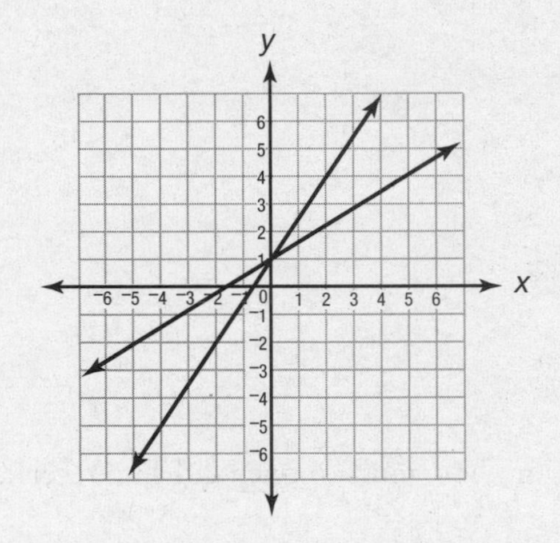

Is there a solution for this system? If so, what is the solution?

STRATEGY **Find where the lines intersect.**

STEP 1 Determine if the lines are parallel or intersecting.

The lines touch one another, so they are intersecting lines.

STEP 2 Find the point at which they intersect.

The point at which they intersect is (0, 1).

SOLUTION **The solution of the system is (0, 1).**

EXAMPLE 2

Look at the system of equations below.

$y = 4 - x$

$y = 2x + 4$

What is the solution for the system?

Strategy **Use substitution to solve the system.**

STEP 1 Isolate one variable in the first equation.

$$y = 4 - x$$

STEP 2 Substitute that expression into the second equation.

$$y = 2x + 4$$
$$4 - x = 2x + 4$$

STEP 3 Solve for x.

$$4 - x = 2x + 4$$
$$4 - x - 4 = 2x + 4 - 4$$
$$^{-}x = 2x$$
$$^{-}x - 2x = 2x - 2x$$
$$^{-}3x = 0$$
$$x = 0$$

STEP 4 Substitute the known value of x into your first equation and solve for y.

$$y = 4 - x$$
$$y = 4 - 0$$
$$y = 4$$

SOLUTION **The solution of the system is (0, 4).**

COACHED EXAMPLE

Look at the system of equations below.

$$y = 3 - x$$
$$2x - 3y = -4$$

What is the solution for the system?

THINKING IT THROUGH

What expression represents y? ___________

When you substitute this expression for y in the second equation, you get the following equation: ___________.

Solving for x gives $x =$ ___________.

When you substitute this value for x in the first equation, you get the following equation: ___________.

Solving for y gives $y =$ ___________.

They intersect at the point ___________.

Lesson Practice

Choose the correct answer.

1. Look at the graph below.

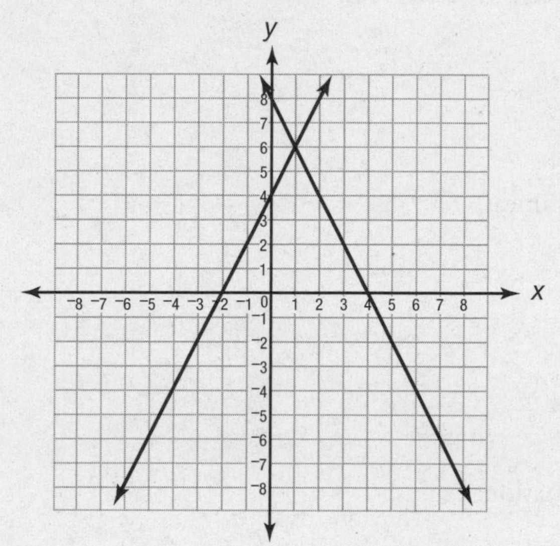

Which of these statements describes the relationship between the two lines?

A. The lines never intersect.

B. They intersect at the point (1, 6).

C. They intersect at the point (6, 1).

D. They intersect at the point (8, 4).

2. Look at the graph below.

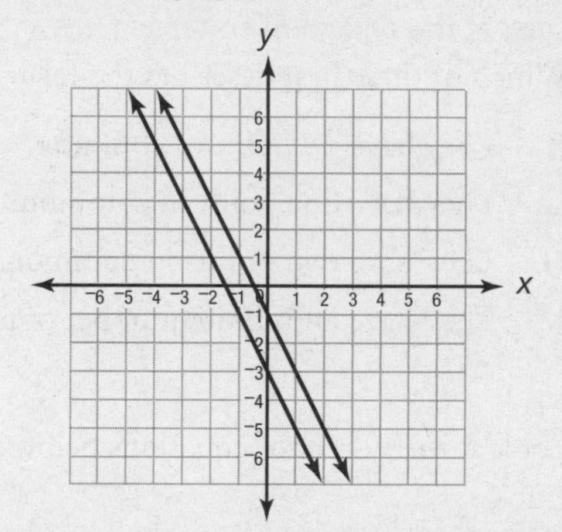

Which of these statements describes the relationship between the two lines?

F. The lines never intersect.

G. They intersect at the point $(0, ^-1)$.

H. They intersect at the point $(0, ^-3)$.

J. They intersect at the point $(^-1, ^-3)$.

3. Look at the system of equations below.

$y = x - 3$

$y = {}^-3x + 5$

Which of these describes this system?

A. two parallel lines

B. two equations of the same line

C. two lines that intersect only at $(2, ^-1)$

D. two lines that intersect only at (2, 1)

4. Look at the system of equations below.

$y = 5x - 6$

$\frac{1}{3}y = \frac{5}{3}x - 2$

Which of these best describes the relationship between the two lines?

F. They have no point in common.

G. They have one point in common.

H. They have two points in common.

J. They have an infinite number of points in common.

5. Look at the system of equations below.

$y = x - 4$

$y = {}^{-}2x - 4$

Which of these graphs represents this system of equations?

A.

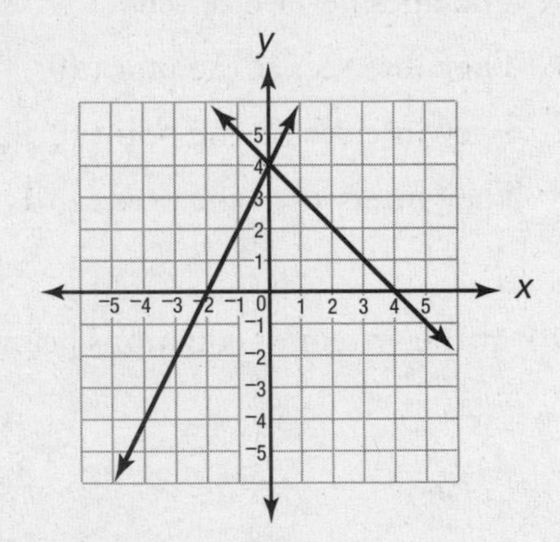

C.

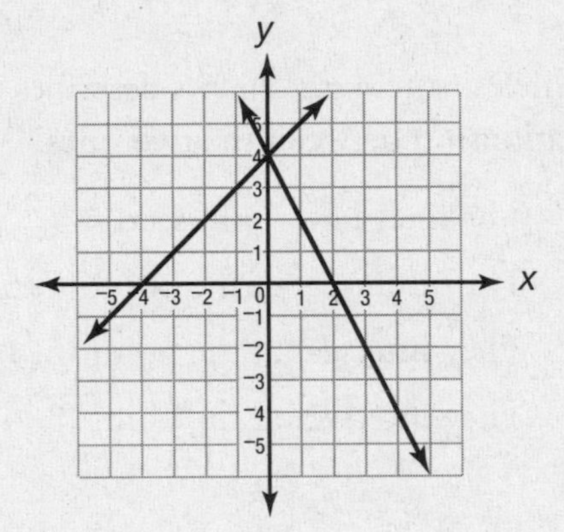

B.

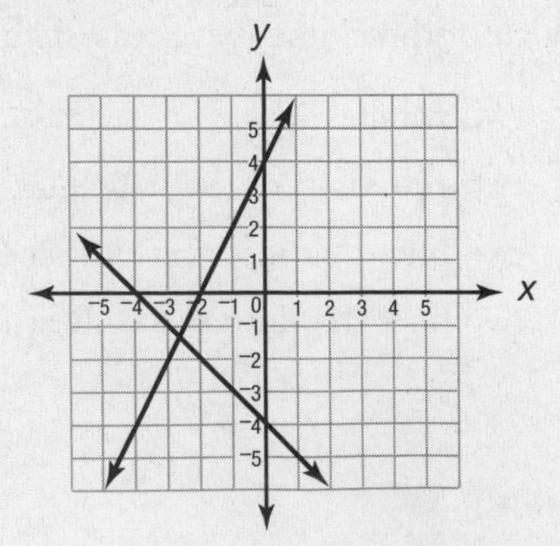

D.

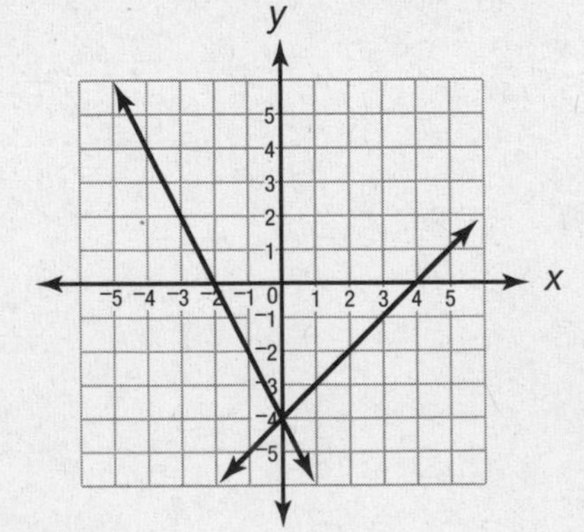

6. The graph below shows the cost of purchasing a movie ticket at Sienna's Cinema for members of the movie club and for non-member customers.

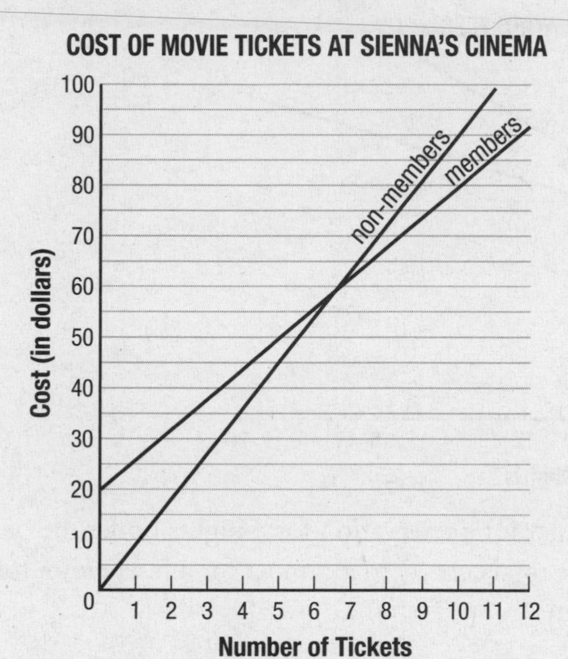

According to the graph, which of these statements is true?

F. Non-members pay less for 5 movie tickets.

G. Members pay less for 6 movie tickets.

H. Members and non-members pay the same for 7 movie tickets.

J. Non-members pay less for 8 movie tickets.

Use the Response Grid to complete Number 7.

7. The graph below shows the monthly cost of using Jared's Pool. Pool members pay a membership fee and get a discount for a monthly pass. Non-members pay the regular rate for a monthly pass.

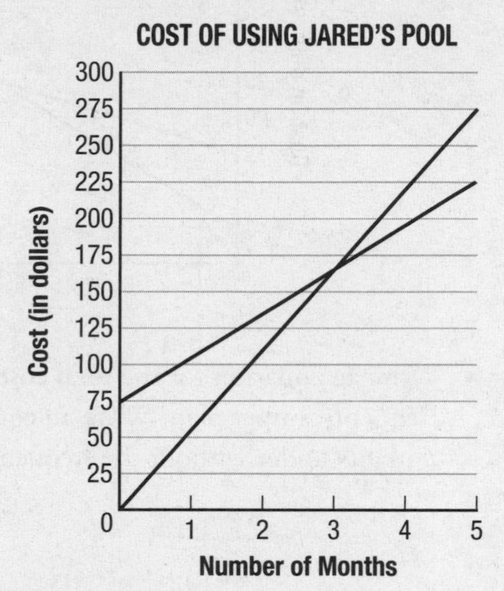

What is the cost in dollars of a membership fee for Jared's Pool?

8. **ECR** At a state park, a frequent-camper pass costs $15 and lets you camp at a reduced price each night. Without the pass, you must pay $5 to camp plus the regular price per night. The graph below compares the two fee plans for campsite reservations.

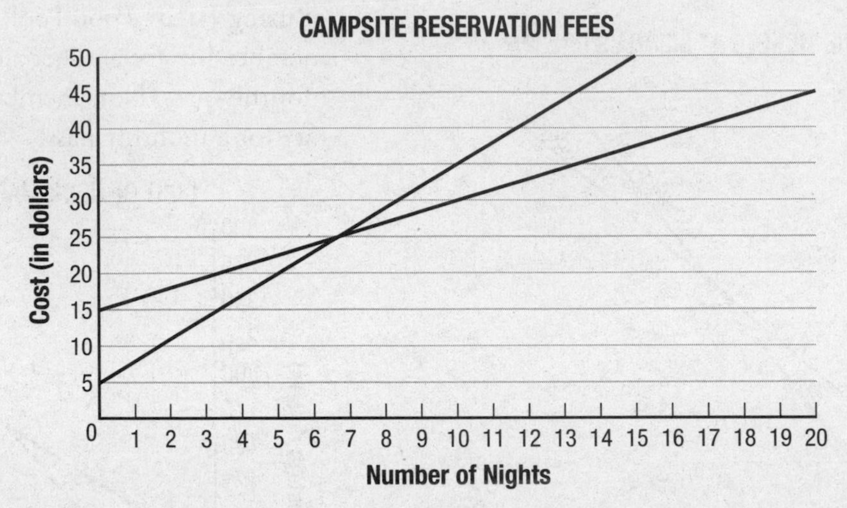

- Write an equation for the total cost (c) to a camper for a reservation for n nights under the frequent-camper plan. Write an equation for the total cost (c) to a camper for a reservation for n nights under without the frequent camper plan.

- How many nights would you have to camp for the total cost of reservation fees under both fee plans to be equal? Use mathematics to explain how you determined your answer. Use words, symbols, or both in your explanation.

- A camper wants to make a reservation for 7 nights. Should she buy the frequent camper pass? Use mathematics to justify your answer.

Interpreting Graphs of Non-Linear Functions

The graph of a **non-linear** equation is not a straight or continuous line. You can still use the *x*- and *y*-axes to find data points, but you cannot use a linear equation to graph the data. Even though the function might not be a continuous line, regions within the graph can have positive or negative slope. When interpreting graphs of any kind of data, be sure to note the scale, units, and titles of the axes.

EXAMPLE

The graph below shows a company's yearly profit from 1997 to 2007.

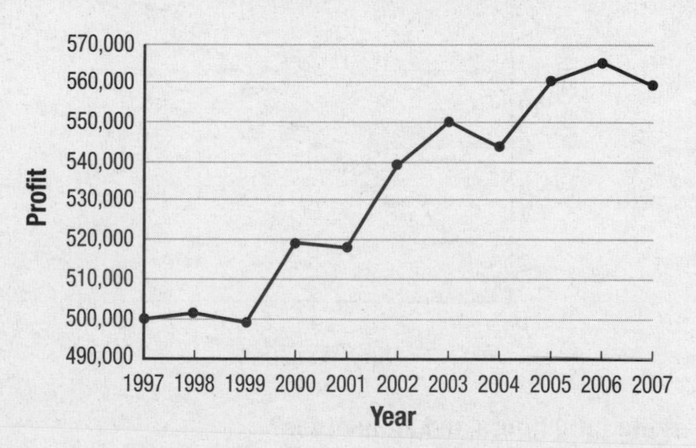

Based on the graph, how many times did the company's yearly profit have a negative rate of change?

STRATEGY **Examine slope.**

STEP 1 Think about positive and negative slope.

A slope is positive when the values increase as you go from left to right along the *x*-axis.

A slope is negative when the values decrease as you go from left to right along the *x*-axis.

STEP 2 Find the regions of the graph where the slope is negative.

The slope is negative:

- from 1998 to 1999
- from 2000 to 2001
- from 2003 to 2004
- from 2006 to 2007

SOLUTION **The company's yearly profits had a negative rate of change 4 times.**

COACHED EXAMPLE

The graph below shows the cost of parking in a parking lot for various lengths of time.

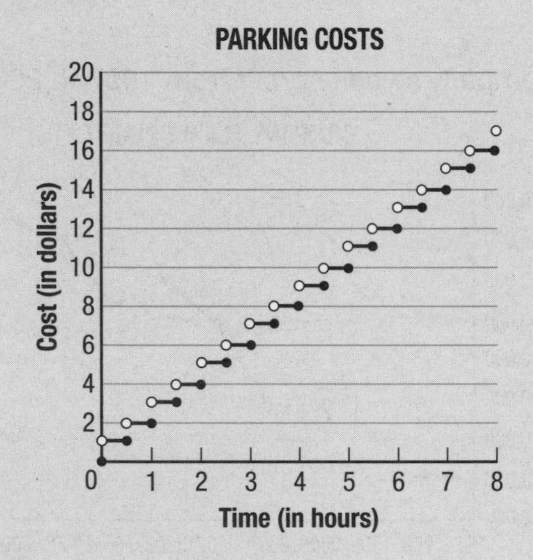

What is the cost of parking for 4 hours and 20 minutes?

THINKING IT THROUGH

The cost of parking for exactly 4 hours is ____________.

The cost of parking for exactly $4\frac{1}{2}$ hours is ____________.

The cost of parking any time in between 4 and $4\frac{1}{2}$ hours is ____________.

The cost of parking for 4 hours and 20 minutes is ____________

Lesson Practice

Choose the correct answer.

1. Lenny and Lucy took a 12-hour road trip. The car's computer kept track of their speed over the length of the trip. They started the trip at 10:00 A.M. and arrived at their final destination at 10:00 P.M.

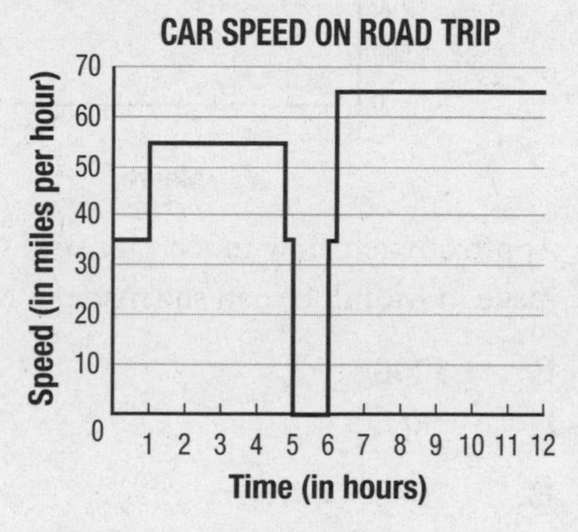

At one point during the trip, they stopped for an hour-long meal. Based on the graph, when was their meal?

A. from 10:00 A.M. to 11:00 A.M.

B. from 12:00 P.M. to 1:00 P.M.

C. from 3:00 P.M. to 4:00 P.M.

D. from 5:00 P.M. to 6:00 P.M.

2. A subway travels into a 100-meter tunnel. The graph below shows the distance (in centimeters) between the subway car and the wall of the tunnel as the car travels through the tunnel.

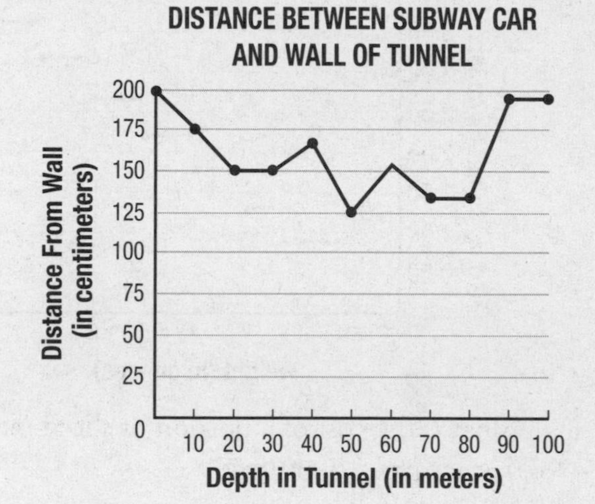

How deep into the tunnel is the subway car when it is closest to the wall of the tunnel?

F. 0 meters

G. 50 meters

H. 90 meters

J. 125 meters

3. A deli charges by the ounce for sliced deli meats. Each ounce (or fraction of an ounce) of deli meat costs $0.45 as shown in the graph below.

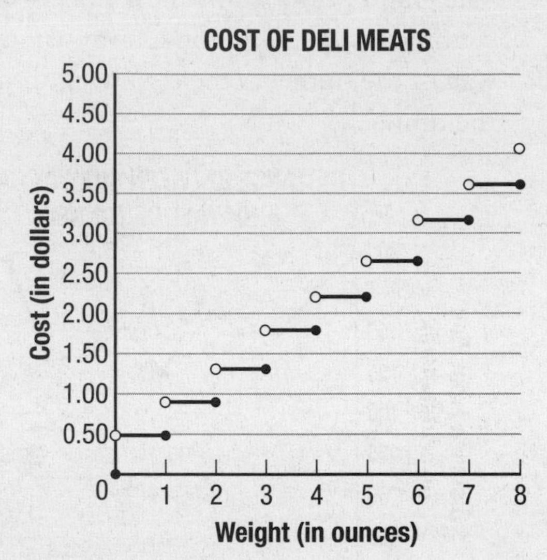

What is the cost of a portion of sliced meat that weighs 5.7 ounces?

A. $2.25

B. $2.70

C. $3.15

D. $3.60

4. Celia makes a graph of the total amount of money she makes in tips each month as a waitress. The graph is shown below.

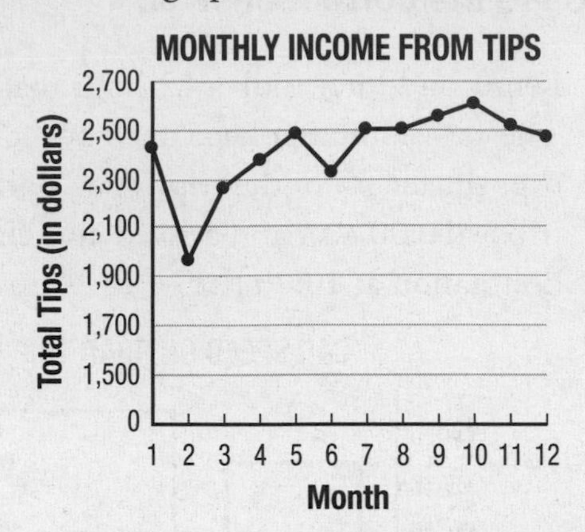

Approximately how much more did Celia make in Month 8 than she made in Month 3?

F. $200

G. $500

H. $600

J. $5,000

5. The graph below shows the speed of a roller coaster car as it travels along its track over 200 seconds.

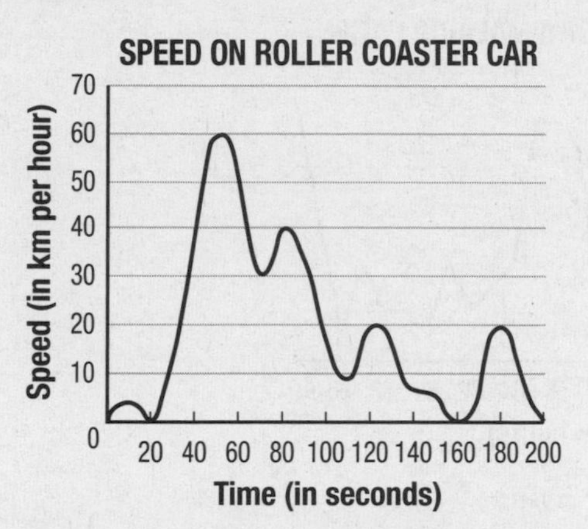

Approximately how many seconds into the ride did the car travel the fastest?

A. 50 seconds

B. 60 seconds

C. 105 seconds

D. 200 seconds

6. The graph below shows the temperature of a sample of ice water as it is gradually heated over time.

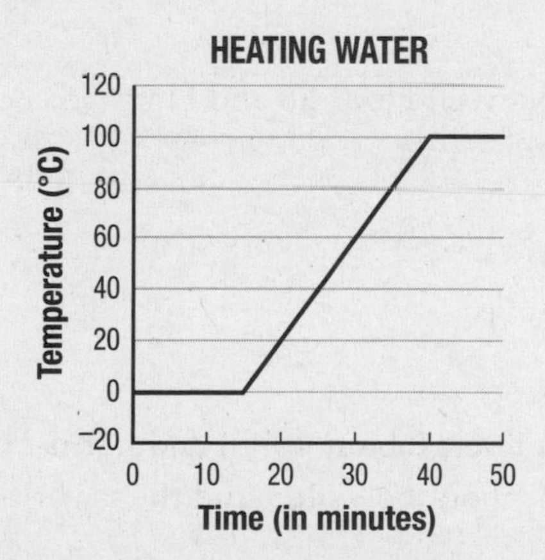

During which time period did the temperature increase at a steady rate?

F. from 0 to 15 minutes

G. from 10 to 20 minutes

H. from 15 to 40 minutes

J. from 40 to 50 minutes

Use the Response Grid to complete Number 7.

7. The graph below shows the estimated population of Baltimore, Maryland each year from 2000 to 2005.

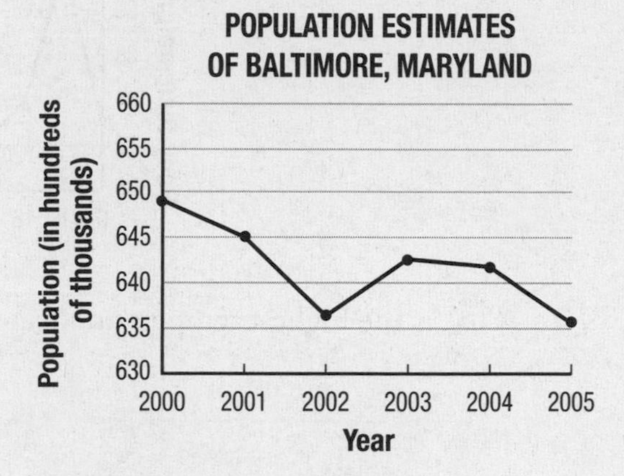

According to the graph, in what year did the population of Baltimore reach its lowest number?

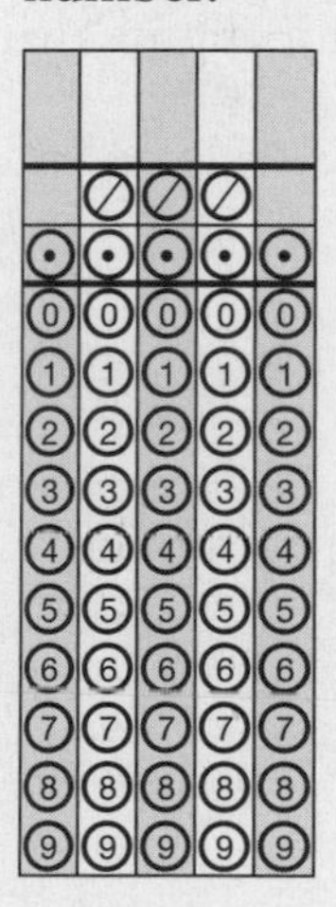

8. The graph below shows the body temperature (in degrees Celsius) of a patient with malaria over
ECR a period of 104 hours.

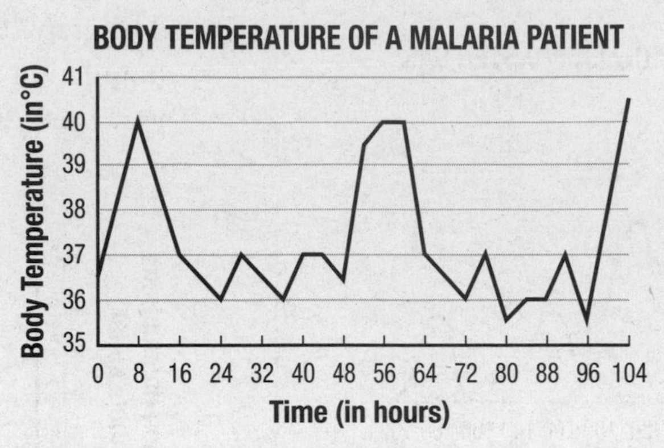

- What is the highest temperature that the patient has?

- What is the lowest temperature that the patient has?

- Did the patient's temperature increase or decrease between Hour 48 and Hour 56?

- Malaria patients typically experience a cycle of high fevers (about 40°C) and normal body temperatures (about 37°C). According to the graph, about how often did the malaria patient experience a high fever?

Lesson

Inequalities

An **inequality** shows that two numbers or mathematical expressions are not always equal. The symbol $<$ means "is less than" and the symbol $>$ means "is greater than." The symbol $\leq$ means "is less than or equal to" and the symbol $\geq$ means "is greater than or equal to." When simplifying inequalities, treat them as you would an equation, performing the same operation on both sides of the inequality symbol. Multiplying both sides of an inequality by a negative number reverses the sign, changing $<$ to $>$ and $>$ to $<$.

EXAMPLE 1

Draw a number line to show the solution set of the inequality $15 - 3x \leq 45$.

STRATEGY **Solve the inequality for *x*.**

STEP 1 Solve as you would an equation.

$15 - 3x \leq 45$

$15 - 3x - 15 \leq 45 - 15$

$^{-}3x \leq 30$

$(^{-}\frac{1}{3})(^{-}3x) \geq 30(^{-}\frac{1}{3})$

$x \geq {}^{-}10$

Note that multiplying both sides of the $\leq$ sign by a negative number changes it to $\geq$.

STEP 2 Draw a number line.

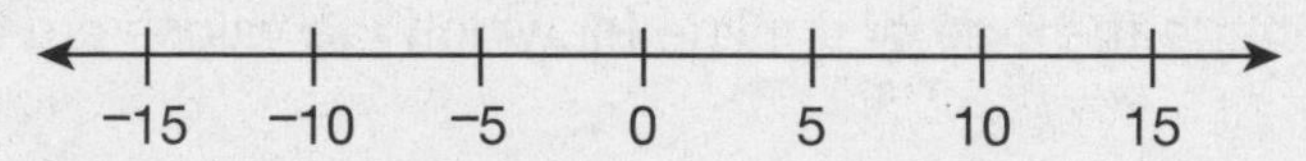

STEP 3 Identify the point that defines one end of the solution set.

Use a solid dot because it "is greater than **or equal to.**"

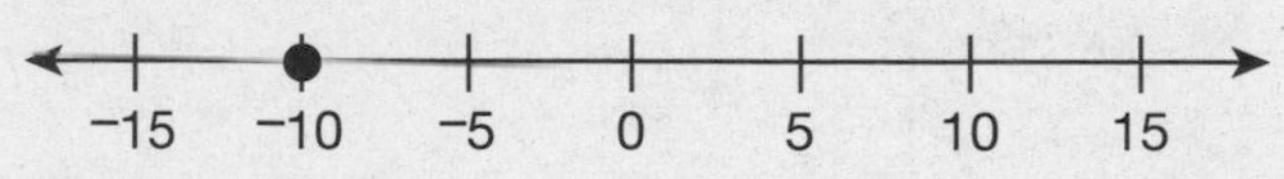

STEP 4 Shade the line to show the inequality.

SOLUTION

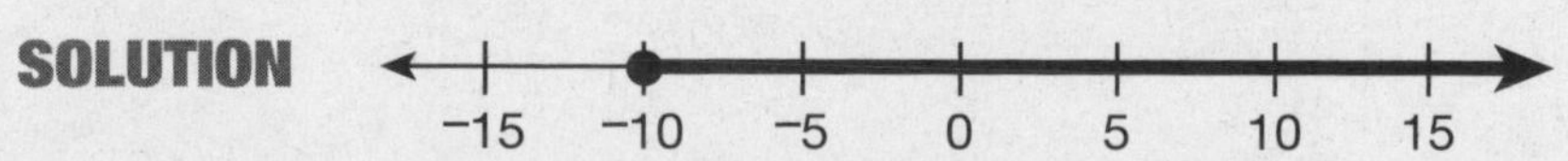

EXAMPLE 2

What is the graph of the solution set for the inequality $y \geq 2x + 3$?

STRATEGY **Graph the inequality as you would a linear equation.**

STEP 1 Identify the y-intercept and slope.

$y \geq 2x + 3$

$m = 2$

$b = 3$

STEP 2 Graph the line defined by the inequality.

Draw a solid line because it "is greater than or equal to."

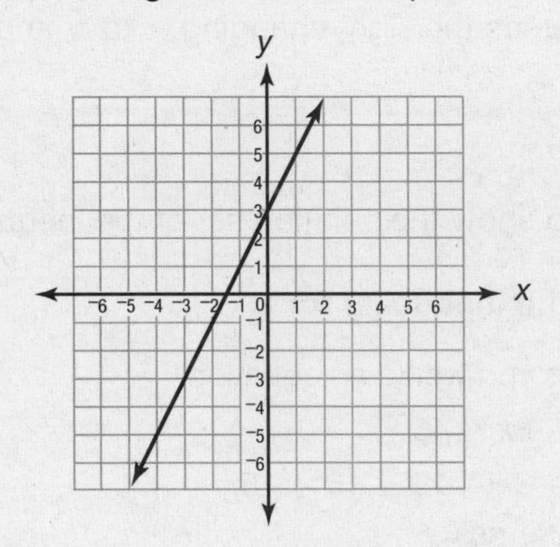

STEP 3 Choose a point and check that the x and y values are true for the inequality.

For point (0, 0):

$y \geq 2x + 3$

$0 \geq 2 \times 0 + 3$

$0 \geq 3$ → This is not true. $0 \leq 3$

STEP 4 Shade the side of the line for which the values are true.

SOLUTION

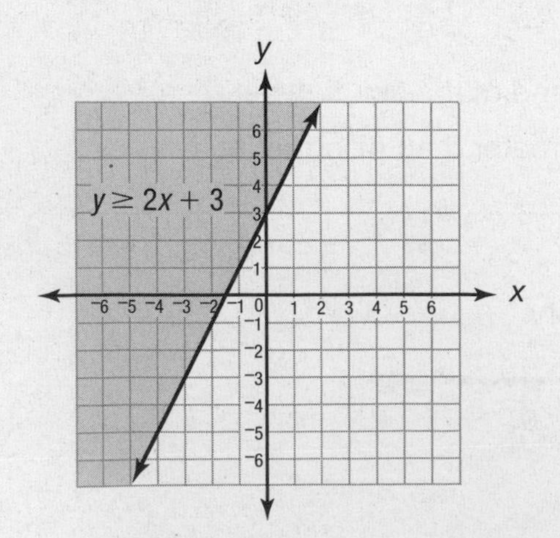

COACHED EXAMPLE

Brian has $10 to spend on pens and pencils. The pens are on sale for $1.20 each, and the pencils are on sale for $0.49 each. What is the maximum number of pencils Brian can buy if he buys 3 pens?

THINKING IT THROUGH

How much money can Brian spend? ____________

How much does a single pen cost?____________

How much do 3 pens cost? ____________

How much money does he have left after buying 3 pens? ____________

Divide that amount by the cost of a pencil to get ____________.

Round down to the nearest whole number to get ____________, the maximum number of pencils Brian can buy.

Lesson Practice

Choose the correct answer.

1. Look at the inequality below.

$2x + 13 \geq 21$

Which of these number lines shows the solution to this inequality?

A. 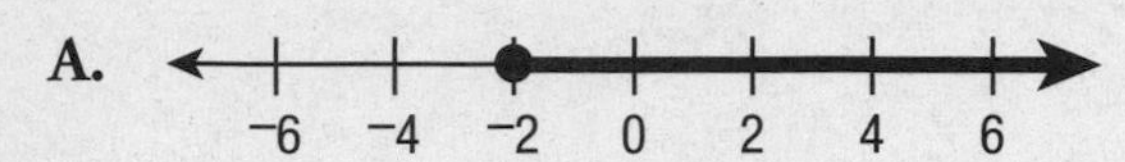

B. 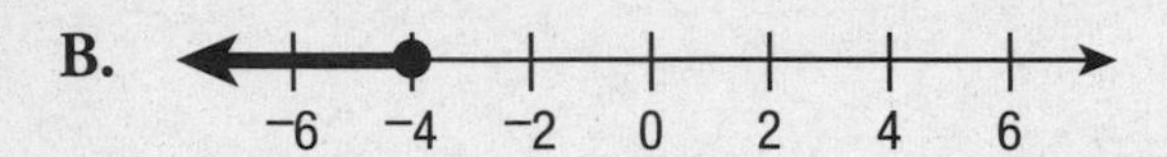

C.

−6 −4 −2 0 2 4 6

D. 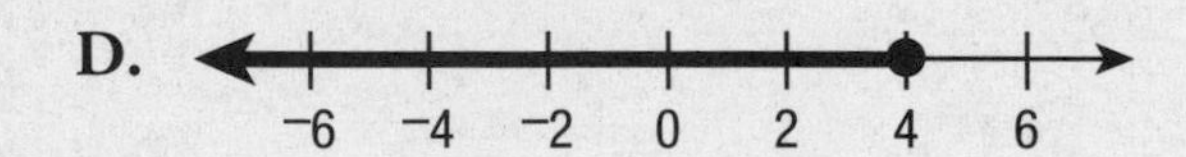

2. Look at the number line below.

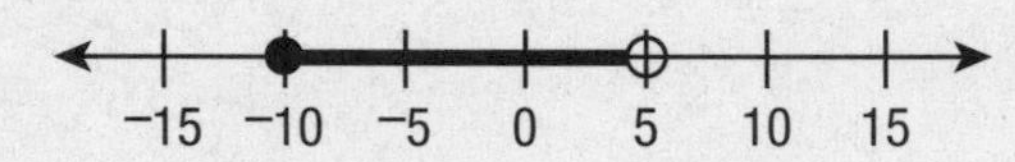

Which of these inequalities has the solution set that is shown on the number line?

F. $^{-}10 \leq x \leq 5$

G. $^{-}10 < x < 5$

H. $^{-}10 \leq x < 5$

J. $^{-}10 < x \leq 5$

3. Which of these graphs represents the solution set of the inequality $x + y \leq 0$?

A.

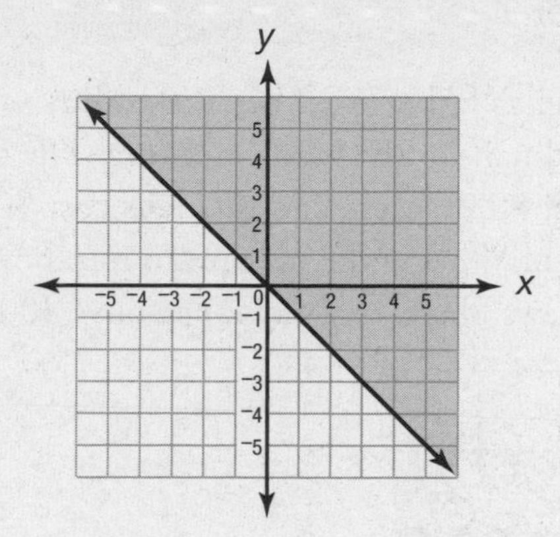

C.

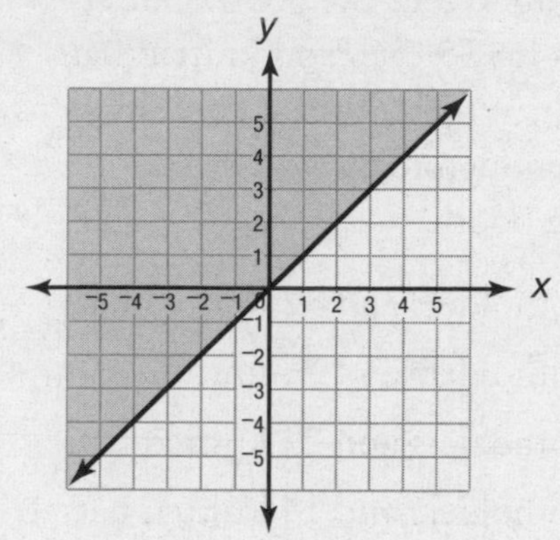

B.

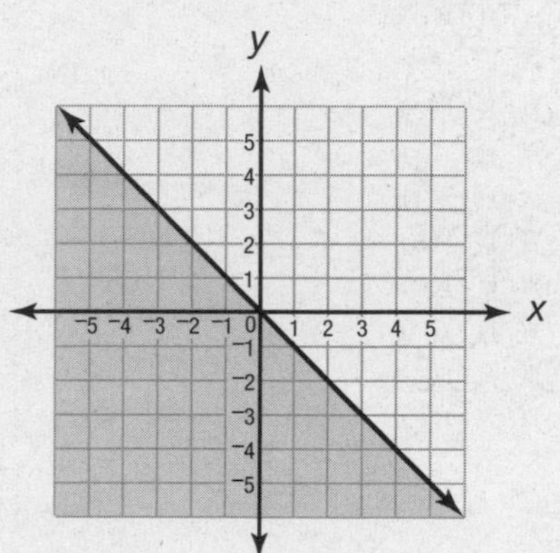

D.

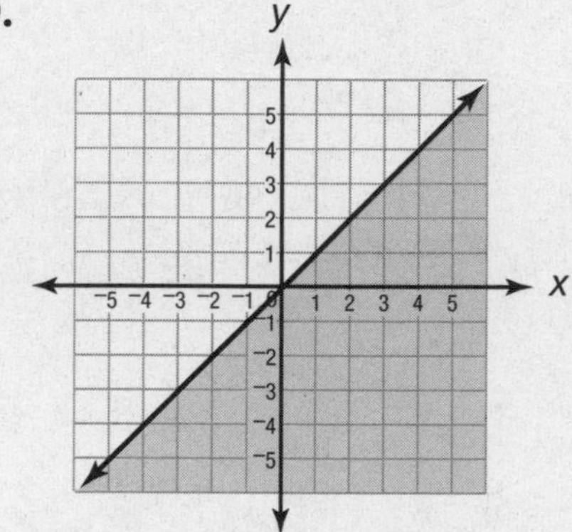

4. Look at the graph below.

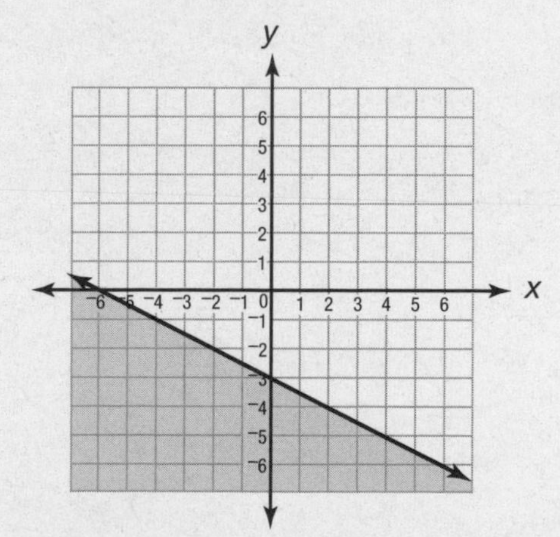

Which of these inequalities best describes this graph?

F. $y \leq -\frac{1}{2}x - 3$

G. $y \geq -\frac{1}{2}x - 3$

H. $y \leq \frac{1}{2}x - 3$

J. $y \geq \frac{1}{2}x - 3$

5. At a school bake sale, the honor society sells brownies (b) and cookies (c). The honor society makes \$2.00 for each brownie sold and \$1.25 for each cookie sold. The president of the honor society wants to earn at least \$100 from the bake sale. Which of these inequalities represents this situation?

A. $1.25b + 2c \leq 100$

B. $1.25b + 2c \geq 100$

C. $2b + 1.25c \leq 100$

D. $2b + 1.25c \geq 100$

6. Aida wants to rent a booth at a craft fair. It costs $500 to rent the booth. She sells potholders for $5 each and knitted hats for $8 each. Which of these combinations would be enough to cover the cost of renting the booth?

F. 49 potholders and 32 knitted hats

G. 61 potholders and 24 knitted hats

H. 56 potholders and 27 knitted hats

J. 77 potholders and 14 knitted hats

Use the Response Grid to complete Number 7.

7. Sheila's father gives her $20 to buy screws and nails at the hardware store. The screws cost $0.26 each, and the nails cost $0.15 each. What is the maximum number of screws Sheila can buy if she buys 50 nails?

8. A company's accountant budgets $500 to spend on printing paper and ink cartridges each month.
ECR Boxes of printing paper cost $40 each and the ink cartridges cost $25 each, including tax.

- Write an inequality that represents the situation above, where p represents the number of boxes of printing paper and i represents the number of ink cartridges.

- What is the **maximum** number of boxes of paper the accountant can buy if she buys 9 ink cartridges? Use mathematics to explain how you determined your answer. Use words, symbols, or both in your explanation.

- List all the number combinations of boxes of paper and ink cartridges the accountant can buy to spend **exactly** $500, assuming she buys both each month. Use mathematics to justify your answer.

Lesson

Matrices

A **matrix** is a rectangular table of numbers displayed in brackets. The row titles and column titles of a matrix show how the numbers are related. If you perform an operation on one number in the matrix, you must perform the same operation on all numbers in that row and change the row title. The same is true for the numbers in a column. Or, you can perform an operation on all of the numbers in the matrix. You can also add or subtract matrices of the same dimension by adding or subtracting the corresponding numbers in each matrix.

EXAMPLE

The matrices below show the jersey sizes ordered for the co-ed softball team during 2000 and 2001.

2000

	S	M	L
Girls	8	4	3
Boys	1	7	10

2001

	S	M	L
Girls	5	6	4
Boys	0	8	10

Make a matrix that shows the **change** in the number of jerseys ordered from 2000 to 2001.

STRATEGY **The word "change" indicates a difference, which involves subtraction. Subtract each set of corresponding number in the matrices.**

STEP 1 Make a larger matrix that shows the subtraction operations.

2001–2000

	S	M	L
Girls	5 − 8	6 − 4	4 − 3
Boys	0 − 1	8 − 7	10 − 10

STEP 2 Perform the operations within the matrix.

SOLUTION

2001–2000

	S	M	L
Girls	⁻3	2	1
Boys	⁻1	1	0

COACHED EXAMPLE

When employees at a chain of stores work overtime, they get paid "time and a half," which is 1.5 times their normal hourly wage. The matrix below shows the normal hourly wages for employees at two stores.

HOURLY WAGE

	Store 1	Store 2
Manager	30	31
Regular Staff	20	22

Make a matrix that represents the hourly wage when the employees are paid "time and a half."

THINKING IT THROUGH

Managers at Store 1 normally get paid 30.

1.5 × the normal wage of managers at Store 1 is 45.

Managers at Store 2 normally get paid 31.

1.5 × the normal wage of managers at Store 2 is 46.5.

Regular staff at Store 1 normally get paid 20.

1.5 × the normal wage of regular staff at Store 1 is 30.

Regular staff at Store 2 normally get paid 22.

1.5 × the normal wage of regular staff at Store 2 is 33.

The matrix that represents "time and a half" is:

OVERTIME HOURLY WAGE

	Store 1	Store 2
Manager	45	46.5
Regular Staff	30	33

Lesson Practice

Choose the correct answer.

1. A juice shop sells four different kinds of juice in three different sizes.

PRICE OF JUICES (in dollars)

	S	M	L
Orange	0.90	1.00	1.10
Carrot	1.00	1.10	1.20
Apple	0.85	0.95	1.05
Pineapple	1.00	1.10	1.20

How much does a large carrot juice cost?

A. $0.90

B. $1.00

C. $1.10

D. $1.20

2. A company has three departments: Shipping, Stockroom, and Factory. The matrix below shows the costs of wages, stock, and operations for all three departments.

COMPANY COSTS (in dollars)

	Wages	Stock	Operations
Shipping	3,562	1,999	1,495
Stockroom	4,125	2,580	659
Factory	6,500	5,895	5,450

What is the total cost for wages in all three departments?

F. 3,562

G. 6,500

H. 7,056

J. 14,187

3. Two stores in the same chain sell three different brands of salsa: Rita's, El Salsa, and Hot Ta Molly. The matrices below show the number of bottles of mild, medium, and hot salsa of each brand in stock at the two different stores.

STORE 1

	Mild	Medium	Hot
Rita's	25	35	42
El Salsa	12	22	27
Hot Ta Molly	28	38	32

STORE 2

	Mild	Medium	Hot
Rita's	40	41	38
El Salsa	19	21	20
Hot Ta Molly	42	39	25

Which of these matrices represents the total number of mild bottles of salsa in stock in both stores?

A.

	Mild
Rita's	15
El Salsa	7
Hot Ta Molly	14

B.

	Mild
Rita's	25
El Salsa	12
Hot Ta Molly	28

C.

	Mild
Rita's	40
El Salsa	19
Hot Ta Molly	42

D.

	Mild
Rita's	65
El Salsa	31
Hot Ta Molly	70

4. Misty took a poll of her schoolmates' preference for different flavors of ice cream. The matrix below shows the results of her poll.

ICE CREAM FLAVOR PREFERENCE

	Girls	Boys
Chocolate	25	15
Vanilla	5	8
Strawberry	18	12
Other	10	20

How many students were polled in all?

F. 8

G. 40

H. 58

J. 113

5. In three chemistry labs, the lab workers wear protective gloves that come in three different sizes. The matrices below show the number of pairs of small, medium, and large protective gloves ordered for lab workers in all three labs during two different years.

2006

	S	M	L
Lab A	3	9	5
Lab B	4	7	6
Lab C	13	18	19

2007

	S	M	L
Lab A	3	9	5
Lab B	3	10	7
Lab C	12	15	20

Which of these matrices represents the combined numbers of gloves ordered for both years?

A.

	S	M	L
Lab A	0	0	0
Lab B	−1	3	1
Lab C	−1	−3	1

B.

	S	M	L
Lab A	0	0	0
Lab B	1	−3	−1
Lab C	1	3	−1

C.

	S	M	L
Lab A	6	18	10
Lab B	7	17	13
Lab C	25	33	39

D.

	S	M	L
Lab A	17	17	0
Lab B	17	20	−3
Lab C	50	47	3

6. The matrix below shows the number of votes tallied in a poll two days before the election for the student council president.

RESULTS OF POLL BEFORE ELECTION

	Girls	Boys
Rhonda	36	29
Hillary	39	45
Toby	18	20
Jamal	45	38

Mitch predicts that on the actual day of the election, there will be approximately 12% more votes for each candidate. Which of the following matrices represents Mitch's predicted numbers of votes for each candidate?

A.

	Girls	Boys
Rhonda	4	4
Hillary	5	5
Toby	2	2
Jamal	5	5

B.

	Girls	Boys
Rhonda	40	32
Hillary	39	45
Toby	18	20
Jamal	45	38

C.

	Girls	Boys
Rhonda	40	32
Hillary	44	50
Toby	20	22
Jamal	50	43

D.

	Girls	Boys
Rhonda	432	348
Hillary	468	540
Toby	216	240
Jamal	540	456

Use the Response Grid to complete Number 7.

7. The matrices below show the number of large and small snow cones sold at a snow cone stand during two different summer months.

JUNE

	Small	Large
Cherry	140	115
Grape	201	190
Lime	99	45

JULY

	Small	Large
Cherry	208	305
Grape	350	472
Lime	143	215

How many more small and large **lime** snow cones were sold in July than in June?

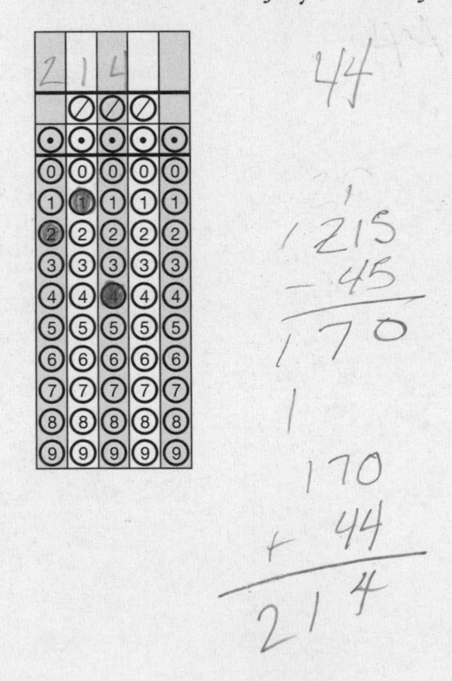

8. The matrix below shows the amount of money spent on wages for employees at a dry cleaner.

ECR

BUDGET SPENT ON WEEKLY WAGES FOR EMPLOYEES

	Washers	Dryers	Ironers	Clerks	Drivers
Managers	$1,200	$550	$0	$600	$0
Regular Staff	$1,200	$700	$1,000	$900	$400

- What is the total amount the dry cleaner spent weekly on wages for employees?

6,550

- The owner decides to increase everyone's wages by 2%. What matrix represents the new wages with the salary increase?

$$\begin{bmatrix} 1224 & 561 & 0 & 612 & 0 \\ 1224 & 714 & 1020 & 918 & 408 \end{bmatrix}$$

- What is the total amount that the dry cleaners will spend weekly on the new wages for employees?

6,681

Lesson 16 Using Formulas

A **formula** describes a relationship among different quantities. Formulas usually come in the form of an equation with variables that represent unknown quantities. At the back of this workbook, you can find a formula reference sheet that gives the formulas for calculating area and volume for various shapes and solids. To use a formula, plug in the number values for the different known quantities and solve for the unknown. Be sure that all of the units are correct.

EXAMPLE

The rectangular crate below has a volume of 45 cubic feet, a length of 6 feet, and a width of 3 feet.

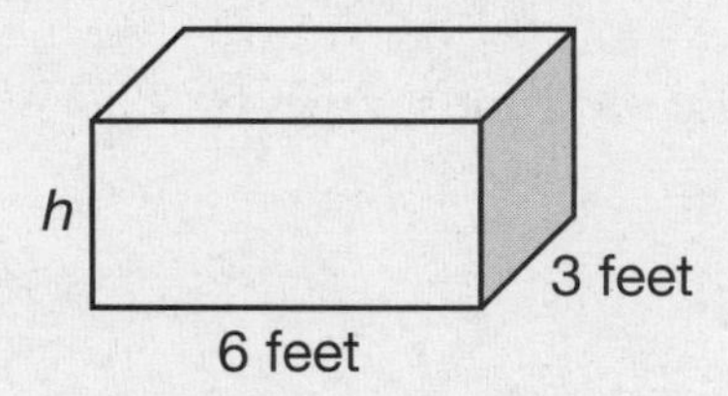

What is the height (h) of the rectangular crate?

STRATEGY **Use the formula for volume and solve for height.**

STEP 1 Find the formula for volume of a rectangular prism.

$$V = lwh$$

STEP 2 Plug the known quantities into the formula.

$$V = lwh$$
$$45 = 6 \times 3 \times h$$

STEP 3 Solve for height.

$$45 = 6 \times 3 \times h$$
$$45 = 18 \times h$$
$$\left(\frac{1}{18}\right)45 = 18 \times h\left(\frac{1}{18}\right)$$
$$2.5 = h$$

SOLUTION **The height of the crate is 2.5 feet.**

COACHED EXAMPLE

The formula for distance traveled is $d = rt$, where r is rate and t is time. How long does it take a car traveling at a rate of 40 miles per hour to travel 130 miles?

THINKING IT THROUGH

The rate, r, is __________.

The distance, d, is __________.

The formula for distance traveled is $d =$ __________.

Plugging the known quantities into this formula gives the equation __________.

It took the car __________ hours.

Lesson Practice

Choose the correct answer.

1. The formula below can be used to calculate simple interest (I) on a loan.

   $I = prt$

   (p = principal, r = interest rate, t = time)

   What is the simple interest over a period of 9 months at a rate of 0.5% a month for a principal of $1,000?

   A. $5
   B. $45
   C. $500
   D. $4,500

2. The rectangular box below has a volume of 75,000 cubic centimeters, a height of 100 centimeters, and a length of 30 centimeters.

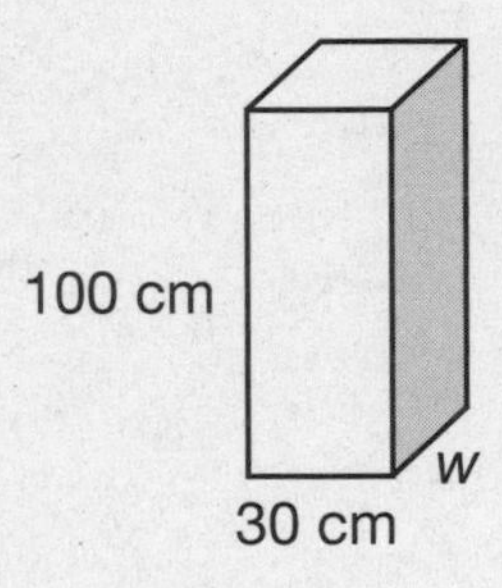

   What is the width (w) of the rectangular box?

   F. 25 cm
   G. 30 cm
   H. 75 cm
   J. 100 cm

3. A sphere has a radius of 4 inches. Using 3.14 for π, what is the surface area of the sphere in square inches?

   A. 50.24
   B. 66.99
   C. 200.96
   D. 267.95

4. Juanita throws a basketball up in the air. The equation below describes the height of the basketball $f(t)$, in feet, as a function of time (t) in seconds.

   $f(t) = {}^{-}16t^2 + 10t + 5$

   What is the height of the basketball after 0.6 seconds?

   F. 0.60 feet
   G. 1.40 feet
   H. 5.24 feet
   J. 10.00 feet

5. Kenny drops a rock down a well and times how long it falls before he hears a splash. He uses the formula for the height of a falling object, shown below, to calculate the depth of the well.

$$d = 16t^2$$

In the formula, d is the distance the object fell in feet and t is the time it took to travel that distance in seconds. He drops the rock and it takes 5 seconds before he hears a splash. How many feet deep is the well?

A. 41 feet

B. 80 feet

C. 160 feet

D. 400 feet

6. Ralph went on vacation to Europe with his family. Europeans use the Celsius scale to report temperature, while Ralph is used to the Fahrenheit scale. Ralph uses the following formula to convert from degrees Celsius (T_C) to degrees Fahrenheit (T_F).

$$T_F = \left(\frac{9}{5}\right) \times T_C + 32$$

What is the temperature in degrees Fahrenheit when the weather forecast reports a temperature of 25 degrees Celsius?

F. 46

G. 57

H. 77

J. 103

Use the Response Grid to complete Number 7.

7. The formula for average acceleration is given below.

$$A_{ave} = \frac{v_{final} - v_{starting}}{t}$$

($v_{starting}$ = starting velocity,
v_{final} = final velocity, t = time)

In the last lap of a car race, the driver has an initial velocity of 152 miles per hour. He crosses the finish line at 187 miles per hour. If his last lap takes 50 seconds, what is the driver's average acceleration for his last lap (in miles per hour per second)?

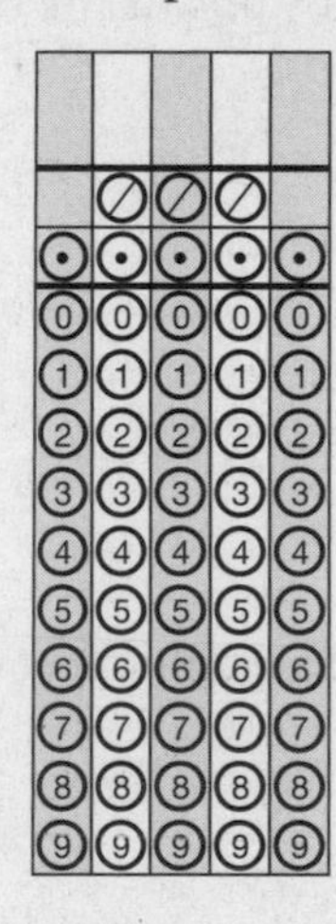

8. A farmer has a water storage tank shaped like a cylinder. The tank has a height of 20 feet and a base radius of 8 feet.

BCR

- The farmer wants to seal the entire inside surface of the tank with paint. To calculate how much paint he needs, he needs to know the surface area of the tank. What is the surface area of the tank in square feet?

- The farmer wants to paint just the vertical walls of the outside of the tank. What is the surface area of just the vertical walls of the tank (without the roof and base)?

- What volume of water in cubic feet can the storage tank hold?

- The farmer notices that the storage tank has only 5 feet of water in it. What is the volume of water, in cubic feet, in the storage tank?

HSA Review

1 **Alethea's mother gives her \$20 to buy chips and drinks for a party. Chips cost \$3.95 per bag and drinks cost \$2.39 per bottle. Which of these equations represents how many dollars she will have left (d) if she buys 3 bottles of drinks and b bags of chips?**

A $d = (3.95)(3) - 2.39b$

B $d = (2.39)(3) + 3.95b$

C $d = 20 - 2.39 - 3.95b$

D $d = 20 - (2.39)(3) - 3.95b$

2 **A gas station pump puts out gas at a rate of 2.5 gallons per minute. Hank's truck already has 3.2 gallons of gas in its tank. He fills the tank for an additional 5 minutes. What is the total number of gallons of gas in Hank's tank?**

F 12.5

G 15.7

H 16.0

J 18.5

3 **There are 64 students in the marching band. The number of boys in the marching band is eight less than three times the number of girls. How many girls are in the marching band?**

A 14

B 18

C 46

D 50

4 **Which of these equations represents a line with an x-intercept of $^{-}1$ and a y-intercept of 3?**

F $y = {^{-}3}x - 3$

G $y = {^{-}3}x + 3$

H $y = 3x - 3$

J $y = 3x + 3$

5 Look at the graph below.

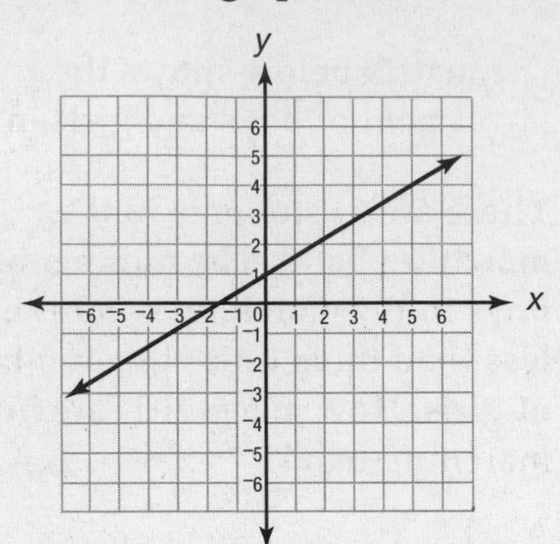

What is the slope of the line?

A $^-1$

B $\frac{3}{5}$

C 1

D $\frac{5}{3}$

6 Look at the system of equations below.

$$y = x + 4$$

$$y = {}^-2x + 4$$

Which of these describes this system?

F two parallel lines

G two equations of the same line

H two lines that intersect only at $(0, {}^-4)$

J two lines that intersect only at (0, 4)

7 The graph below shows the population of a herd of cattle over a period of 12 months.

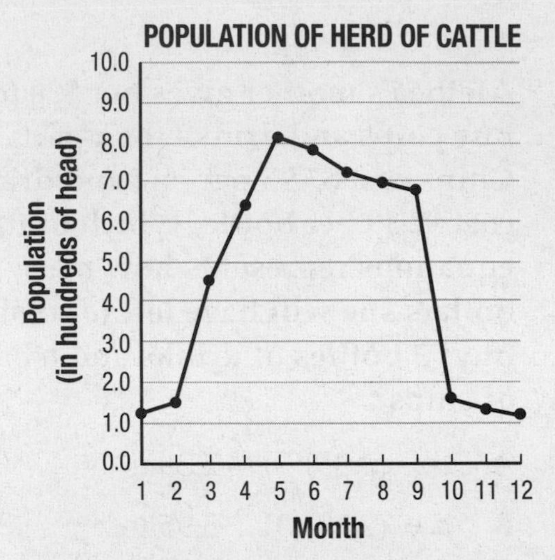

The rancher who owns these cattle usually sells about 80% of his herd once a year, reducing its population drastically. Based on the graph, between which two months did this sale take place?

A 3 and 4

B 4 and 5

C 8 and 9

D 9 and 10

8 Look at the graph below.

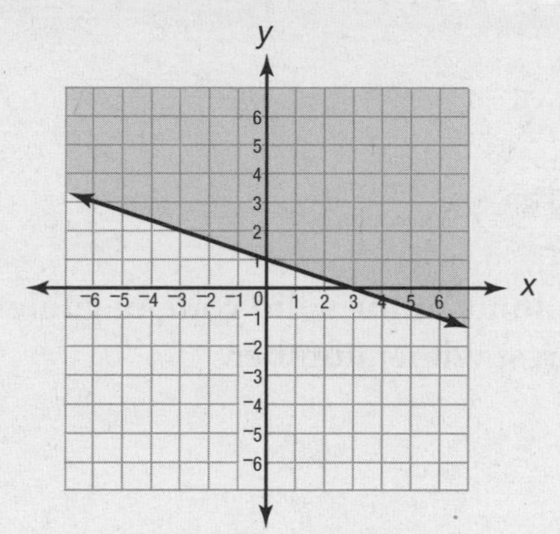

Which of these inequalities <u>best</u> describes this graph?

F $y \le -\frac{1}{3}x + 1$

G $y \ge -\frac{1}{3}x + 1$

H $y \le \frac{1}{3}x + 1$

J $y \ge \frac{1}{3}x + 1$

Use the Response Grids to complete Numbers 9 and 10.

9 The matrix below shows the enrollment of boys and girls in different school sports teams.

ENROLLMENT IN SCHOOL SPORTS

	Girls	Boys
Soccer	33	32
Basketball	29	35
Volleyball	18	0
Swimming	12	18
Football	0	45

According to the matrix, how many girls are enrolled in a sport?

10 **The solid cone below has a radius of 3 centimeters and a height of 6 centimeters.**

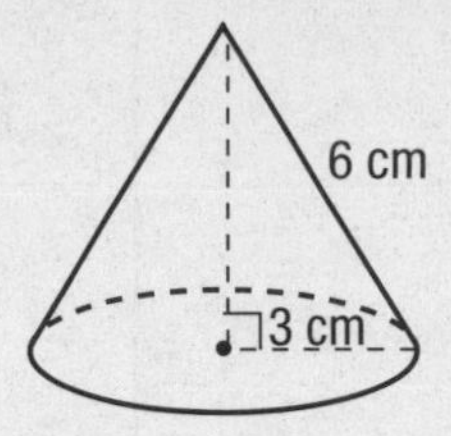

Using 3.14 for π, what is the approximate volume of the solid cone in cubic centimeters? Round your answer to the nearest whole number.

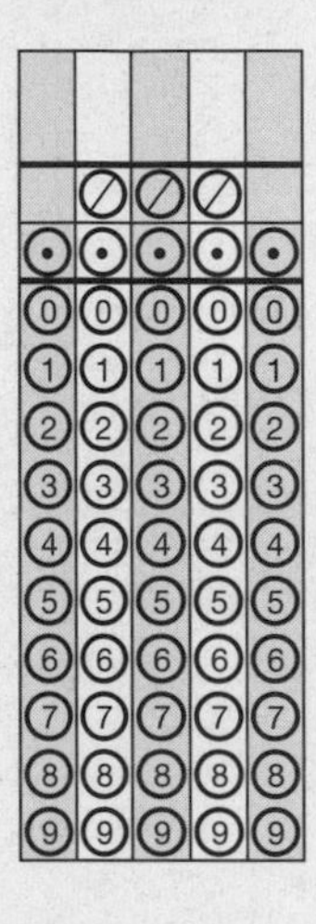

11
BCR **A factory has a storage container shaped like a rectangular prism. The container has a width of 8 feet, a length of 20 feet, and a depth of 15 feet.**

- **What is the maximum volume, in cubic feet, that the storage container can hold?**

- **The storage container is currently filled to a depth of 8 feet. What additional volume, in cubic feet, could the storage container hold?**

CHAPTER

Goal 3, Expectation 3.1

Working with Data: Statistics and Probability

Lesson

Mean, Median, and Mode

You can analyze the numbers in a data set by identifying the mean, median, and mode. These numbers are called the **measures of central tendency,** and they are used to summarize a data set.

- The **mean** is the average of a set of values, or the total sum of the values divided by the number of values in the set.
- The **median** is the middle value when the values are arranged in order from least to greatest. When there are two middle values, the median is the mean of those two values.
- The **mode** is the value that occurs most often in the set.

EXAMPLE 1

For the school charity event, Ms. Wang's class collected cash donations. A total of 15 students collected $25 each, 3 students collected $75 each, and the other students collected $37, $42, $51, and $40. What is the mean amount collected per student?

STRATEGY **Find the total and divide by the number of individuals.**

STEP 1 Find the total amount of cash collected by the class.

$$(15 \times \$25) + (3 \times \$75) + \$37 + \$42 + \$51 + \$40 = \$770$$

STEP 2 Count the total number of students in the class.

$$15 + 3 + 4 = 22$$

STEP 3 Divide the total amount of cash by the total number of students.

$$\frac{\$770}{22} = \$35$$

SOLUTION **The mean amount collected per student is $35.**

EXAMPLE 2

Renata made the following scores on the first seven math exams for the semester: 91, 77, 90, 85, 93, 72, and 88. Her median score is 88. If she earned a 95 on her eighth exam, would this change her median score? Use mathematics to justify your answer.

STRATEGY **Rearrange the numbers in ascending order.**

STEP 1 Write the scores in order from least to greatest, including the eighth exam grade.

72, 77, 85, 88, 90, 91, 93, 95

STEP 2 Eliminate the highest and lowest scores until only one or two scores remain.

~~72~~, ~~77~~, ~~85~~, 88, 90, ~~91~~, ~~93~~, ~~95~~

STEP 3 Find the mean of the two remaining scores.

$\frac{88 + 90}{2} = 89$

SOLUTION **Her median score would increase to 89.**

EXAMPLE 3

Sheila had 5 bags of jellybeans. She calculated that the mean number of jellybeans per bag was 69. When she checked her numbers, she found that one of the bags had 15 more jellybeans than she originally thought. What is the actual mean number of jellybeans per bag?

STRATEGY **Find the actual total number.**

STEP 1 Find the original total number that she calculated.

$69 \times 5 = 345$

STEP 2 Add the extra jellybeans to get the correct total number.

$345 + 15 = 360$

STEP 3 Divide the correct total number by the number of bags.

$360 \div 5 = 72$

SOLUTION **The actual mean number of jellybeans per bag is 72.**

COACHED EXAMPLE

Chris scored the following points during the first 9 basketball games this season: 24, 30, 18, 5, 20, 29, 34, 16, and 24. If his mean score per game for the season is 22, how many points did he score in the tenth and final game of the season?

THINKING IT THROUGH

What is the total number of games that he played this season? ___________

His mean score multiplied by the total number of games is ___________, all the points he earned over the season.

The sum of all his scores in the first nine games is ___________ points.

Subtracting the number of points he earned in the first nine games from the total number of points earned over the season gives ___________.

So, his score in the final game was ___________ points.

Lesson Practice

Choose the correct answer.

1. Felix makes the following scores in a game: 12, 24, 7, 9, 15, 14, 25, 12, 10, and 12. What are Felix's mean and median scores?

   A. mean: 7, median: 15.5

   B. mean: 12, median: 12

   C. mean: 14, median: 12

   D. mean: 25, median: 18

2. Collette's club sold baked goods at the fair. The table below shows the number of items they sold at each of five different prices. What is the mode price?

Price	Number Sold
25¢	9
50¢	6
75¢	4
$1.00	11
$1.25	3

   F. 25¢

   G. 75¢

   H. $1.00

   J. $1.25

3. Katrice counts how many peanuts are found in a single shell. She opens 18 peanut shells and marks how many peanuts are in each shell on the following line plot. What is the median number of peanuts in a single shell?

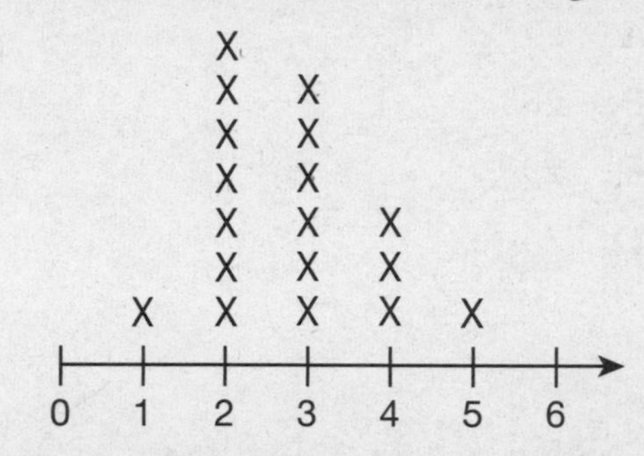

   A. 2

   B. 3

   C. 5

   D. 6

4. Ling made the following grades on the first five biology tests for the semester: 75, 82, 74, 95, and 89. If her mean grade for the semester was 85, what did she make on the sixth and final test?

   F. 83

   G. 85

   H. 89

   J. 95

5. In his job helping the principal look at attendance records for 6 classes, Quentin found that the mean class size was 28 students. Later he realized that one of the classes had 6 more students then he originally counted. What is the correct mean class size?

A. 22

B. 28

C. 29

D. 34

6. To determine Jane's final score in the dominoes tournament, the judges drop the highest and lowest scores she made in the preliminary rounds. Then they take the mean of the remaining scores. Jane made the following scores in the preliminary rounds: 60, 35, 48, 44, 57, 55, and 51. What is Jane's final score?

F. 48

G. 51

H. 50

J. 55

7. **BCR** Natalia recorded the number of cans collected by each member of the Recycle Club. She recorded her data in the table below.

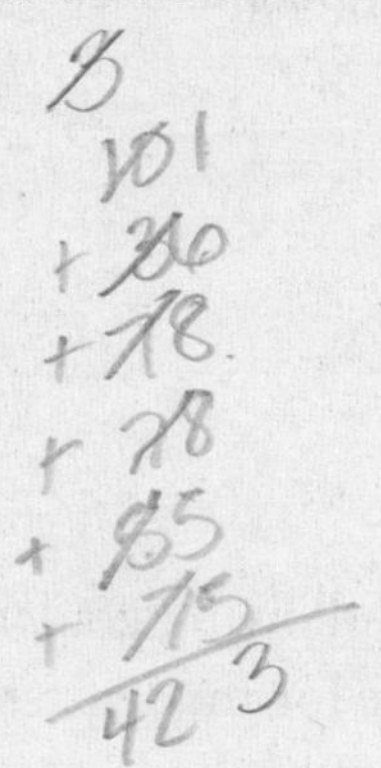

Member	Number of Cans
Donell	75
Eleanor	78
Felicia	101
Natalia	67
Raymundo	36
Sandra	55
Tony	78

- What are the measures of central tendency for this data?

- Two students joined the club late. Amy brought 24 cans and Dan brought 62. If Natalia added their numbers to the data above, would this change the measures of central tendency? Use mathematics to justify your answer.

- Natalia decided not to include her own number, nor Amy's nor Dan's, in the data. How does dropping her number of cans affect the measures of central tendency of the data shown in the table above?

Lesson

Range and Quartiles

You can compare the numbers in two data sets by looking at their **measures of variability.** Measures of variability include range, interquartile range, and quartiles.

- The **range** is the difference between the least and greatest values in a set.
- If you divide the full set of data into four equal parts, these mini sets of data are separated by three **quartiles**. The second quartile is equal to the median. The first and third quartiles are the midpoints of the two halves of the data set. The middle 50% of the data is bound on either side by the first and third quartiles.
- The **interquartile range** is the difference between the values of the first and third quartiles. It is the range of the middle 50% of the data.

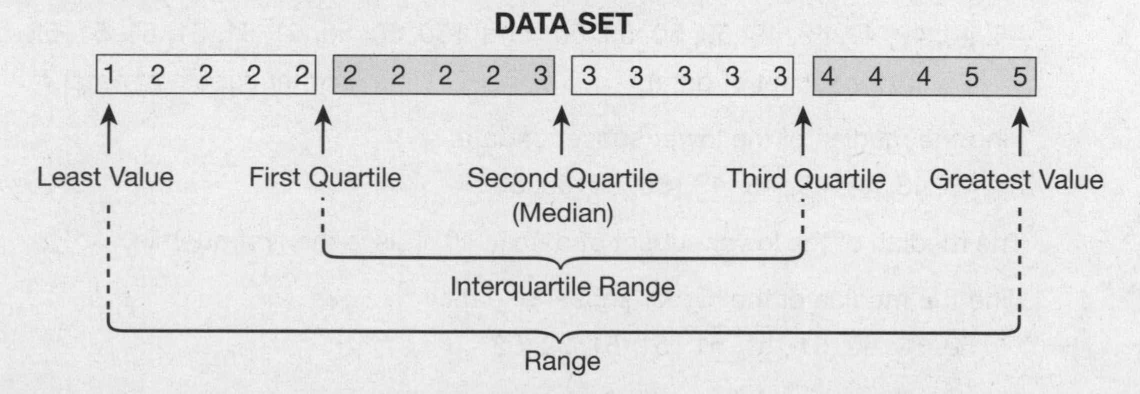

EXAMPLE 1

Shelby collected the following set of data in an investigation.

Data: 49, 50, 51, 50, 50, 50, 49, 48, 46, 50, 51, 51, 52, 49, 52, 50, 50, 51, 51, 49

What is the range for this data set?

STRATEGY **Subtract the least value from the greatest value.**

STEP 1 Find the greatest value.

The greatest value is 52.

STEP 2 Find the least value.

The least value is 46.

STEP 3 Find the difference between the greatest and least values.

$52 - 46 = 6$

SOLUTION **The range of the data set is 6.**

EXAMPLE 2

What are the quartiles for the data set given in the example above?

STRATEGY **Divide the data into two subsets and find their medians.**

STEP 1 Make a list of each value in the data set in order from least to greatest.

46, 48, 49, 49, 49, 49, 50, 50, 50, 50, 50, 50, 50, 51, 51, 51, 51, 51, 52, 52

STEP 2 Find the median and use it to divide the data set into two subsets.

46, 48, 49, 49, 49, 49, 50, 50, 50, [50, 50,] 50, 50, 51, 51, 51, 51, 51, 52, 52

The median of the entire data set is 50. This is also the second quartile.

The two subsets of data are:

46, 48, 49, 49, 49, 49, 50, 50, 50, 50 (lower subset of data) and 50, 50, 50, 51, 51, 51, 51, 51, 52, 52 (higher subset of data)

STEP 3 Find the median of the lower subset of data.

46, 48, 49, 49, [49, 49,] 50, 50, 50, 50

The median of the lower subset of data is 49. This is the first quartile.

STEP 4 Find the median of the higher subset of data.

50, 50, 50, 51, [51, 51,] 51, 51, 52, 52

The median of the higher subset of data is 51. This is the third quartile.

SOLUTION **The first quartile is 49, the second quartile is 50, and the third quartile is 51.**

COACHED EXAMPLE

What is the interquartile range of the following list of values?

3, 5, 9, 9, 10, 12, 12, 14, 15, 15, 15, 15, 15, 16, 19, 21, 21, 22, 23, 25

THINKING IT THROUGH

The median of the data is ___________.

The first quartile of the data is ___________.

The third quartile of the data is ___________.

Subtract the first quartile from the third quartile to get the interquartile range.

The interquartile range is ___________.

Lesson Practice

Choose the correct answer.

1. Look at the monthly earnings shown below.

MONTHLY EARNINGS (IN DOLLARS)

Month	Earnings
Jan	2,540
Feb	2,145
Mar	2,645
Apr	2,173
May	2,090
Jun	3,100
Jul	2,195
Aug	2,300
Sep	2,301
Oct	2,145
Nov	2,149
Dec	2,299

Which of these is the range of the monthly earnings?

A. \$241

B. \$555

C. \$1,010

D. \$2,145

2. Manuel's club sold souvenirs at the carnival. The table below shows the number of items they sold at each of five different prices. What is the range of these prices?

Price	Number Sold
25¢	12
50¢	7
75¢	18
\$1.00	3
\$1.25	4

F. \$0.25

G. \$0.75

H. \$1.00

J. \$1.25

3. Mike's juggling team is competing in a local tournament. Each team in the tournament is awarded points for successfully completing tricks and for overall style. The scores for each of the teams in the tournament are listed below.

55, 42, 75, 49, 50, 50, 72, 57, 51, 43, 61, 48, 42, 55, 49, 46

The teams whose scores are greater than or equal to the third quartile get to go on to the state finals. What is the minimum score Mike's team would have to have to go on to the state finals?

A. 55

B. 56

C. 59

D. 61

4. The table below shows the number of sales made by eight salespeople at a car dealership last year.

CARS SOLD LAST YEAR

Salesperson	Cars Sold
Bob	180
Jim	172
Sandeep	149
Lena	185
Min	149
Paula	125
Rick	150
Tito	179

Which salesperson achieved a number of sales lower than the first quartile?

F. Paula
G. Min
H. Bob
J. Lena

5. What is the interquartile range of the following list of grades?

93, 45, 89, 79, 89, 91, 52, 94, 75, 65, 65, 75, 73, 86, 98, 52, 82, 82, 83, 85

A. 16
B. 20
C. 53
D. 82

6. A scientist is studying four groups of mice. She weighs each of the mice in her study. A summary of her data is shown below. Weights are shown in grams.

Group	Least Weight	First Quartile	Median Weight	Third Quartile	Greatest Weight
A	15	16	19	21	22
B	13	14	17	18	19
C	16	18	19	20	21
D	14	19	20	21	22

Which group of mice has the widest spread in the middle 50% of their weights?

F. Group A
G. Group B
H. Group C
J. Group D

Use the Response Grid to complete Number 7.

7. The table below lists the ages of teens who participated in a race and the frequency of those ages. What is the range of ages of teens who participated in the race?

Age	Frequency
13	5
14	16
15	25
16	40
17	39
18	37
19	25

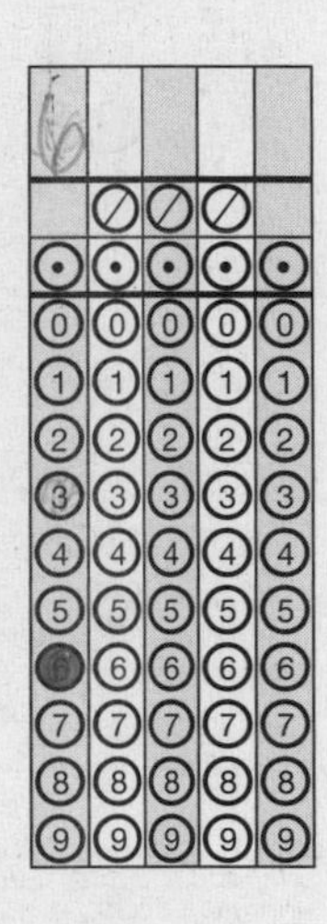

8. Harold's school basketball team, the Pumas, played 18 games last season. The graph below plots
BCR the scores that they made in each game of the season.

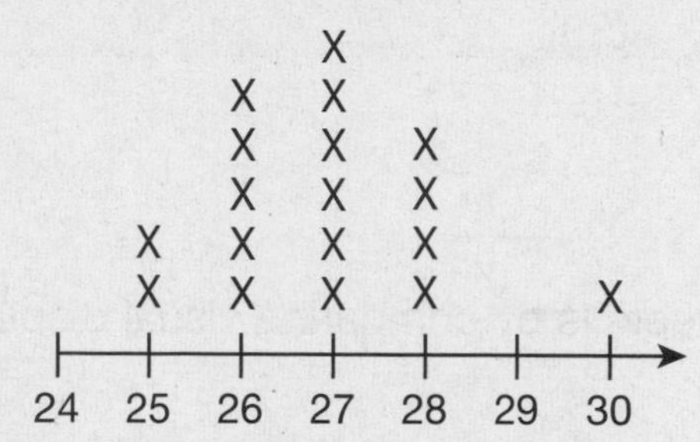

NUMBER OF POINTS SCORED IN A BASKETBALL GAME
X = 1 basketball game

- What is the range of the scores?

5

- What are the quartiles of this data set?

1st: 26 3rd: 28

median: 27

- What is the interquartile range of this data set?

2

- In how many games did the Pumas score a number of points greater than or equal to the first quartile value and less than or equal to the third quartile value? In how many games did they score less than the first quartile amount or greater than the third quartile amount?

26, 28, 27
1st 3rd Med

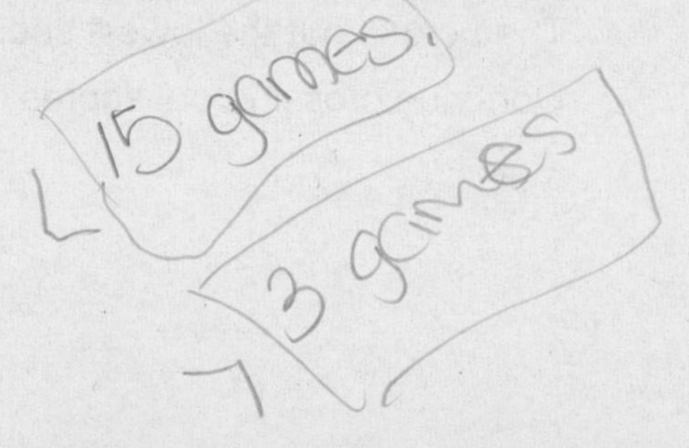

Lesson 19 Displaying Data

Another way to compare data sets is by comparing visual displays of the data and their measures of variability.

- A **histogram** is a bar graph that compares the frequency of values as bars of different heights.
- A **frequency table** is a table that lists the frequencies of values as numbers.
- A **stem-and-leaf plot** is a table that lists the values as numbers categorized by place value.
- A **box-and-whisker plot** is a graph in the form of a number line that shows the measures of variability (least value; first, second, and third quartiles; and greatest value).

EXAMPLE 1

Find the median score for the following stem-and-leaf plot:

TEST SCORES

Stem	Leaf
9	1, 2, 3, 5, 5, 5, 8
8	0, 0, 3, 3, 7
7	1, 2, 9
6	5, 5, 7
5	9

KEY
6 | 5 = 65

STRATEGY **Cross out the highest and lowest scores.**

STEP 1 Cross out the highest and lowest scores one at a time.

Start by crossing out the highest score, 91.

Then cross out the lowest score, 59.

Continue crossing out scores until you have only one (or two) left.

TEST SCORES

Stem	Leaf
9	~~1~~, ~~2~~, ~~3~~, ~~5~~, ~~5~~, ~~5~~, ~~8~~
8	~~0~~, ~~0~~, ~~3~~, 3, ~~7~~
7	~~1~~, ~~2~~, ~~9~~
6	~~5~~, ~~5~~, ~~7~~
5	~~9~~

KEY
6 | 5 = 65

STEP 2 Use the key to determine the score.

According to the key, 8 | 3 = 83.

SOLUTION **The median score is 83.**

EXAMPLE 2

Draw a box-and-whisker plot for the following set of grades.

93, 45, 89, 79, 89, 91, 52, 94, 75, 65, 65, 75, 73, 86, 98, 52, 82, 82, 83, 85

STRATEGY **Find the greatest and least grades, the median grade, and the first and third quartiles. Then draw the box-and-whisker plot.**

STEP 1 Rewrite the grades from least to greatest.

45, 52, 52, 65, 65, 73, 75, 75, 79, 82, 82, 83, 85, 86, 89, 89, 91, 93, 94, 98

STEP 2 Identify the greatest and least grades.

least : 45

greatest : 98

STEP 3 Find the median grade.

45, 52, 52, 65, 65, 73, 75, 75, 79, [82, 82,] 83, 85, 86, 89, 89, 91, 93, 94, 98

median grade: 82

STEP 4 Find the first and third quartiles.

45, 52, 52, 65, [65, 73,] 75, 75, 79, 82, 82, 83, 85, 86, [89, 89,] 91, 93, 94, 98

first quartile: 69

third quartile: 89

STEP 5 Draw a box-and-whisker plot.

- Draw a number line that includes the full range of grades.
- The ends of the "whiskers" are the greatest and least grades.

- The lesser part of the box is bordered on the left side by the first quartile and on the right side by the median.
- The greater part of the box is bordered on the left side by the median and on the right side by the third quartile.

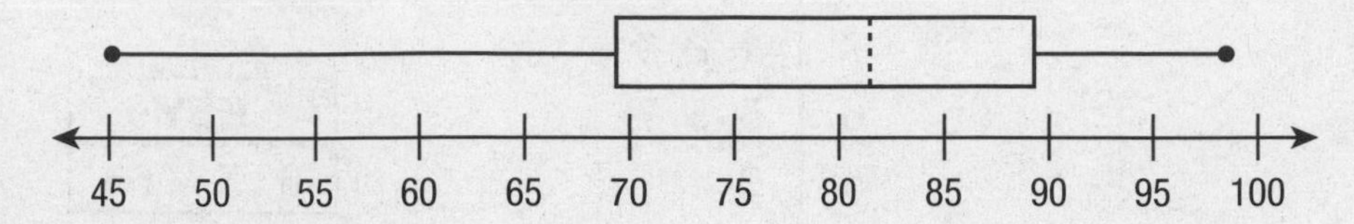

COACHED EXAMPLE

Frankie counted the numbers of blue and red jellybeans in 50 bags of candy.

He made the following frequency tables to organize his data.

Number of Red Jelly Beans	Frequency
15	1
16	5
17	7
18	12
19	8
20	13
21	4

Number of Blue Jelly Beans	Frequency
15	9
16	5
17	14
18	18
19	3
20	1
21	0

Which data set has the greater mode?

THINKING IT THROUGH

Which number of red jellybeans has the greatest frequency? ________

This is the mode of the data set.

Which number of blue jellybeans is the mode? ________

The data set for the ________ jelly beans has the greater mode.

Lesson Practice

Choose the correct answer.

1. A company accountant wants to find out which group of employees uses the most paper. He makes the stem-and-leaf plots below to compare the number of pages in each printed document for the employees who work the nightshift and the employees who work the dayshift.

NIGHTSHIFT

Stem	Leaf
0	1, 2, 4, 4, 6, 9, 9
1	0, 1, 2, 3, 3, 9
2	5
3	
4	5

KEY
4 | 5 = 45

DAYSHIFT

Stem	Leaf
0	1, 1, 2, 2
1	3
2	0, 1, 2
3	3, 3, 3, 3, 3
4	0, 2

What conclusion can you draw based on the data?

A. The nightshift employees use more paper.
B. The nightshift employees print more documents.
C. The dayshift employees print more documents that are only 3 pages long.
D. The dayshift employees print more documents that are over 20 pages long.

2. Manuela is in Mrs. Green's class and her brother is in Mr. Brown's class. She claims that her test scores are lower than her brother's because Mrs. Green grades harder. Look at the histograms below. What conclusion based on these graphs supports Manuela's claim?

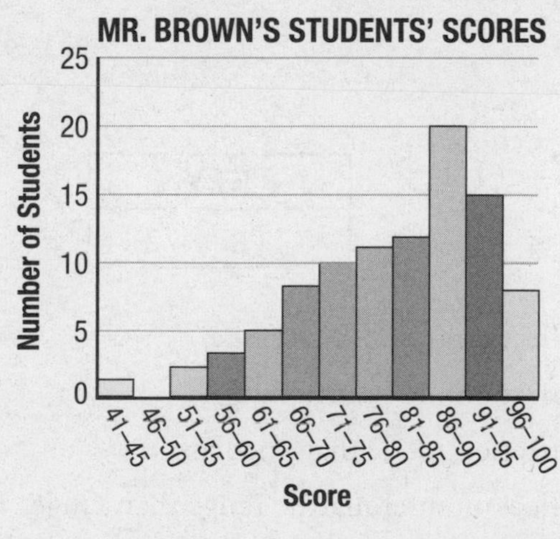

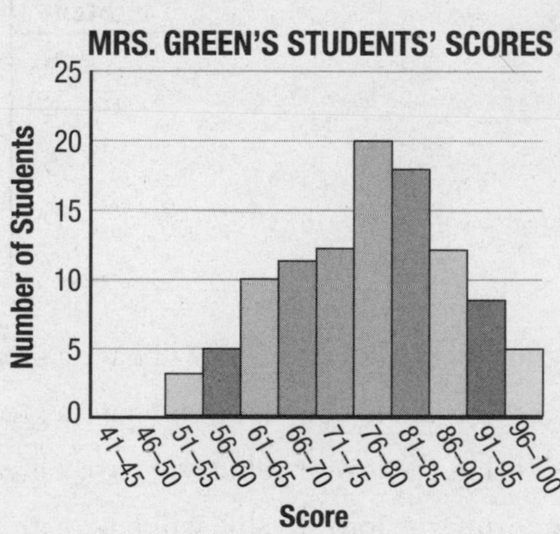

F. The median score is higher in Mrs. Green's classes.
G. The mode test score is lower in Mrs. Green's classes.
H. The range of test scores is greater in Mr. Brown's classes.
J. More people make grades less than 56 in Mrs. Green's classes.

3. For a science project, Gerald compared the numbers of seeds in 20 oranges and 20 apples. He made the histograms below to display his data.

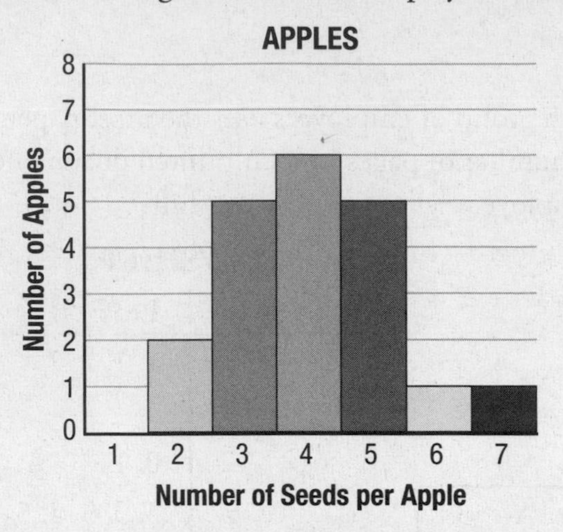

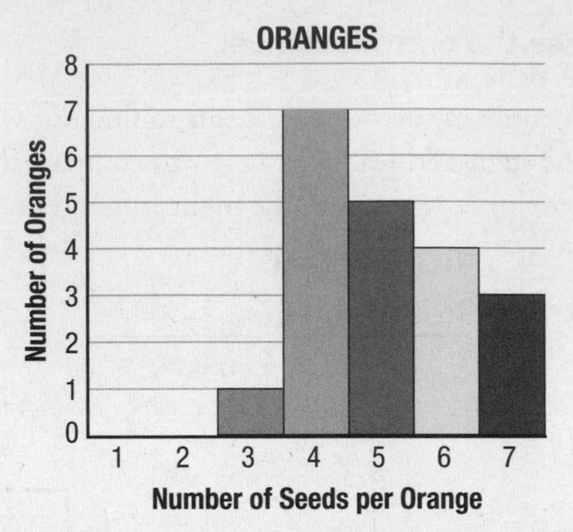

Which conclusion can Gerald draw based on the data?

A. The mode for the orange data set is greater.

B. The range for the orange data set is greater.

C. The quartiles for the orange data set are higher.

D. The interquartile range for the orange data set is greater.

4. Judy is examining the following set of data. She notices that one value is significantly lower than the other values in the set. She is considering throwing out the data point before she calculates the measures of central tendency. What effect will ignoring the lowest value have on her calculations?

Stem	Leaf
3	2
4	
5	8, 9, 9, 9
6	0, 2, 3, 3, 5, 9
7	2, 3, 5, 6, 8, 9, 9

KEY
7 | 2 = 72

F. Ignoring the lowest value will have a greater effect on mean than mode.

G. Ignoring the lowest value will have a greater effect on mode than range.

H. Ignoring the lowest value will have a greater effect on mode than median.

J. Ignoring the lowest value will have a greater effect on interquartile range than range.

5. The box-and-whisker plots below show the average daily temperatures for four cities.

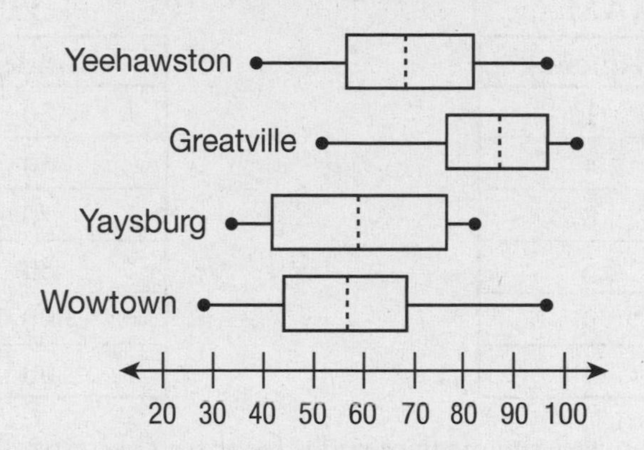

Which location has the widest spread in the middle 50% of its average daily temperatures?

A. Greatville

B. Wowtown

C. Yaysburg

D. Yeehawston

6. Peter coaches a Little League baseball team. The box-and-whisker plots below show the scores that Peter's team made this year and last year.

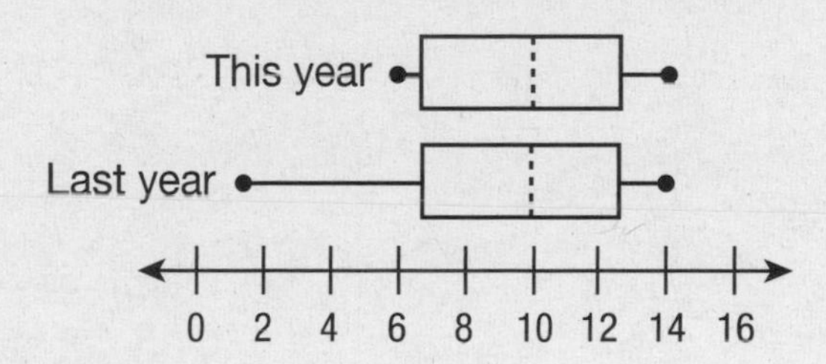

How have the team's scores changed since last year?

F. The range is smaller this year.

G. The median score is greater this year.

H. The highest score is greater this year.

J. The interquartile range is smaller this year.

Use the Response Grid to complete Number 7.

7. A teacher compares the grades that students received on two different exams in the following tables.

MIDTERM EXAM

Grade	Frequency
50	1
60	4
70	8
80	15
90	9
100	3

FINAL EXAM

Grade	Frequency
50	0
60	2
70	4
80	11
90	7
100	16

What is the difference between the median grades for these two tests?

1	0			
	⊘	⊘	⊘	
⊙	⊙	⊙	⊙	⊙
0	0	0	0	0
1	1	1	1	1
2	2	2	2	2
3	3	3	3	3
4	4	4	4	4
5	5	5	5	5
6	6	6	6	6
7	7	7	7	7
8	8	8	8	8
9	9	9	9	9

8. Rick held a contest for who could sell the most candy bars to benefit the marching band. He recorded his data in the following table.

ECR

Student	Number of Candy Bars
Reynaldo	75
Kate	78
Donnell	90
Karen	67
Rick	51
Kirk	55
Juan	78
Fiona	77

- What are the range, quartiles, and interquartile range?

- Draw a box-and-whisker plot for this data.

- Rick decided not to include his own number in the data. How does dropping his number of candy bars affect the range of this data? Use mathematics to justify your answer.

Data Sampling and Detecting Bias

When you collect data about a group, it is often easier to collect information about only part of that group rather than about every member of that group. A **sample** is a part of a group that is representative of the whole group. But the way you collect the data, or the samples that you choose to collect, can affect the outcome of the investigation. **Bias** is a sampling error that favors certain outcomes. To avoid bias, you can increase sample size, perform random sampling, and take representative samples.

EXAMPLE

A teacher is conducting a survey to find out how many of the students at his school plan to go to college. It is possible for him to survey 5, 50, or 500 students selected at random from the school. Which sample size will likely give him the most reliable data?

STRATEGY **Examine sample size.**

STEP 1 Compare the sample sizes given.

The sample sizes are 5, 50, or 500 students, all selected at random.

STEP 2 Determine which is greatest.

The larger the sample size chosen, the less bias in the sampling method.
The sample of 500 students will be the least biased.

SOLUTION **The largest sample size, 500 students, will likely give him the most reliable data.**

COACHED EXAMPLE

Carl wants to find out how often students at his school take their books home to study. He decides to survey 35 students to find out. He randomly selects 35 students from two of his honors classes. In what way has he introduced bias into his sampling methods?

THINKING IT THROUGH

What is Carl's sample size? ___________

Did he use random sampling within the two honors classes? ___________

What population does he want to know about? ___________

Is his sample representative of that population? ___________

Lesson Practice

Choose the correct answer.

1. Greg wants to conduct a survey to find out how often students at his school go to the movie theater. Which of these methods provides Greg with the most representative sample of students?

   A. Survey students as they exit the movie theater.

   B. Survey students who live near the movie theater.

   C. Survey students who pass by the movie theater.

   D. Survey students as they leave school in the afternoons.

2. Greg wants to conduct a second survey to find out what types of movies are enjoyed by students who see movies often. Which of these methods provides Greg with the most representative sample of these students?

   F. Survey students as they exit the movie theater.

   G. Survey students who live near the movie theater.

   H. Survey students who pass by the movie theater.

   J. Survey students as they leave school in the afternoons.

3. The owner of a chain of sandwich shops wants to find out how long it takes his employees to get to work each day. He plans to survey 50 of his 500 employees. Which of the following methods of sampling would give the most representative random sample of his employees?

   A. Select at random 50 employees who are managers.

   B. Randomly select 50 employees from his downtown shops.

   C. Randomly select 25 stores and ask the manager of each store to select 2 employees.

   D. Use a random number generator to generate 50 random numbers and use these to select 50 employees from a numerical list of all employees.

4. The owner of a bread factory wants to test the quality of the loaves of bread the factory bakes. The factory produces 5,000 loaves each day. Which of the following methods gives a sample that is more representative of the loaves of bread?

   F. Randomly choose 5 loaves throughout the day and test their quality.

   G. Randomly choose 500 loaves throughout the day and test their quality.

   H. Choose the first 1,000 loaves that are produced each day and test their quality.

   J. Choose the last 1,000 loaves that are produced each day and test their quality.

5. The mayor of a small town wants to conduct a random survey to find out how many people visit a downtown park on a regular basis. Which of these methods would provide the mayor with a simple random, representative sample of 100 people?

A. Select 100 people from a list of people who donate to wildlife charities.

B. Choose every 5th person who visits the park on Saturday until 100 people are chosen.

C. Choose the name of every 20th person in the town phonebook until 100 names are chosen.

D. Randomly select 10 people from each of 10 different states.

6. Fred's mother owns an ice cream shop. She wants to add three new flavors to the selection of flavors that she sells in her shop. She is considering the four options below for collecting data on what flavors might attract new customers. Which option gives her the most representative sample of potential new customers?

F. Spend seven days outside her own ice cream shop and ask every person who exits what flavors they like.

G. Spend five days outside of a randomly selected ice cream shop and ask every person who exits what flavors they like.

H. Spend one day outside of eight randomly selected ice cream shops and ask ten randomly selected people who exit each ice cream shop what flavors they like.

J. Spend one day outside of five randomly selected ice cream shops in nearby cities and ask the first 100 people who exit each ice cream shop what flavors they like.

Use the Response Grid to complete Number 7.

7. The principal wants to find out how often her students go to the school counselor. She is trying to decide whether to survey 25, 50, 100, or 200 students selected at random. Which sample size will likely give her the most reliable data?

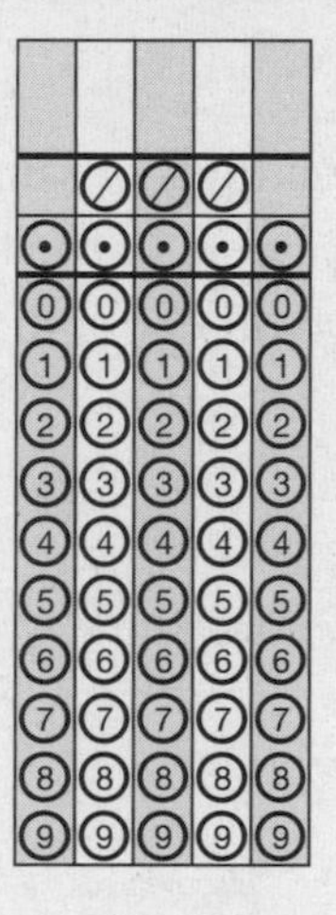

8.
ECR

The soccer league president wants to find out how much parents of soccer players are willing to pay for tournament entry fees. He asks one of the league coaches to gather data for him. The coach is going to survey 100 parents of soccer players in the league. Consider the methods of sampling shown below.

Method 1: randomly select 100 parents of soccer players from the 5 most successful teams.
Method 2: use a random number generator to generate 100 random numbers and use these to select 100 parents from a numerical list of the soccer players.
Method 3: randomly select 10 soccer teams and ask the coaches of each team to select 10 parents.

Which of the above methods of sampling would give the most representative random sample of the parents of soccer players in the league? Use mathematics to justify your answer. Include in your justification why you chose that method and why you did not choose each of the other two methods.

Lesson

Probability

- **Probability** is a ratio that represents the likelihood that a certain event will occur. It can be expressed as a fraction, a decimal or a percent.

$$P = \frac{\text{number of favorable outcomes}}{\text{all possible outcomes}}$$

- The numerator of the probability ratio is the number of favorable outcomes representing the specified event.
- The denominator of the probability ratio is the number of all possible outcomes.
- The probability of an event is always a number between 0 (impossible that the event will happen) and 1 (certainty that the event will happen).

EXAMPLE 1

The spinner below is divided into 4 equal sections.

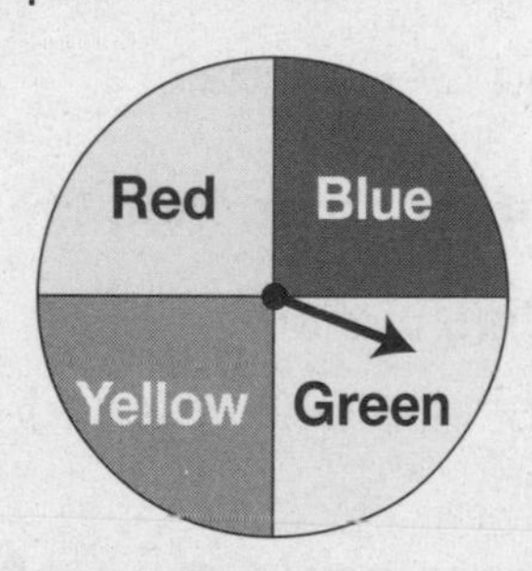

If the arrow lands on a color, what is the probability that it will land on red or blue?

STRATEGY **Set up a ratio and simplify.**

STEP 1 Identify the favorable outcomes specified in the question.

Favorable outcomes: arrow landing on blue or red

STEP 2 Identify the number of all possible outcomes.

There are 4 different colors, so there are 4 possible outcomes.

STEP 3 Identify the number of those outcomes that are the favorable outcomes.

Only 2 of those outcomes, landing on red or blue, are the favorable outcomes.

STEP 4 Set up a ratio and simplify.

$$P = \frac{\text{number of favorable outcomes}}{\text{all possible outcomes}}$$

$$P = \frac{\text{landing on blue or red}}{\text{landing on a color}}$$

$$P = \frac{2}{4}$$

$$P = \frac{1}{2}$$

The fraction $\frac{1}{2}$ is equal to the decimal 0.5.

SOLUTION **The probability of the arrow landing on red or blue is 1 in 2, $\frac{1}{2}$, or 0.5.**

EXAMPLE 2

The following table shows the results of the election for student council president.

RESULTS OF STUDENT COUNCIL ELECTION

	Girls	Boys
Rhonda	36	29
Hillary	39	45
Toby	24	20
Jamal	45	38

What is the probability that a girl voted for Rhonda?

STRATEGY **Delete unnecessary information, then create and simplify a probability ratio.**

STEP 1 Delete the unnecessary information.

The question asks about girls who voted for Rhonda, so the "Boys" column is unnecessary information.

RESULTS OF STUDENT COUNCIL ELECTION

	Girls	~~Boys~~
Rhonda	36	~~29~~
Hillary	39	~~45~~
Toby	24	~~20~~
Jamal	45	~~38~~

STEP 2 Find the total number of the girls who voted.

$36 + 39 + 24 + 45 = 144$

STEP 3 Identify the favorable outcome.

The favorable outcome is a girl voting for Rhonda. 36 girls voted for Rhonda.

STEP 4 Set up the ratio and simplify.

$P = \frac{\text{number of favorable outcomes}}{\text{all possible outcomes}}$

$P = \frac{\text{girls voting for Rhonda}}{\text{girls who voted}}$

$P = \frac{36}{144}$

$P = \frac{1}{4}$

The fraction $\frac{1}{4}$ is equal to the decimal 0.25.

SOLUTION **The probability that a girl voted for Rhonda is 1 in 4, $\frac{1}{4}$, or 0.25.**

COACHED EXAMPLE

A six-sided die has the numbers 1 through 6 printed on its faces. What is the probability of rolling an even number?

THINKING IT THROUGH

How many sides does the die have? ___________

How many of the numbers are even? ___________

The ratio of even numbers to numbers on the die is ___________, which simplifies to ___________.

The probability of rolling an even number is ___________.

Lesson Practice

Choose the correct answer.

1. A deck of 52 playing cards has 13 cards of each suit: diamonds, hearts, spades, and clubs. If you draw a single card at random, what is the probability that it is a diamond?

   A. $\frac{1}{2}$

   B. $\frac{1}{4}$

   C. $\frac{1}{13}$

   D. $\frac{1}{52}$

2. A twelve-sided die has the letters A through L printed on its faces. What is the probability of rolling a vowel?

   F. $\frac{1}{2}$

   G. $\frac{5}{12}$

   H. $\frac{1}{4}$

   J. $\frac{1}{12}$

3. As part of a contest, Selena spins the spinner below, which is divided into 8 equal sections. Whatever prize the arrow lands on, she will win.

   What is the probability that the arrow will land on an amount of money?

   A. $\frac{1}{8}$

   B. $\frac{1}{4}$

   C. $\frac{3}{8}$

   D. $\frac{1}{2}$

4. The table below shows the numbers of participants in a 5K race.

PARTICIPANTS IN THE 5K RACE

	Men	Women
Ages 18 and under	50	52
Ages 19 to 35	125	110
Ages 36 to 50	99	89
Ages 51 and over	75	79

   What is the probability that a participant is between the ages of 19 and 50?

   F. $\frac{136}{188}$

   G. $\frac{99}{188}$

   H. $\frac{136}{679}$

   J. $\frac{423}{679}$

5. Heidi surveys students about their favorite vegetable. The survey results are shown in the table below.

SURVEY RESULTS

Vegetable	Number of Students
Green Beans	14
Broccoli	12
Peas	8
Brussels Sprouts	2

Based on the survey results, what is the probability that a randomly selected student prefers broccoli?

A. $\frac{7}{18}$

B. $\frac{1}{3}$

C. $\frac{1}{12}$

D. $\frac{1}{36}$

6. At a school carnival, the debate team is selling raffle tickets. The team sells 65 tickets that are numbered from 100 to 164. At the end of the carnival, the team president draws one ticket from the hat. What is the probability that the ticket drawn is an odd number?

F. $\frac{1}{65}$

G. $\frac{2}{65}$

H. $\frac{32}{65}$

J. $\frac{33}{65}$

Use the Response Grid to complete Number 7.

7. Half of the students in Mr. Smith's class are girls. Half of the girls in the class have brown hair. If Mr. Smith randomly chooses a student, what is the probability that the student is a girl with brown hair?

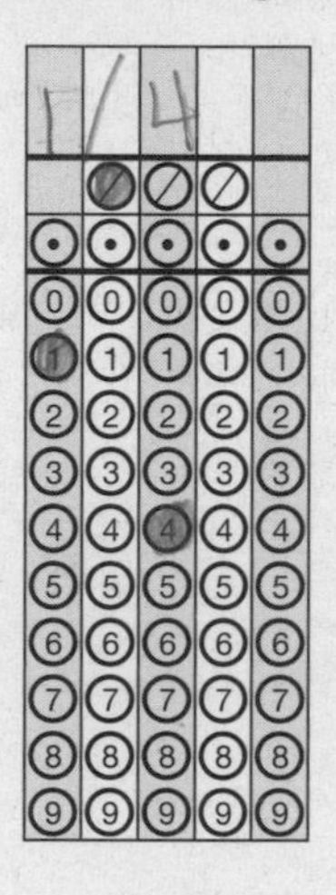

8. A cloth bag holds 20 blue marbles, 15 red marbles, 15 white marbles, and 40 black marbles.

ECR

- If a marble is chosen at random, what is the probability that it is a red marble?

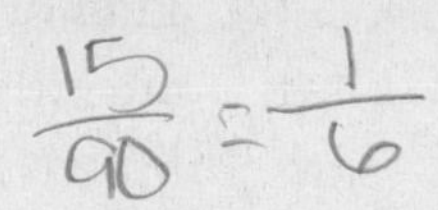

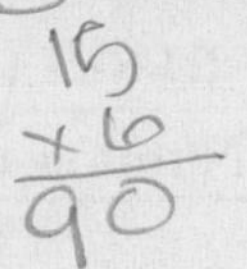

- If a marble is chosen at random, what is the probability that it is a red or a white marble?

- If a marble is chosen at random, what is the probability that it is **not** a black marble?

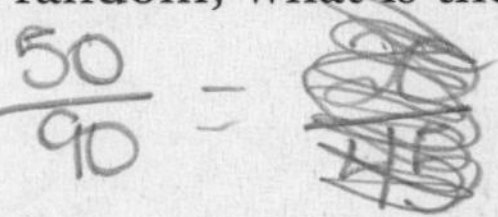

- If a marble is chosen at random, what is the probability that it is a purple marble?

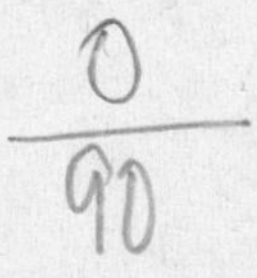

HSA Review

1 **Kelly made the following grades on her first four math tests for the semester: 79, 86, 98, 89. Her mean grade for the semester is 90. What did she make on the fifth and final test?**

A 88

B 90

C 92

D 98

2 **Harry makes the following measurements in a study of average daily temperature: 79, 77, 74, 77, 75, 80, 83, 84, 82, 80, 80, 77, 79, 77, and 81. What are the mode and median temperatures?**

F mode: 77, median: 79

G mode: 79, median: 79

H mode: 79, median: 80

J mode: 80, median: 79

3 **The stem-and-leaf plots below show the daily high temperatures for 24 days in June and 24 days in July.**

JUNE DAILY HIGHS

Stem	Leaf
10	
9	1, 2, 4, 4, 5
8	1, 1, 2, 3, 5, 5, 8, 8, 8, 8, 9
7	0, 1, 2, 5, 5, 8
6	9, 9

KEY
6 ǀ 9 = 69

JULY DAILY HIGHS

Stem	Leaf
10	0
9	1, 1, 1, 2, 2, 3, 5, 8, 9
8	1, 1, 2, 5, 5, 8, 8, 8, 8
7	1, 2, 5, 9, 9
6	

What conclusion can you draw based on the data?

A The mode temperature for the July data is greater.

B The range of temperatures for the June data is greater.

C The median temperature for the July data is greater.

D The interquartile range for the July data is greater.

4 **Mr. Hernandez made a box-and-whisker plot to compare two sets of test scores.**

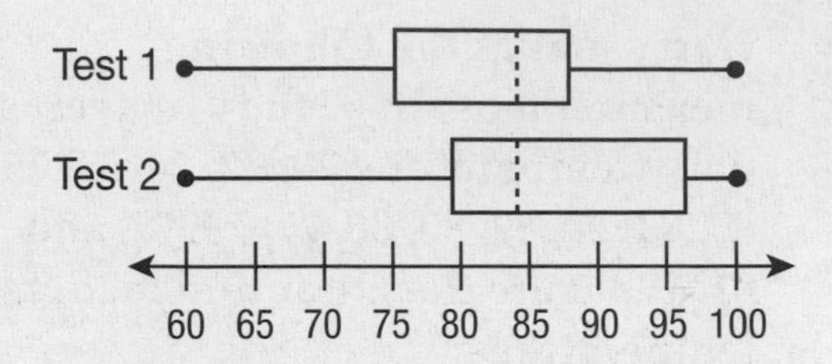

What conclusion can you draw based on the plots?

G The range was greater on Test 1.

F The median score was higher on Test 2.

H As a group, the middle 50% scored higher on Test 1.

J There was greater variability of scores in the middle 50% on Test 2.

5 **Cynthia is conducting a survey to find out what percentage of the student population at her school bring their lunches from home. Which of these methods provides her with the most representative sample of students?**

A Survey students from all of the honors classes.

B Survey students as they leave school in the afternoon.

C Survey students as they exit the lunch line of the cafeteria.

D Survey students as they buy drinks from the vending machines.

6 **Cynthia is conducting a second survey to find out whether students who buy drinks from the vending machines prefer soda or juice. Which of these methods provides her with the most representative sample of these students?**

F Survey students from all of the honors classes.

G Survey students as they leave school in the afternoons.

H Survey students as they exit the lunch line of the cafeteria.

J Survey students as they buy drinks from the vending machines.

7 **The spinner below is divided into 6 equal sections.**

If the arrow lands on a number, what is the probability that it will land on an odd number?

A $\frac{1}{6}$

B $\frac{1}{5}$

C $\frac{1}{3}$

D $\frac{1}{2}$

8 Janet writes the names of each of her classmates on slips of paper. She places each slip of paper in a hat. There are 32 students in her class. 14 of them are boys and the rest are girls. She chooses a slip of paper from the hat at random. What is the probability that she draws a girl's name?

F $\frac{7}{16}$

G $\frac{1}{2}$

H $\frac{9}{16}$

J $\frac{7}{9}$

Use the Response Grids to complete Numbers 9 and 10.

9 The table below lists the points scored during a competition and the frequency of those scores. What is the range of scores?

Score	Frequency
14	7
15	2
16	5
17	0
18	8
19	6

10 What is the interquartile range, in dollars, of the following list of prices?

\$1.75, \$1.99, \$1.19, \$1.25, \$2.00, \$2.10, \$1.75, \$1.58, \$1.64, \$1.73, \$1.85, \$1.95

11
ECR

Helen, Troy, and Paris enter a raffle at a charity event. Helen buys 13 raffle tickets, Troy buys 15 raffle tickets, and Paris buys 7 raffle tickets. There are a total of 100 raffle tickets sold that evening.

- **If a raffle ticket is chosen at random from the 100 tickets, what is the probability that it is Helen's?**

- **If a raffle ticket is chosen at random from the 100 tickets, what is the probability that it is Troy's?**

- **If a raffle ticket is chosen at random from the 100 tickets, what is the probability that it is either Helen's, Troy's, or Paris's?**

- **Two raffle tickets have already been drawn and removed from the raffle. Neither of them was Paris's. If a third raffle ticket is chosen at random from the remaining tickets, what is the probability that it is Paris's?**

CHAPTER

Goal 3, Expectation 3.2

Using Statistics and Probability in Real-World Situations

Lesson

Making Predictions Based on Data

If a sampling method is unbiased, then a sample can represent a larger group. You can use a proportion to make predictions based on data. In a **proportion,** equivalent ratios are compared in an equation.

ratio of sample group = ratio of larger group

For example, consider the situation in which 10 people in a sample group of 50 representative people prefer apples to oranges. You can set up an equation with equivalent ratios to find out how many people in a larger group of 500 prefer apples.

$\frac{10}{50} = \frac{?}{500}$

$\frac{10}{50} = \frac{100}{500}$

EXAMPLE

A scientist conducted an experiment 200 times. The table below shows the results of the experiment and the number of times each result occurred.

EXPERIMENTAL RESULTS

Result	Frequency
25.1	6
25.2	44
25.3	99
25.4	39
25.5	12

Using the information in the table, predict how many times a result of "25.2" would occur in 500 trials of the experiment.

STRATEGY **Set up equivalent ratios.**

STEP 1 Find the ratio of the sample group.

The result "25.2" occurs 44 times out of 200.

The ratio for the sample group is $\frac{44}{200}$.

STEP 2 Find the ratio of the larger group using an unknown.

The ratio of the larger group is $\frac{x}{500}$.

STEP 3 Set the ratios equal to one another in an equation.

$$\frac{44}{200} = \frac{x}{500}$$

STEP 4 Solve for the unknown.

$$\frac{44}{200} = \frac{x}{500}$$

$$500 \times \frac{44}{200} = 500 \times \frac{x}{500}$$

$$500 \times \frac{44}{200} = x$$

$$x = 110$$

SOLUTION A result of "25.2" would occur 110 times in 500 trials of the experiment.

COACHED EXAMPLE

The spinner shown below is spun 18 times.

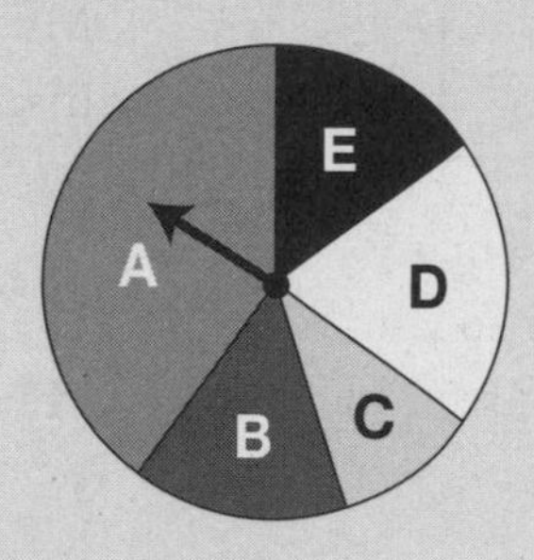

The results of the spins are shown below.

A	B	D	A	A	D
E	B	A	C	E	E
D	B	D	A	C	A

Based on these results, how many times would A be expected to appear in 90 spins?

THINKING IT THROUGH

How many times did the spinner already spin? ___________

How many times will the spinner spin next? ___________

The simplified ratio of the number of times the spinner has been spun to the number of times it will spin is ___________.

How many times has A already appeared? ___________

Set up a proportion showing the ratio of the number of times the spinner has been spun to the number of times it will spin, equal to the ratio of the number of times A has already appeared to x, the unknown number of times A is expected to appear. ___________

Solve this equation for x. $x =$ ___________

In 90 spins, A would appear ___________ times.

Lesson Practice

Choose the correct answer.

1. Kate spun a toy spinner 80 times and recorded her results in the table below. The spinner had six sections, each labeled with a different animal.

EXPERIMENTAL RESULTS

Animal	Frequency
Chicken	31
Cow	15
Duck	12
Goat	6
Horse	5
Pig	11

Based on the results in the table, how many times should Kate expect the spinner to land on the section labeled "Horse" or the section labeled "Cow" if she spins the spinner 400 times?

A. 20

B. 25

C. 75

D. 100

2. The owner of Fink's Inks wants to order bottles of four different colors of ink for her store. She takes a survey of 25 customers to find out what color ink they would buy. The table below shows her results.

INK COLOR VOTES

Color	Number of Votes
Black	10
Blue	8
Red	5
Green	2

Ms. Fink will order 650 bottles of ink. How many bottles of green ink should she order?

F. 13

G. 26

H. 50

J. 52

3. An ice cream factory has a defective machine that sometimes does not add chocolate chips to the ice cream. Every hour for 5 hours, an inspector examined a batch of 20 containers of chocolate chip ice cream made by the machine. The table below shows the number of containers that were missing chocolate chips in each batch.

ICE CREAM CONTAINERS MISSING CHOCOLATE CHIPS

Batch Number	Number of Containers Missing Chocolate Chips
1	5
2	6
3	4
4	3
5	4

How many containers of ice cream missing chocolate chips would be expected if the inspector examined a batch of 8,000 containers?

A. 88

B. 1,600

C. 1,760

D. 2,000

4. The spinner shown below is spun 15 times.

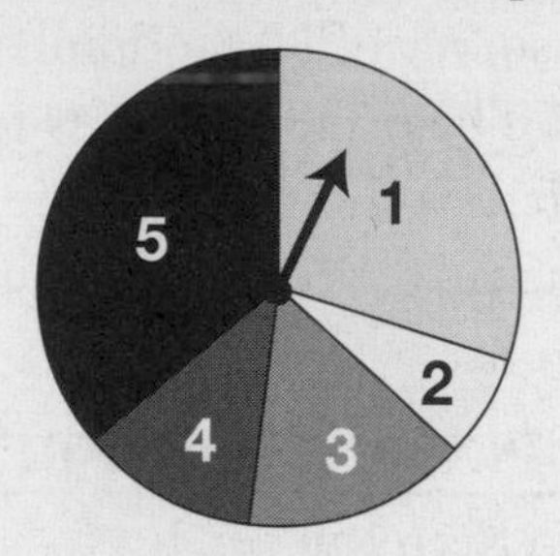

The results of the spins are shown below.

5	1	1	2	3
4	5	2	1	1
5	4	3	5	5

Based on these results, how many times would 2 be expected to appear in 60 spins?

F. 2

G. 4

H. 8

J. 20

5. A cheese maker surveyed 35 customers to find out whether she should sell her cheeses in smaller portions. Of the customers surveyed, 15 favored the change to smaller portions. Her cheese shop gets a total of 400 customers each week. According to the survey results, which of these is a reasonable prediction of the total number of customers each week that would favor this change?

A. 60

B. 125

C. 140

D. 171

6. The principal of a school conducted an opinion survey of 80 randomly selected students. The principal wants to determine if the cafeteria should continue selling milk. The survey results are shown in the table below.

OPINION SURVEY RESULTS

Want to Keep Milk	45
Do Not Want to Keep Milk	23
No Opinion	12

There are 1,950 students in the school. How many students would be expected to want the cafeteria to continue selling milk? Round the answer to the nearest whole number.

F. 449

G. 561

H. 876

J. 1,097

Use the Response Grid to complete Number 7.

7. Mike conducted a random survey of 30 households in his neighborhood to determine how many of his neighbors would support the construction of a sport facility in a local park. The survey results are shown in the table below.

NEIGHBORS' CHOICE OF SPORT FACILITY

Sport Facility	Number of Neighbors
swimming pool	9
bike trail	12
tennis court	3
soccer field	6

There are 500 houses in the neighborhood. Based on the survey results, how many neighbors would be expected to choose to build a bike trail?

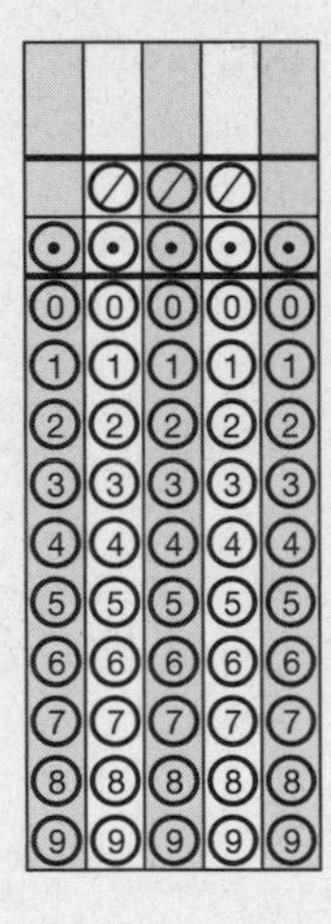

8. The table below shows the number of participants enrolled in a triathlon last year. The 1,500 participants are grouped according to their age.

ECR

LAST YEAR'S TRIATHLON PARTICIPATION INFORMATION

Age	**Number of Participants**
Ages 18 and under	216
Ages 19 to 35	589
Ages 36 to 50	426
Ages 51 and over	269

- The triathlon officials expect to have 2,000 participants this year. Based on last year's participation information, approximately how many participants this year will be ages 19 to 35? Use mathematics to explain how you determined your answer. Use words, symbols, or both in your explanation.

- Using last year's participation information, one official claims that this year, there will be only twice as many people 19 to 35 years old as people ages 18 and under. Is the official correct? Use mathematics to justify your answer.

- One official surveyed 50 people who plan to participate this year. Would you expect the age-group participation information from the triathlon last year or from this group of 50 people to give a more reliable prediction of this year's age group participation? Use mathematics to justify your answer.

Lesson

23 Interpolating and Extrapolating From Data

A **scatter plot** is a graph of data points that relates two variables. When you graph data points on a scatter plot, sometimes you can identify a trend among the points. This trend is illustrated by a line or a curve of best fit. A **line of best fit** is the straight line that most closely represents the relationship between the two variables. A **curve of best fit** is a curved line that does the same thing. You can make an educated guess about information outside of your data set by following the line or curve of best fit.

EXAMPLE

The graph below shows the percentage of students in Mona's school that have had cell phones each year. The line of best fit is drawn.

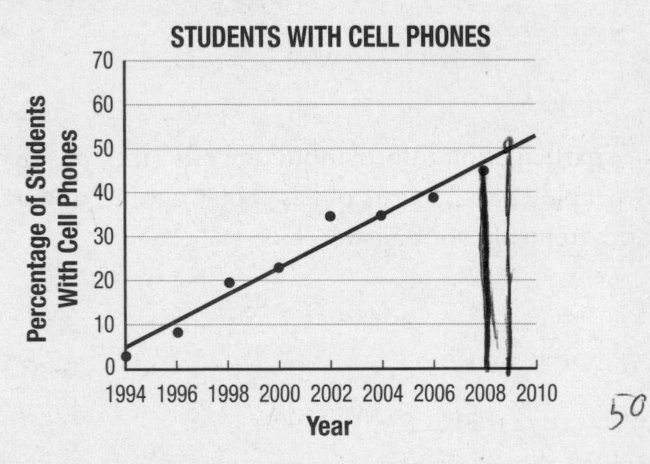

Using the line of best fit, what percentage of students in Mona's school can be expected to have a cell phone in the year 2009?

STRATEGY **Find the desired coordinates.**

STEP 1 Find the year 2009 on the *x*-axis of the graph.

The year 2009 is almost at the far right side of the graph, halfway between 2008 and 2010.

STEP 2 Follow that gridline up from the axis until you reach the line of best fit.

The line of best fit touches the gridline for 2009 at a horizontal gridline.

STEP 3 Identify the y-value of that point.

The line of best fit touches the gridline for 2009 at the horizontal gridline for $y = 50$.

SOLUTION **In 2009, 50% of students will have cell phones.**

COACHED EXAMPLE

The graph below relates the diameter and volume of spherical piñatas at a piñata factory.

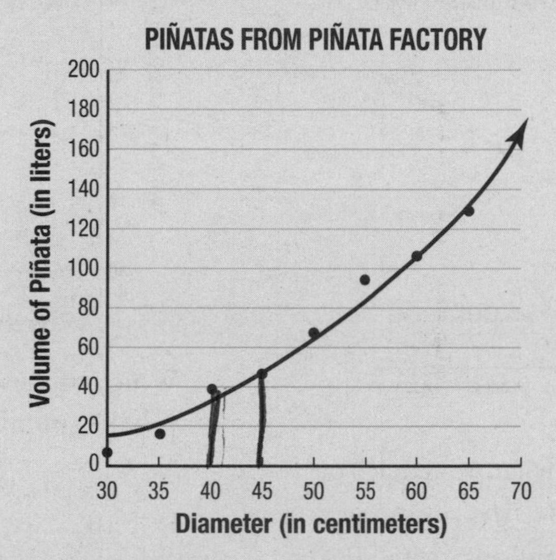

Using the curve of best fit, what would be the expected volume of a piñata that has a diameter of 42 centimeters?

THINKING IT THROUGH

Which axis shows diameter? X

Which axis shows volume? Y

Draw a vertical line for $x = 42$ centimeters.

At what volume does $x = 42$ centimeters? 39-40

A piñata that is 42 centimeters in diameter has a volume of 40 **liters.**

Lesson Practice

Choose the correct answer.

1. The graph below shows the percentage of students at Lila's school who live in households with an Internet connection. The line of best fit is drawn.

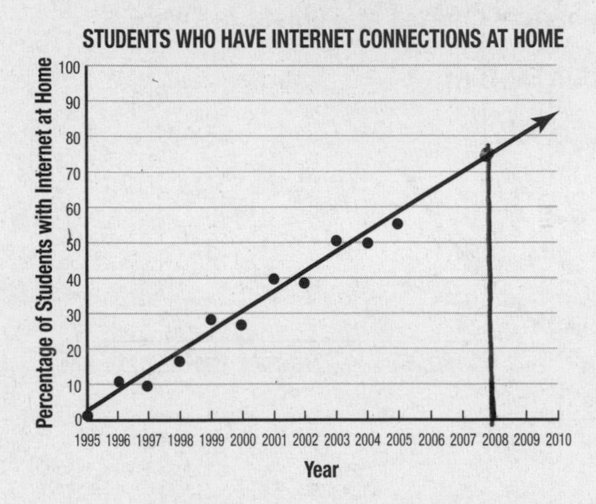

Using the line of best fit, what percentage of students can be expected to have an Internet connection in their homes in the year 2008?

A. 56

B. 60

C. 77

D. 90

2. The graph below models the relationship between temperature and volume of a sample of gas.

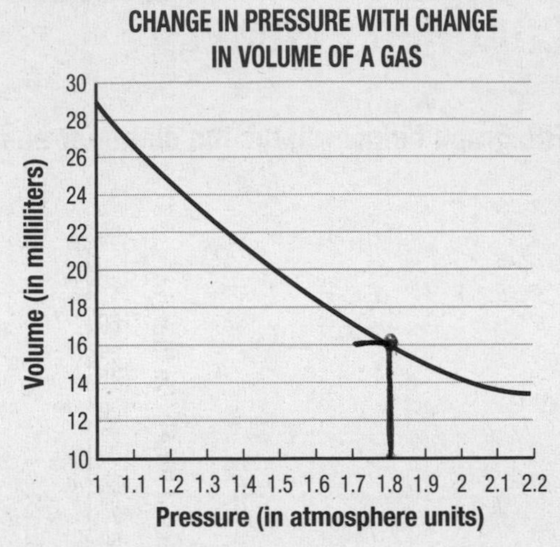

Which of these is the best estimate of the volume (in milliliters) of a sample of gas that has a pressure of 1.8 atmosphere units?

F. 10

G. 13

H. 16

J. 29

3. The scatter plot below shows the average class size at Marjorie's school for the years 1990 through 1999. A curve of best fit has been drawn.

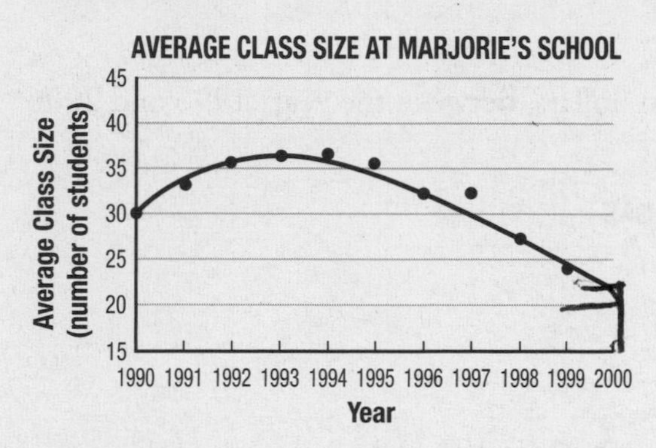

According to the curve of best fit, what was the average class size in 2000?

A. 22
B. 25
C. 29
D. 35

Use the Response Grid to complete Number 4.

4. The graph below shows the population growth of Maryland since 1920. A curve of best fit has been drawn.

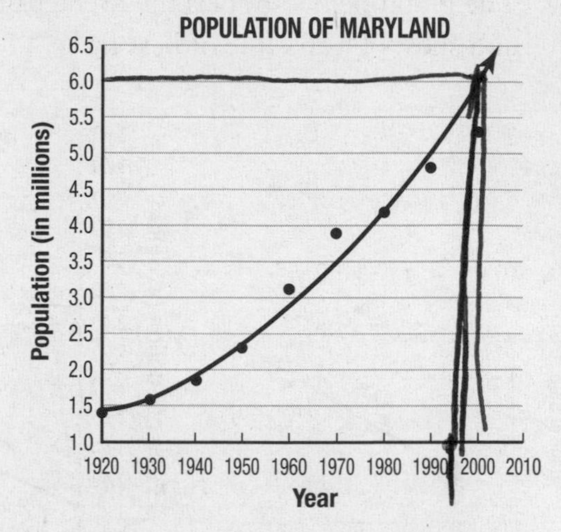

According to the curve of best fit, in what year did the population reach 6 million?

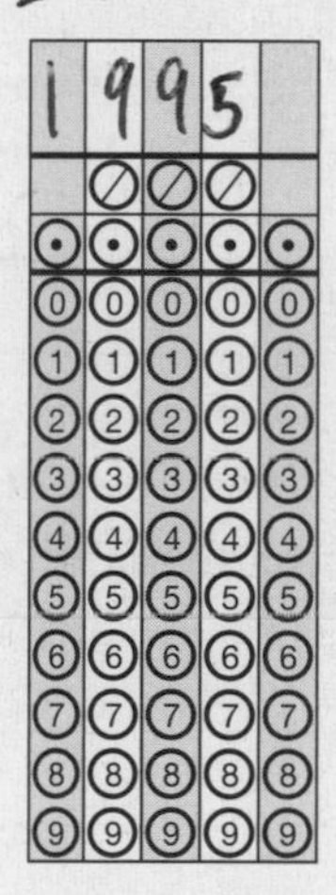

2000

5. **ECR** Dean collected data about the price of a gallon of gas over 10 years. He drew a line of best fit through his data points. He used the equation below to model the average price in dollars (p) of a gallon of gas every year. In Dean's model, m represents the year he recorded each gas price.

$$p = 0.08(m - 1995) + 1.18$$

The graph below models the average price of gas, in dollars, between the years 1996 and 2006 and shows Dean's line of best fit.

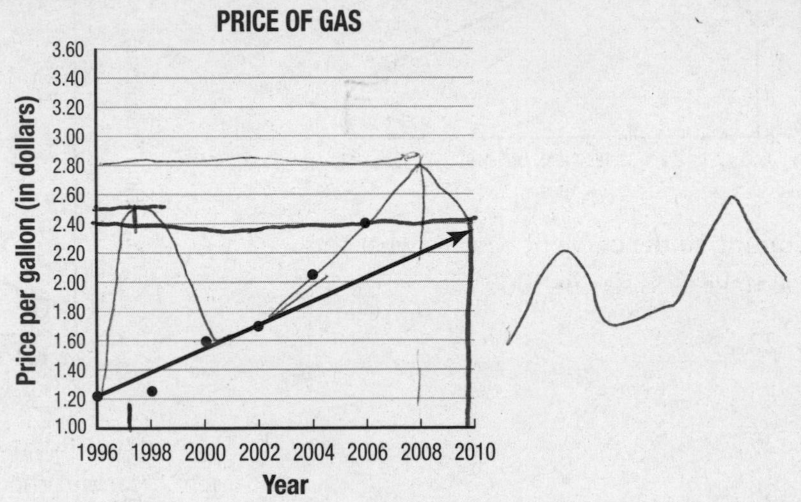

C

- According to the data points in the scatter plot, during which year was the average price of a gallon of gas $2.40?

2006

C

- According to Dean's line of best fit, during which year will the average price of a gallon of gas again be $2.40? Use mathematics to explain how you determined your answer. Use words, symbols, or both in your explanation.

? 2010 because the arrow keeps going up and maches it's tip with 2010.

? 0

- Suppose the average price per gallon of gas were $2.54 in 1997 and $2.80 in 2008. Which would better represent the relationship between the price of a gallon of gas and the year: a curve of best fit or Dean's line of best fit? Use mathematics to explain how you determined your answer. Use words, symbols, or both in your explanation.

? The line would curve up, down, stay constant, go up then down again.

Lesson

Finding a Line of Best Fit

A **line of best fit** is the straight line that most closely represents the relationship between the two variables for data in a scatter plot. When given a set of data points, you can find an approximate equation for the line of best fit by following these steps:

1. Graph the data points in a scatter plot.
2. Draw a straight line that lies as close as possible to all of the data points, with approximately the same number of data points on each side of the line and possibly some data points directly on the line. This is the line of best fit.
3. Identify two points on that line and use those points to find the slope and *y*-intercept. The equation for slope is $m = \frac{y_2 - y_1}{x_2 - x_1}$. To calculate the *y* value of the *y*-intercept, use the same equation but replace one of the data points with (0, *y*).
4. Plug the values for slope, *m*, and *y*-intercept, *b*, into the equation $y = mx + b$ to get the equation for the line of best fit.

EXAMPLE

The table below shows the number of members belonging to the chess club.

CHESS CLUB MEMBERSHIP

Week	Total Members
1	2
2	8
3	12
4	17
5	26
6	33

Write an equation for the line of best fit for this data. Let *x* represent the week and *y* represent the number of club members.

STRATEGY **Graph the data points. Draw a line of best fit. Then use the slope and *y*-intercept to write the equation of the line.**

STEP 1 Graph the data points in a scatter plot.

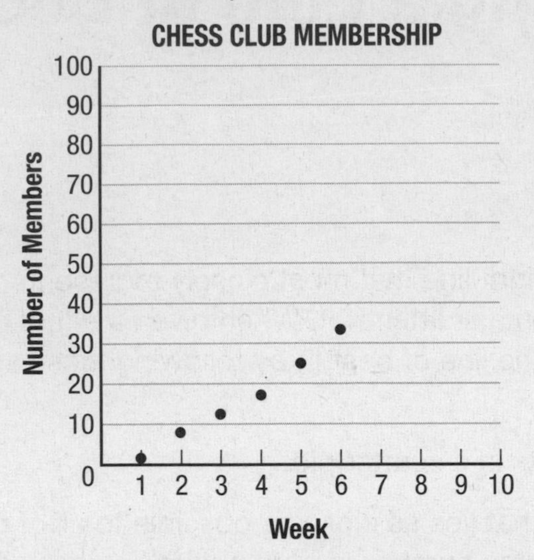

STEP 2 Draw a line of best fit.

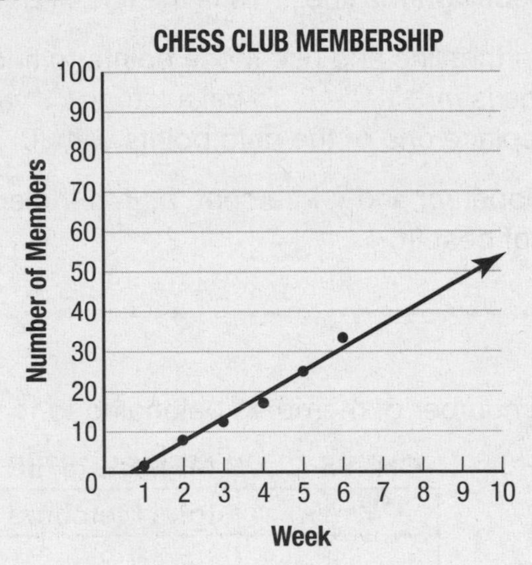

STEP 3 Find the slope.

The two points (1, 2) and (5, 26) lie on the line of best fit.

$m = \frac{y_2 - y_1}{x_2 - x_1}$

$m = \frac{26 - 2}{5 - 1}$

$m = \frac{24}{4}$

$m = 6$

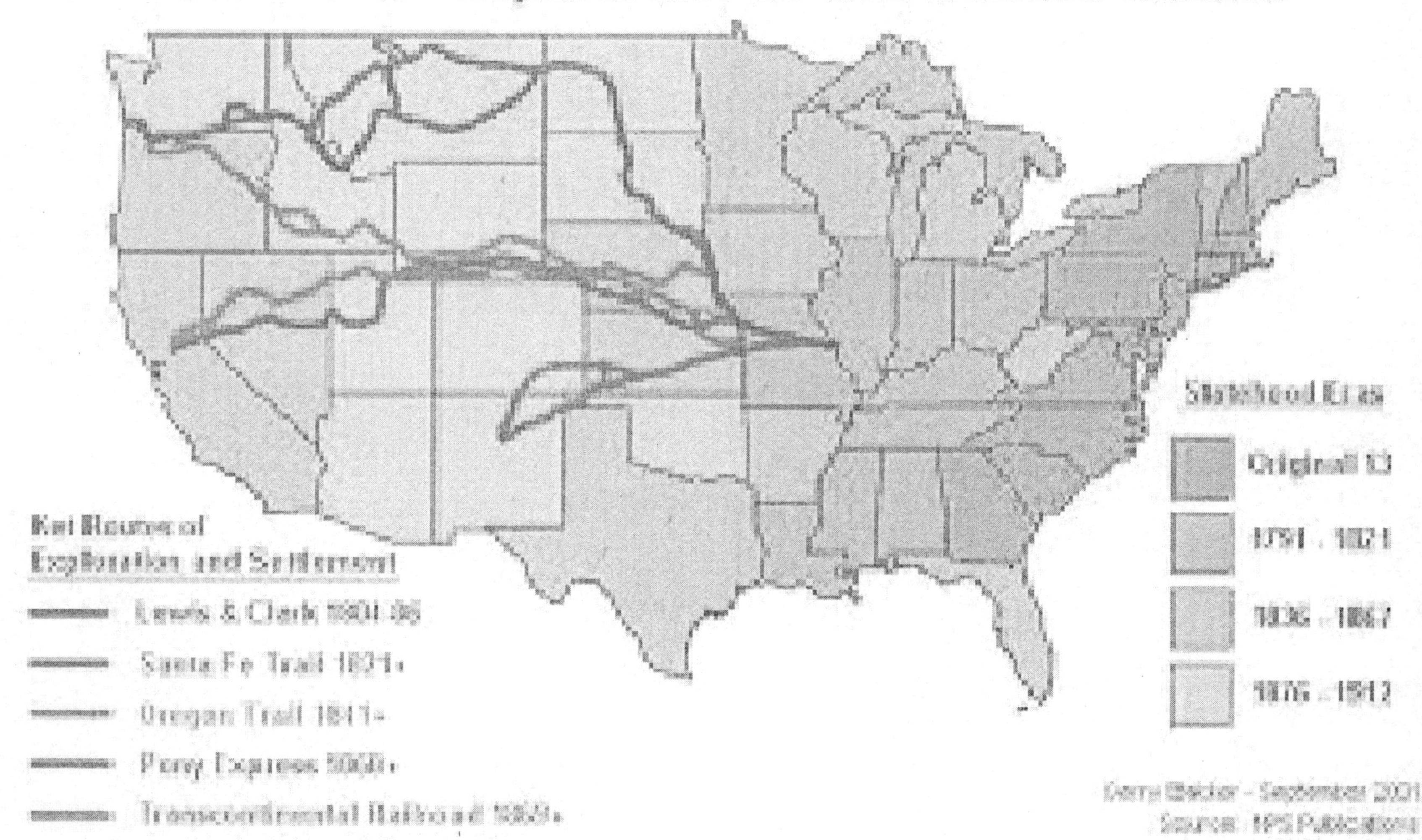
Westward Expansion of the United States
Lewis & Clark
Santa Fe Trail
Oregon Trail
Pony Express
Transcontinental Railroad
Original 13

STEP 4 Find the y-intercept.

The line of best fit crosses the y-axis at $(0, y)$. Use the points $(0, y)$ and $(1, 2)$ in the slope equation.

$$6 = \frac{2 - y}{1 - 0}$$

$$6 = 2 - y$$

$$4 = -y$$

$$y = -4$$

SOLUTION **The line of best fit is $y = 6x - 4$.**

COACHED EXAMPLE

The scatter plot below shows the line of best fit for a set of data points.

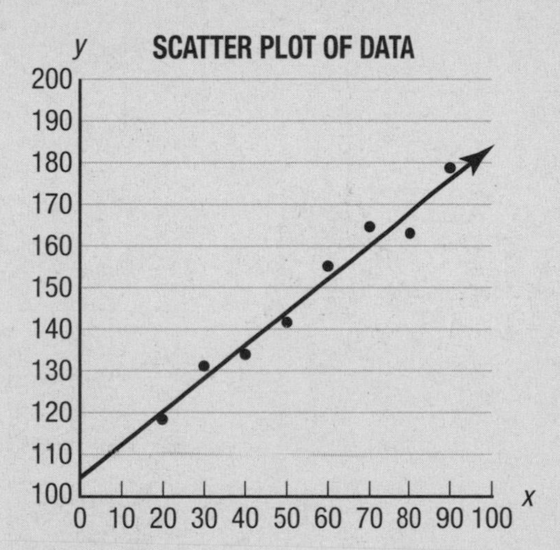

What is the equation for the line of best fit?

THINKING IT THROUGH

The line of best fit passes through the points (20, ___119___) and (70, ___160___).

What is the slope of the line that goes through these points? ___________

What is the y-intercept of that line? ___________

The equation for the line of best fit is $y =$ ___________.

Lesson Practice

Use the table below to answer questions 1 and 2.

The table below shows the relationship between the day of the month and the number of T-shirts that have been sold that month at a sportswear store.

Day	Number of T-shirts sold
2	32
4	48
6	59
8	70
10	72
12	88
14	99
16	111
18	130

1. Which of these equations best represents the line of best fit for the data above?

A. $y = 6x + 20$

B. $y = 8x + 20$

C. $y = 10x + 12$

D. $y = 20x - 10$

2. Suppose there is a sale next month. Why is it not appropriate to use the equation of the line of best fit above to predict sales next month?

F. The slope will become negative during a sale.

G. The rate of sales might be different during a sale.

H. You cannot use any line of best fit for sale figures.

J. The x- and y-axes will change places during a sale.

Use the Response Grid to complete Number 3.

3. Keith collected data in a chemistry experiment. He graphed the data points and drew a line of best fit, as shown below.

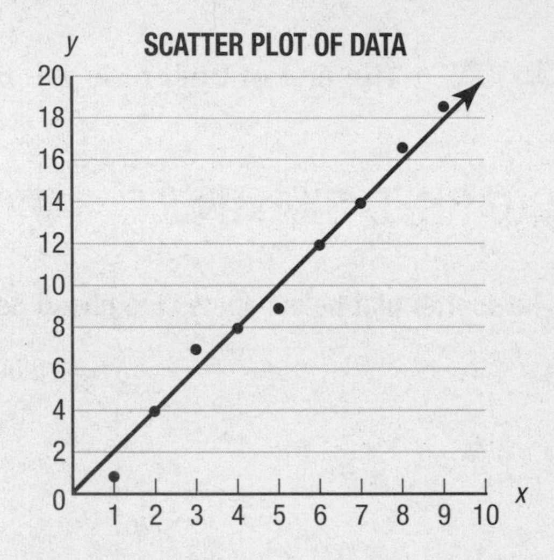

What is the slope of the line of best fit?

4. Students in a biology class decide to measure the length of a vine on different days of the month to determine the rate of growth. The table below shows the length of the vine on different days.

Day	Length (in centimeters)
1	20
4	21
7	22
8	23
9	24
12	25
14	26
17	27
19	28

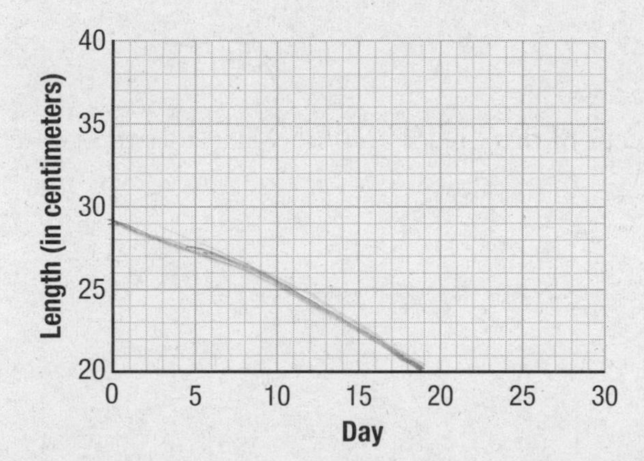

Use the blank coordinate grid to plot these data points and draw a line of best fit. According to your line of best fit, approximately how long will the vine be on Day 30?

A. 20

B. 25

C. 35

D. 45

5. The line of best fit for a set of data is $y = \frac{1}{3}x - 8$. Which of the following is the best estimate of the x-value of a data point in the set with a y-value of 3?

F. -7

G. 4

H. 11

J. 33

6. A deodorant company wants to know how long various sized cans of deodorant spray last. Let x represent the number of months a can was used before running out of deodorant. Let y represent the original weight of the spray can in ounces. An equation for a line of best fit is shown below.

ECR

$$y = 0.5 + 1.2x$$

- What is the slope of this line of best fit? What does the slope mean in the context of this problem?

- What is the y-intercept of this line of best fit? What does the y-intercept mean in the context of this problem?

- Simon has a can of deodorant spray that weighs 6.5 ounces. According to the line of best fit, after how many months will Simon need to replace the can? Use mathematics to explain how you determined your answer. Use words, symbols, or both in your explanation.

Lesson

Evaluating Statistics and Data Interpretation

Consider the following points when evaluating statistics or interpretation of data:

- Was the sample randomly selected? Is there a way the selection could be less biased?
- Look at sample size. A larger sample size often gives more reliable results.
- Think about what the sample represents. Do the conclusions drawn match the information given in the sample? Is the sample representative of the larger group it describes?
- Look at the scale of any graph. When comparing two graphs, be sure they have the same scales on both axes.

EXAMPLE

Melody delivers pizza 10 days out of each month. She made the following graphs to compare her earnings from delivering pizza this month and last.

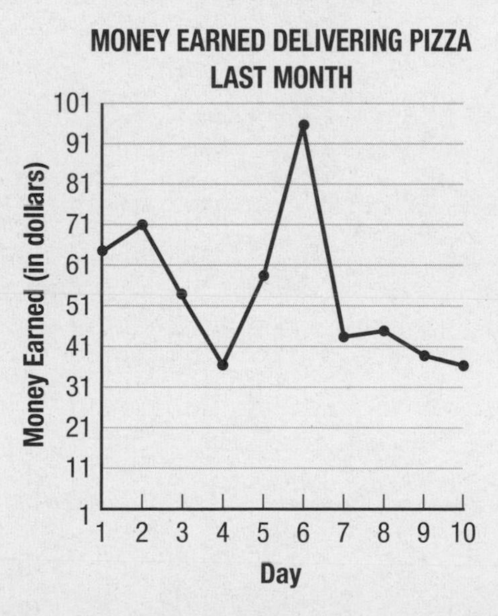

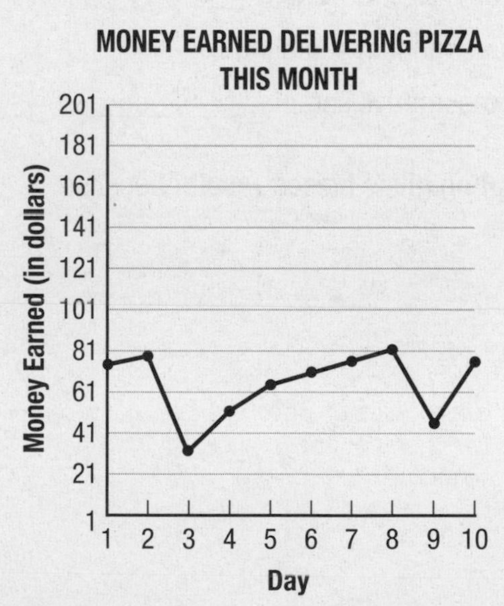

Why is it misleading to compare these two graphs?

STRATEGY **Look at the scale on each of the graphs.**

STEP 1 Compare the titles of the graphs.

These graphs are comparing similar relationships: money earned over a number of days.

STEP 2 Compare the titles of the axes.

The titles of the axes are the same.

STEP 3 Compare the scales of the axes.

The horizontal scales are the same.

The vertical scales are different.

SOLUTION **It is misleading to compare these two graphs because their vertical scales are different.**

COACHED EXAMPLE

Jimmy wants to identify the plants grown in a 100-foot by 100-foot field. He picks a 10-foot by 10-foot square in the middle of the field and identifies 50 plants in that square. Fifteen of these plants have flowers. Jimmy concludes that 30% of the plants in the field have flowers. Why might this type of sampling give biased results?

THINKING IT THROUGH

Has he performed his calculations correctly? ___________

Is the sample size too small? ___________

Does he use random sampling? ___________

Is it a representative sample? ___________

The sampling gives biased results because ___________.

Lesson Practice

Choose the correct answer.

1. Tanika is conducting a survey to find out which is the favorite kind of pet among students in the tenth grade. She decides to survey the students in her first three classes on Friday. Which of these best describes why this type of sampling may give biased results?

A. The sample size is too small.

B. Students are randomly selected.

C. Students from one other class should be selected.

D. The students selected do not represent the whole school.

2. Harold asked 36 of his neighbors whether they would vote Republican. Twelve neighbors responded, "no." Harold concluded that 2,000 of the 6,000 voters in his district will not vote Republican. Which of these explains why his conclusion is invalid?

F. The sample is biased.

G. The sample is not random.

H. The computation is incorrect.

J. The sample size is too large.

3. The table below lists the vehicle types most frequently owned by students at Greg's school.

TYPES OF VEHICLES MOST FREQUENTLY OWNED BY STUDENTS

Rank	Vehicle Type	Number
1	Car	60
2	Van	8
3	Truck	25
4	Motorcycle	7

Greg concludes that 25% of the students at his school own a truck. Why is Greg's conclusion incorrect?

A. Greg did not consider what students used to own before.

B. Greg did not consider the number of doors each car had.

C. Greg did not consider what the students in other schools own.

D. Greg did not consider that there were some students who did not own a vehicle.

4. Helen found that 75% of the members of her book club are willing to spend $10 a month on magazines. She then predicted that since there are 1,200 students in her school, 900 of them are willing to spend $10 a month on magazines. Which of these best describes the reason that her prediction is not valid?

F. She used biased sampling.

G. She interpreted the mean incorrectly.

H. Her prediction was influenced by opinion.

J. The arithmetic in her computation was incorrect.

5. The graphs below show the number of cars sold at Dealership A and Dealership B over the same 12 months last year. The owner of the two dealerships uses the graphs to claim that the overall sales at Dealership A were greater than the overall sales at Dealership B.

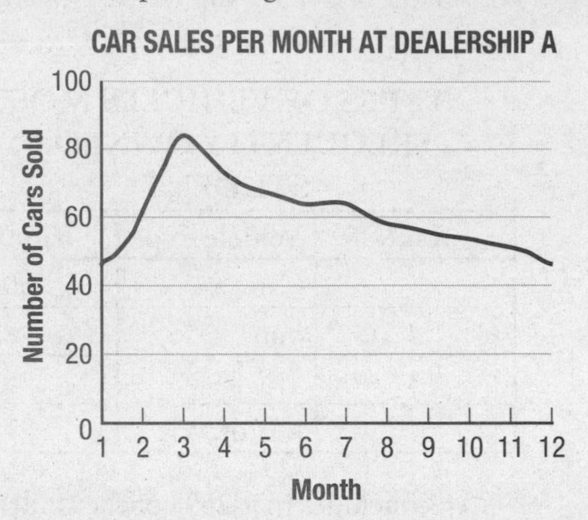

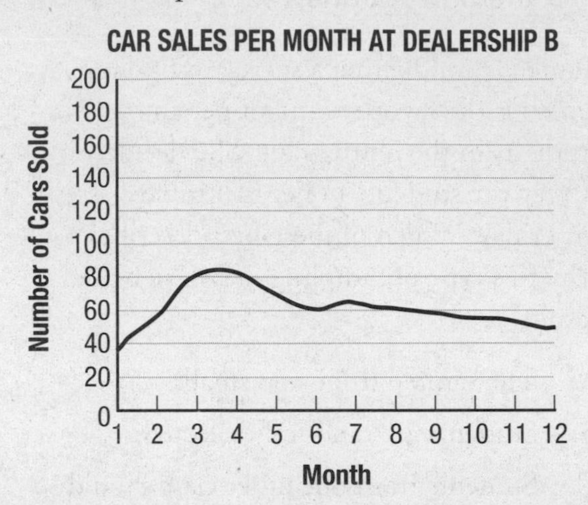

According to the information given, which of these explains why the graphs are misleading?

A. The time periods are different.

B. The types of data are different.

C. The vertical scales are different.

D. The overall numbers of cars sold are different.

6. The graphs below show the grades of students in two different classes. A student uses the graphs to show a teacher that Class B is being graded harder than Class A.

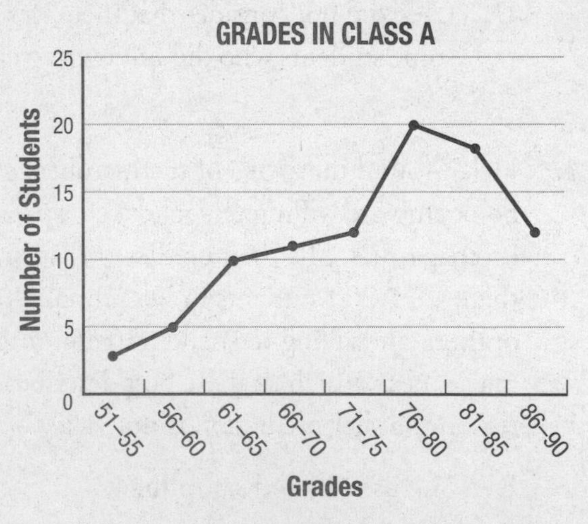

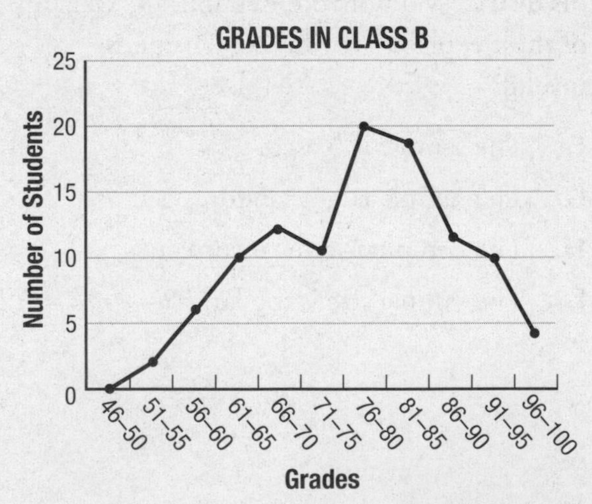

According to the information given, which of these explains why the graphs are misleading?

F. The types of data are different.

G. The overall grades are different.

H. The vertical scales are different.

J. The horizontal scales are different.

Use the Response Grid to complete Number 7.

7. Look at the table of data below.

x	y
25	458
27	525
29	324
31	515
33	601

What is the least maximum value that must appear on the scale's y-axis to include all of the data points?

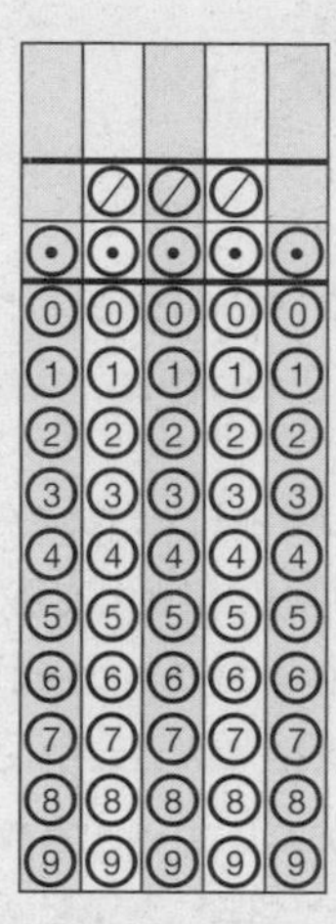

8. The mayor of a small town conducted a survey of 200 randomly selected people to determine
BCR whether or not to build a new library. The survey results are shown in the table below.

USE OF NEW LIBRARY SURVEY

Number of people who said they would use the new library	Number of people who said they would not use the new library
146	54

- Based on this survey, estimate how many of the town's 25,000 residents would use the new library. Use mathematics to explain how you determined your answer. Use words, symbols, or both in your explanation.

- Should a different town use these survey results to predict the number of people who would use a new library in their town? Use mathematics to justify your answer.

HSA Review

Use the Response Grids to complete Numbers 1 and 2.

1 Kiki is learning a foreign language. Her brother gives her a deck of flash cards that have vocabulary words written on them. She chooses a random sample of 25 flash cards from the deck and categorizes the type of word written on each one. The table below shows her results.

	Noun	Verb	Adjective	Adverb
Frequency	10	7	5	3

The total number of flash cards in the deck is 900. Based on the results in the table, how many of the flash cards in the deck are nouns?

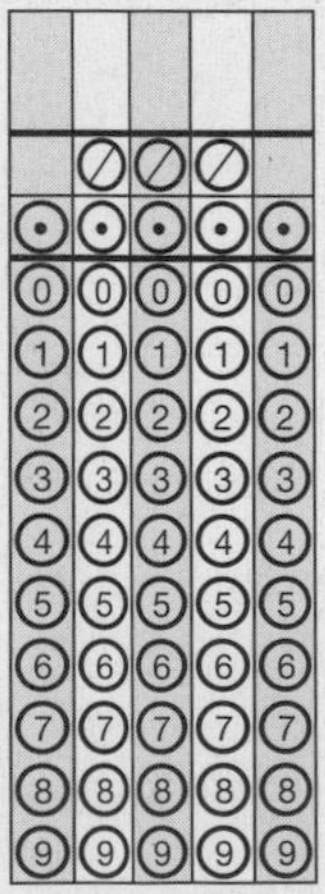

2 A librarian surveyed 75 library members to find out whether the library should start carrying DVDs instead of videotapes. Of the library members surveyed, 45 favored the change. There are a total of 2,500 members of the library. According to the survey results, what is the best prediction of the total number of library members who would favor this change?

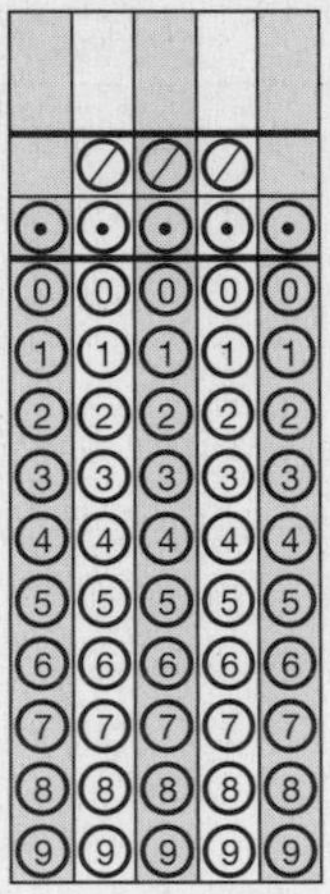

3 The graph below models the amount of money that the debate team raised each year from 1996 to 2006.

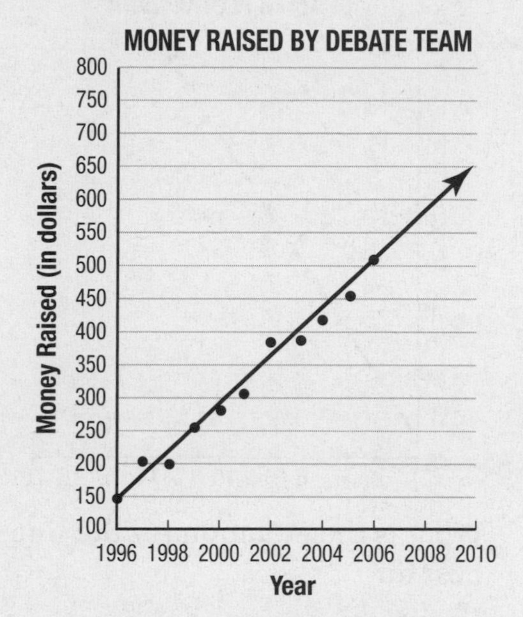

According to the line of best fit, how much would the debate team expect to raise in 2007?

A $510

B $550

C $590

D $650

4 A box factory makes cubic boxes with sides of varying lengths. The graph below models the relationship between volume (in liters) and length (in centimeters) of a box.

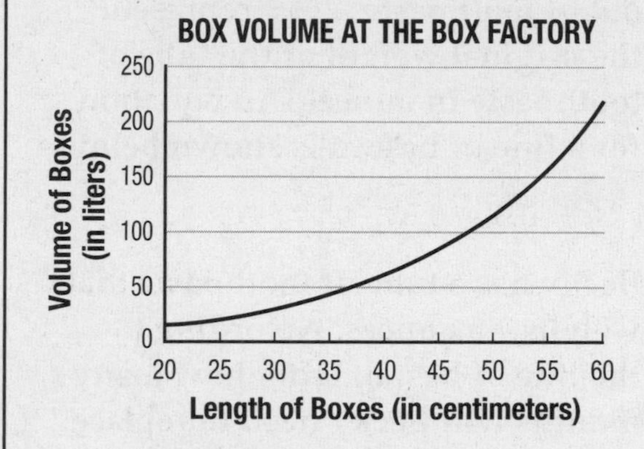

Which of these is the best estimate of the volume (in liters) of a box with sides that are 37 centimeters long?

F 35

G 50

H 125

J 210

5 **A toothpaste company wants to know how long various sized tubes of toothpaste last. Let x represent the number of months a tube was used before running out of toothpaste. Let y represent the original weight of the tube of toothpaste in ounces. An equation for a line of best fit is shown below.**

$$y = 0.3 + 0.6x$$

Becky has a tube of toothpaste that weighs 4.5 ounces. According to the line of best fit, after how many months will Becky need to replace the tube?

A 5

B 6

C 7

D 8

6 **The scatter plot below shows the line of best fit for a set of data points.**

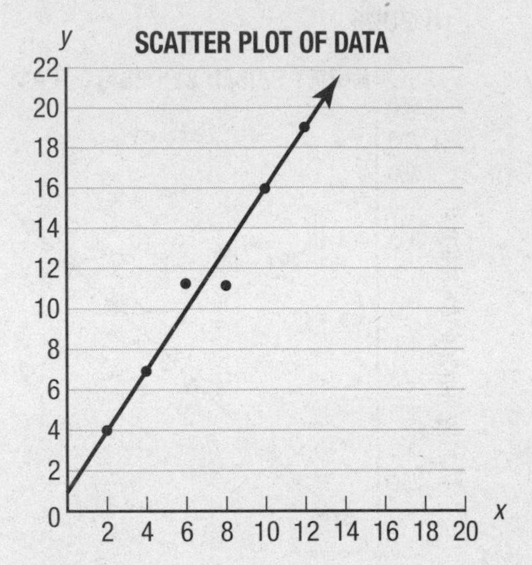

What is the equation for the line of best fit?

A $y = \frac{2}{3}x + 1$

B $y = \frac{3}{2}x + 1$

C $y = 2x + 1$

D $y = 3x + 1$

7 **Kevin and Steve are comparing their salaries over the last 9 years using the graphs below.**

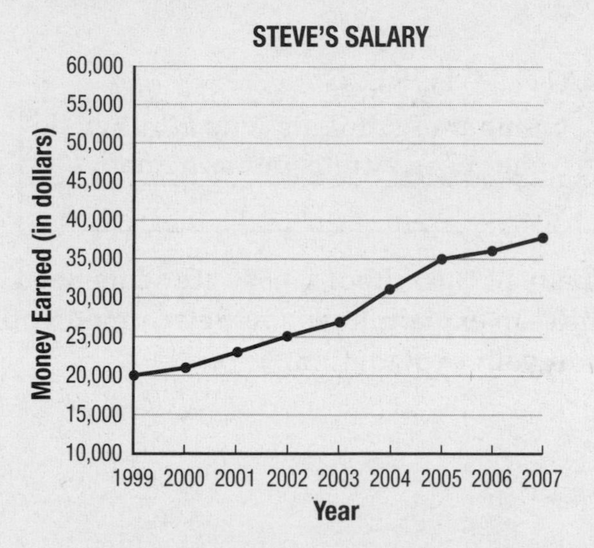

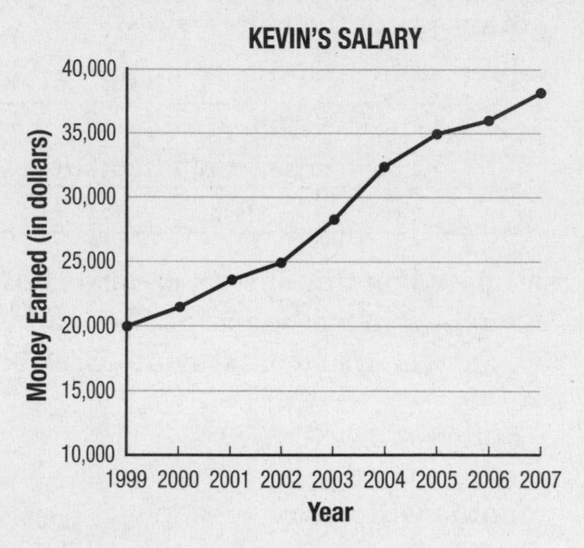

According to the information given, which of these explains why the graphs are misleading?

A The time periods are different.

B The types of data are different.

C The vertical scales are different.

D The horizontal scales are different.

8 **Peter found that 64% of the students in his honors classes did homework every night. He then predicted that since there are 950 students in his school, 608 of them did homework every night. Which of these <u>best</u> describes the reason that his prediction is not valid?**

A He used biased sampling.

B His prediction was influenced by opinion.

C He interpreted the interquartile range incorrectly.

D The arithmetic in his computation was incorrect.

9
BCR **A high-school teacher conducted a survey of 150 randomly selected students to determine whether or not they needed a tutor in mathematics. The survey results are shown in the table below.**

NEED FOR MATH TUTORING

Number of students who say they need a tutor in mathematics	Number of students who say they do not need a tutor in mathematics
114	36

- **Based on this survey, estimate how many of the school's 4,500 students need a tutor in mathematics. Use mathematics to explain how you determined your answer. Use words, symbols, or both in your explanation.**

- **Should a teacher from a middle school use these survey results to predict the number of students there that need a mathematics tutor? Use mathematics to justify your answer.**

Remove Posttest Here

Maryland HSA Coach,
Algebra/Data Analysis, High School

POSTTEST

Name: ______________________________

Session 1

POSTTEST

1 **The table below shows a relationship between *s* and *t*.**

s	$^-3$	$^-1$	1	3	5	7
t	16	24	24	16	0	$^-24$

Which of these equations represents this relationship?

A $t = 25 - s^2$

B $t = 25 + s^2$

C $t = 16 - s^2$

D $t = 16 + s^2$

2 **Nelda notices that the number of brownies on display at a bake sale corresponds to the price for which they sell. When she displays 16 brownies, they sell for $0.40 each. But, when she displays only 8 brownies, she can sell them for $1.20. Which of these graphs shows the relationship between the number of brownies that Nelda displays and the price they sell for in dollars?**

F

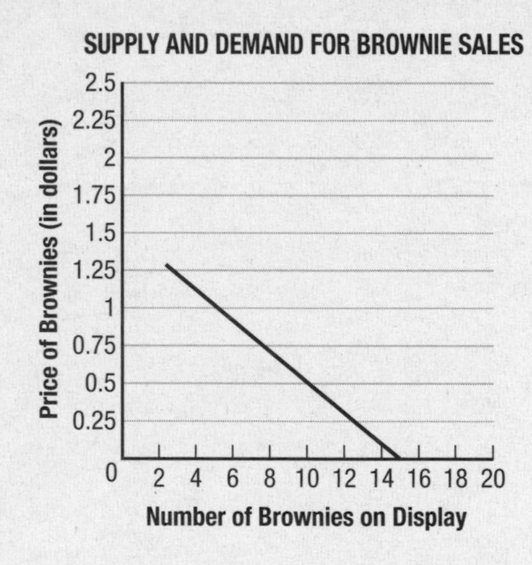

H

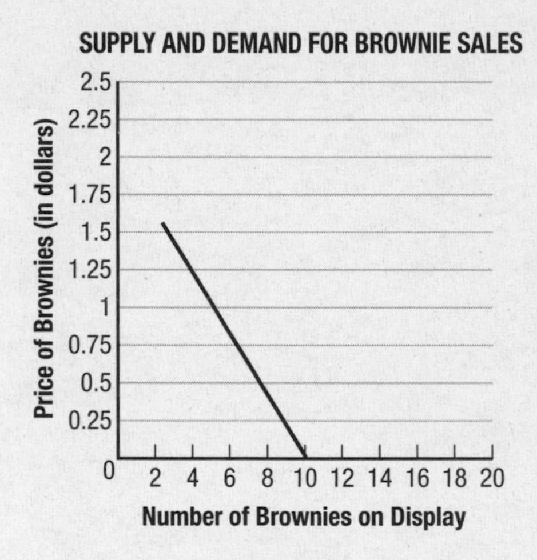

G

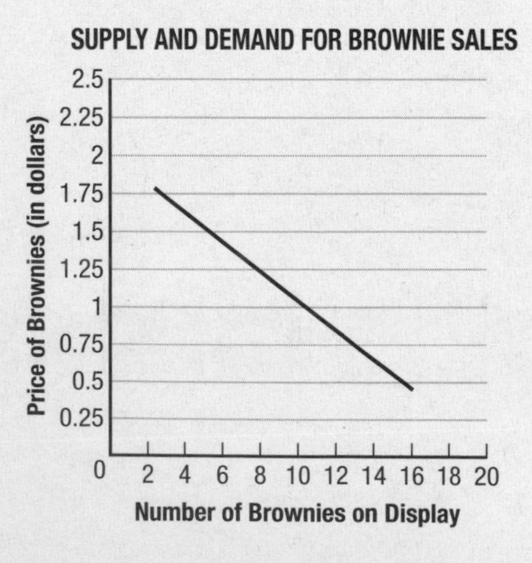

J

GO ON

3 The spinner shown below is spun 30 times.

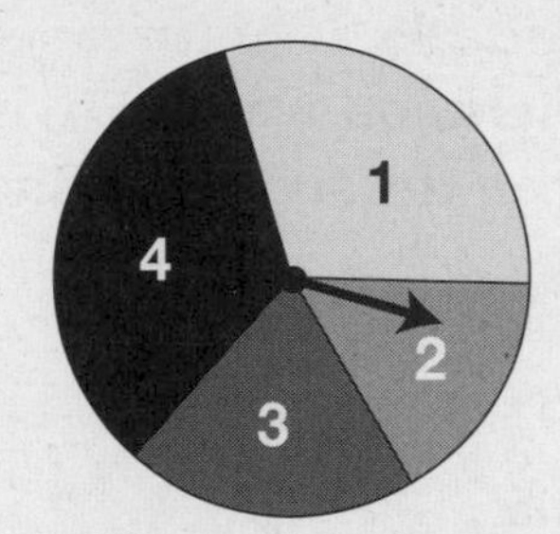

The results of the spins are shown below.

4	4	3	1	1	1
2	1	4	2	3	4
3	4	1	4	1	1
2	4	4	2	1	3
3	2	4	4	1	1

Based on these results, how many times would 3 be expected to appear in 600 spins?

A 30

B 100

C 150

D 200

4 A school nurse wants to find out how often the average student gets sick. Which of these methods provides her with the most representative sample of students?

F Survey students who come to the nurse's office.

G Survey students who participate in school sports.

H Survey students as they arrive at school in the mornings.

J Survey students as they buy their lunches at the cafeteria.

5 Three years ago, Jack bought a new car for $(2d^2 + 3d)$ dollars. Today, he sold the car for $(d^2 + 9)$ dollars. Which expression represents the amount that the car's value decreased?

A $(2d^2 + 3d) + (d^2 + 9)$

B $(2d^2 + 3d) - (d^2 + 9)$

C $\frac{2d^2 + 3d}{d^2 + 9}$

D $(2d^2 + 3d) \times (d^2 + 9)$

POSTTEST

GO ON

POSTTEST

6 **The cylindrical container below holds 274.75 cubic inches of water and has a height of 14 inches. In your calculation, use 3.14 for π.**

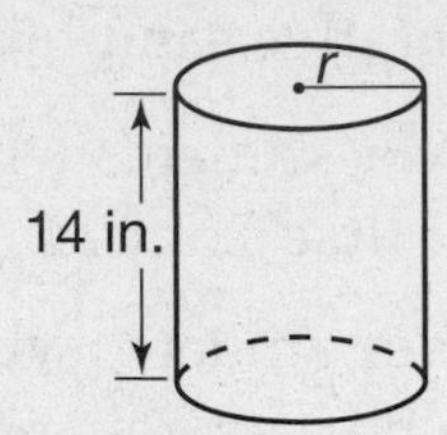

What is the radius (r) of the container's circular base?

F 2.5 in.

G 3.125 in.

H 5 in.

J 6.25 in.

7 **The box-and-whisker plots below show the test grades for four students.**

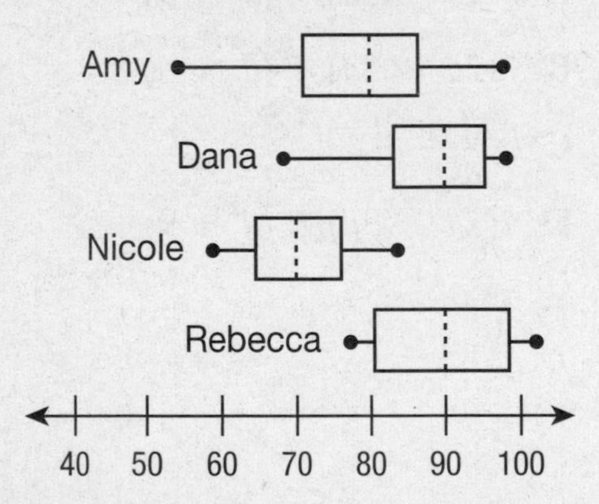

Which student has the widest spread in the middle 50% of her test grades?

A Amy

B Dana

C Nicole

D Rebecca

8 **Hugo made the following scores in five games of bowling: 151, 189, 210, 200, and 195. If his mean score for the afternoon was 205, what did he make on the sixth and final game?**

F 160

G 189

H 205

J 285

9 **The following pattern shows the number of distinct diagonals in polygons of increasing numbers of sides.**

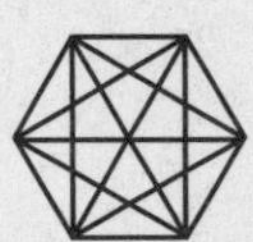

If this pattern continues, how many distinct diagonals will there be in the octagon?

A 6

B 8

C 10

D 20

GO ON

Use the Response Grids to complete Numbers 10 through 12.

10 Ellen rents a pair of ice skates. She pays a flat fee of $6.95 plus $0.75 per hour. She has $10 to spend on skate rental. What is the maximum number of hours Ellen can ice skate?

11 Henry is making a tile mosaic. He pulls colored tiles randomly out of a large sack. The table below shows the colors and numbers of each kind of tile in the sack.

MOSAIC TILES IN SACK

Tile Color	Number
Red	95
Orange	75
Yellow	38
Green	80
Blue	44
Purple	68

Based on the data in the table, what is the probability that a randomly selected tile is green?

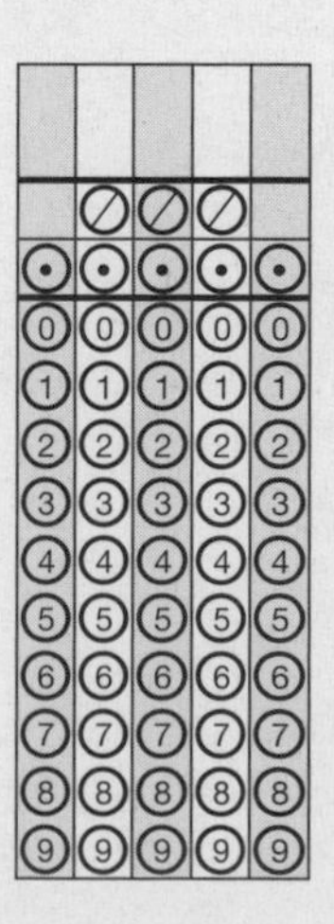

12 The table below shows the number of points scored by a football team last year.

POINTS SCORED AT EACH GAME

Game	Points Scored
1	21
2	28
3	7
4	14
5	42
6	14
7	28
8	21

What is the third quartile for this data set?

GO ON

POSTTEST

13 Look at the graph below.

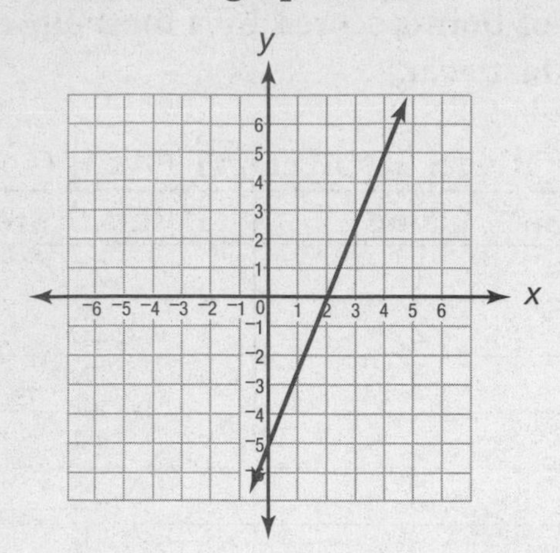

What is the slope of the line?

A $-\frac{5}{2}$

B $-\frac{2}{5}$

C $\frac{2}{5}$

D $\frac{5}{2}$

14 The drawing below shows a plan of a house.

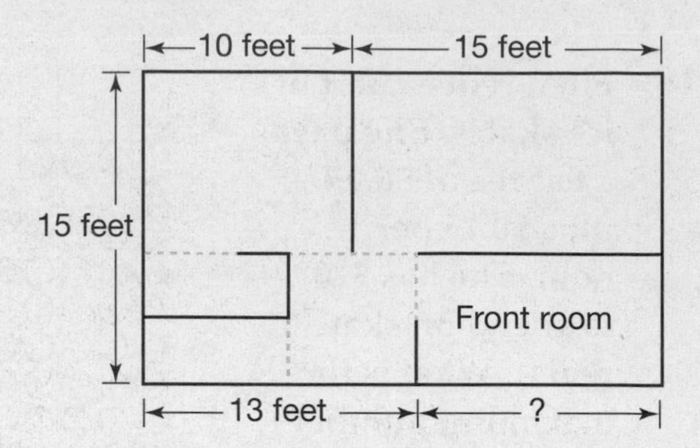

Which of the following expressions represents the length of the front room of the house, in feet?

F $15 - 13$

G $(10 + 15) - 13$

H $10 + 3$

J $(13 + 10) - 15$

GO ON

15 **BCR** The graphs below show the sprint times of two members of the swim team. The swim coach uses the graphs to support his claim that Todd is faster than Wendy.

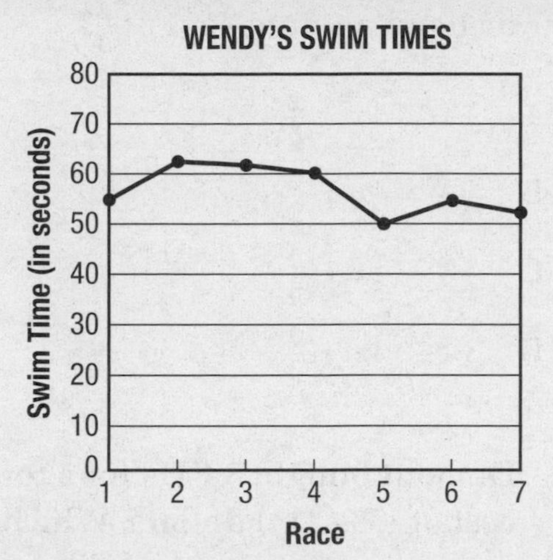

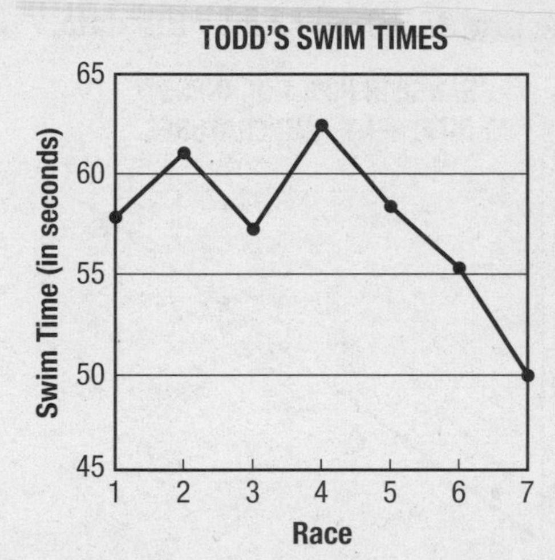

- What is Wendy's fastest swim time? What is Todd's fastest swim time?

- According to the information given, why might these graphs be considered misleading? Use mathematics to explain how you determined your answer. Use words, symbols, or both in your explanation.

16 A scientist measures the thickness of a pipe at different temperatures. The graph below shows his data.

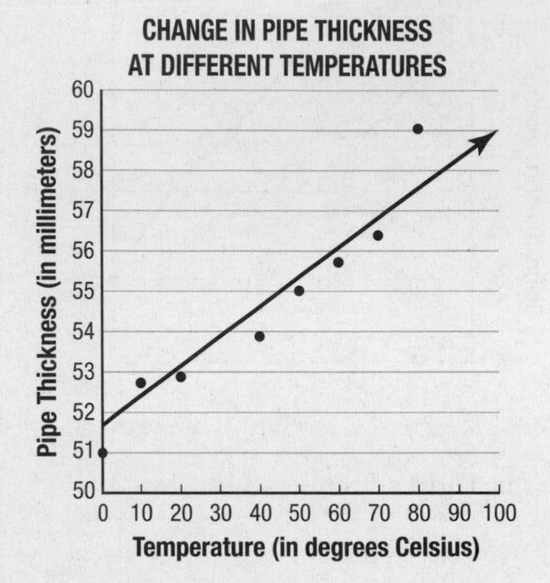

According to the line of best fit, how thick would the pipe be at 95°C?

F 58.0

G 58.5

H 59.0

J 59.5

17 Which of these equations represents a line with an x-intercept of 1 and a y-intercept of $\frac{2}{3}$?

A $y = {}^{-}1x + \frac{2}{3}$

B $y = {}^{-}\frac{2}{3}x + \frac{2}{3}$

C $y = \frac{2}{3}x + \frac{2}{3}$

D $y = 1x + \frac{2}{3}$

18 Demont bought 8 CDs for a total cost of $(33-11n)$ dollars. Which expression represents the average cost of a CD?

F $(33-11n) + 8$

G $(33-11n) - 8$

H $(33-11n) \times 8$

J $(33-11n) \div 8$

19
ECR

Two competing video rental stores have different methods for charging late fees. Arsenio's Videos charges a fee of $0.50 per day that a video is late. Maya's Movies charges $2.00 on the first day the video is late plus $0.25 per day.

TABLE I

Number of days a video is late (d)	Total Fee in Dollars (f)
5	2.50
7	3.50
9	4.50
11	5.50

TABLE II

Number of days a video is late (d)	Total Fee in Dollars (f)
5	3.25
7	3.75
9	4.25
11	4.75

- **Which table represents the late fee that Arsenio's Videos charges its customers? Use mathematics to explain how you determined your answer. Use words, symbols, or both in your explanation.**

- **What equation represents the total fee in dollars (f) charged by Arsenio's Videos when a customer turns in a video d days late?**

- **What equation represents the total fee in dollars (f) charged by Maya's Movies when a customer turns in a video d days late?**

- **If a certain customer tends to return his movies two weeks late every time, which service would save him more money in late fees? Use mathematics to explain how you determined your answer.**

20 **Tomichan has created a website. He keeps track of how many people visit his website each day so that he can predict how many people will visit in the future.**

Day	Number of Visitors
1	16
2	32
3	64
4	128

If he continues to get visitors at this rate, how many people can Tomichan predict will visit his website on the fifteenth day?

F 240

G 256

H 262,144

J 524,288

21 **The table below lists the methods of travel most frequently used by students at Maggie's school.**

METHODS OF TRAVEL MOST FREQUENTLY USED BY STUDENTS

Rank	Method	Number
1	School bus	512
2	Walking	360
3	Car	208

Maggie concludes that 1 out of every 3 students at her school walks. Why is Maggie's conclusion incorrect?

A Maggie did not consider how long it takes students to get to school.

B Maggie did not consider whether students carpooled with students from other schools.

C Maggie did not consider that there were some students who go to school only part time.

D Maggie did not consider students who use other modes of transportation, such as a bike.

Remove Posttest Here

POSTTEST

22 **BCR** **Francisco is in charge of ordering snacks for the soccer team. A month ago he ordered a case of 144 snack bars. He counted the number of snack bars left in the case after each practice and recorded his results in the table below.**

Practice	Number of Snack Bars Left after Practice
1	127
2	110
3	93
4	76

- **If this pattern continues, how many snack bars will be left after the sixth practice?**

- **How many snack bars does the team eat during each practice?**

- **During which practice will the snack bars run out? Use mathematics to explain how you determined your answer. Use words, symbols, or both in your explanation.**

POSTTEST

23 **Hannah took the bus to school. She kept track of the bus's speed over the length of the trip.**

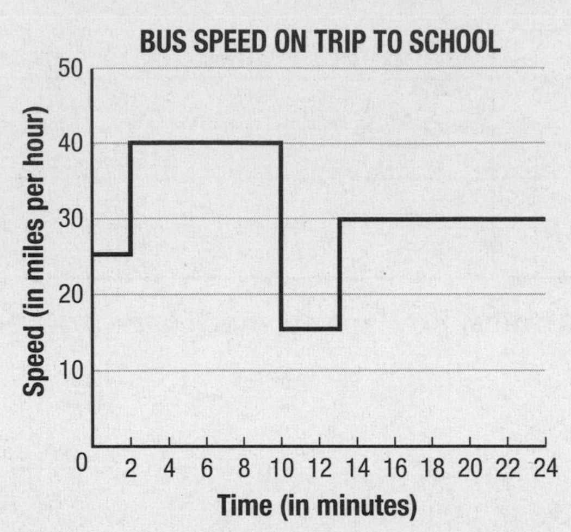

At one point during the trip, the bus went through a school zone with a 15 mile per hour speed limit. Based on the graph, how long did it take to travel through the school zone?

A 2 minutes

B 3 minutes

C 10 minutes

D 24 minutes

POSTTEST

24 Look at the graph below.

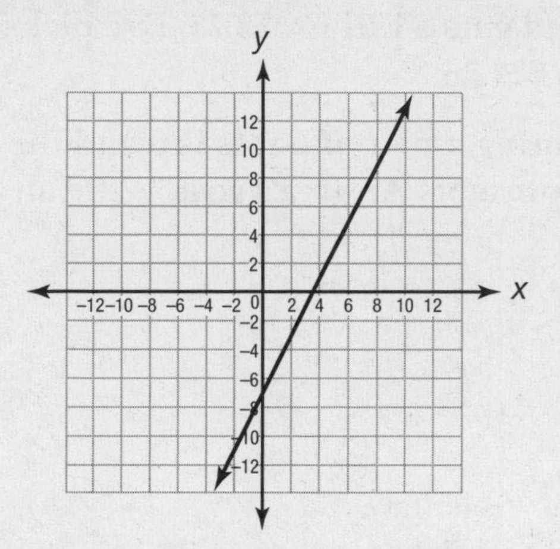

Which of these tables corresponds to the line that is graphed?

F

x	y
0	−7
1	−5
2	−3
3	−1
4	1

G

x	y
0	−6
1	−5
2	−4
3	−3
4	−1

H

x	y
0	3
1	4
2	5
3	6
4	7

J

x	y
0	4
1	5
2	6
3	7
4	8

POSTTEST

25
BCR

Andrea and Dre both pick up clothing at the dry cleaner. Andrea picks up 2 pairs of pants and 3 shirts and gets a bill for $8.75. Dre picks up 4 pairs of pants and 1 shirt. His bill comes to $11.25

- **The cost of dry cleaning a pair of pants is p and the cost of a shirt is s. Write an equation that represents Andrea's cost. Write an equation that represents Dre's cost.**

- **Use mathematics to justify your answers for the cost of cleaning one pair of pants and the cost of cleaning one shirt.**

Session 2

26 **Look at the system of equations below.**

$$y = 2x - 7$$

$$y = 7x - 2$$

Which of these <u>best</u> describes the relationship between the two lines?

F They have no point in common.

G They have one point in common.

H They have two points in common.

J They have infinite points in common.

27 **Look at the graph below.**

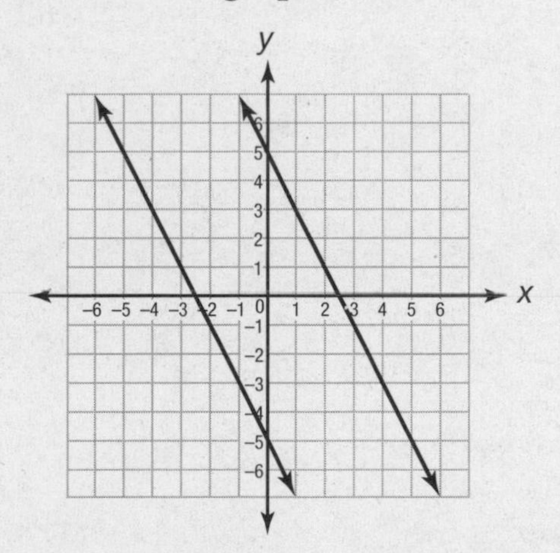

Which of these statements describes the relationship between the two lines?

A The lines never intersect.

B They intersect at the point (0, 5).

C They intersect at the point (5, 0).

D They intersect at the point (5, $^-5$).

28 **An engineer wants to test the performance of the faucets made at a factory. The factory produces 500 faucets each day. Which of the following methods gives a sample that is more representative of the faucets?**

F Randomly choose 10 faucets throughout the day and test their performance.

G Randomly choose 50 faucets throughout the day and test their performance.

H Choose the last 50 faucets that are produced each day and test their performance.

J Choose the first 50 faucets that are produced each day and test their performance.

29 **Look at the function that is graphed below.**

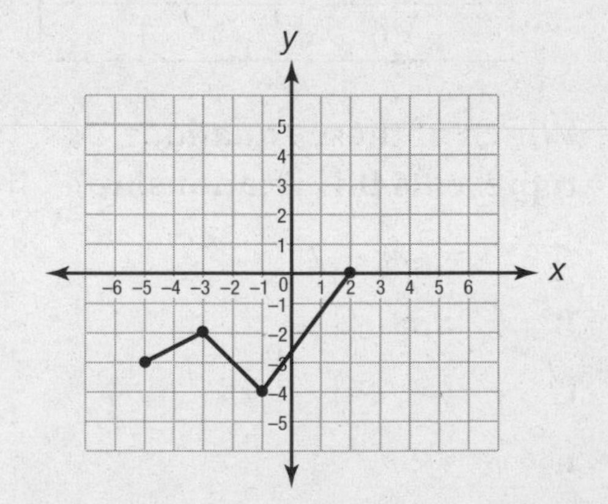

What is the domain of this function?

A $^-5 \le x \le 2$

B $^-4 \le x \le 0$

C $^-1 \le x \le {}^-4$

D $0 \le x \le 2$

POSTTEST

Remove Posttest Here

30 **Neil and Margaret buy pears and peaches at a fruit stand. Neil buys 6 pears and 4 peaches and spends a total of $8.70. Margaret buys 4 pears and 2 peaches and spends a total of $5.30. What is the cost of each pear in dollars?**

F 0.53

G 0.75

H 0.87

J 0.95

31 **The table below shows a relationship between *m* and *n*.**

m	*n*
$^-6$	$^-5$
$^-4$	$^-4$
$^-2$	$^-3$
0	$^-2$
2	$^-1$
4	0
6	1

Which of these equations represents this relationship?

A $n = \frac{1}{2}m - 2$

B $n = m - 1$

C $n = m + 1$

D $n = 2m - \frac{1}{2}$

32 **Look at the function that is graphed below.**

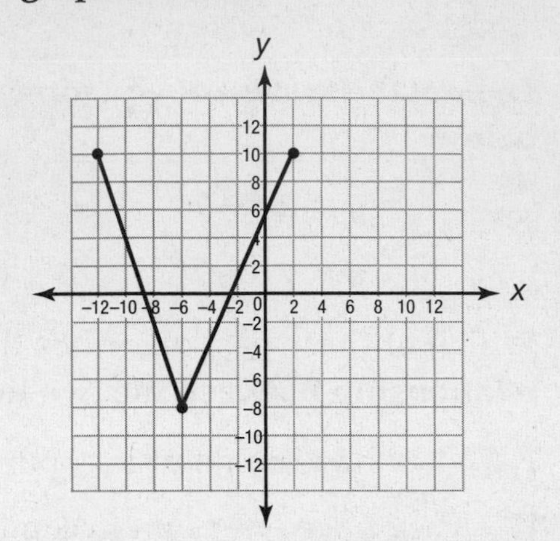

What is the minimum value of this function?

F $^-12$

G $^-8$

H $^-6$

J 10

GO ON

Remove Posttest Here

POSTTEST

33
BCR

Felicia is planning the company holiday party. She wants to conduct a survey to find out what type of band to hire to play music. Consider the methods of sampling shown below.

Method 1: Randomly select 25 employees from the advertising department.

Method 2: Use a random number generator to generate 25 random numbers and use these to select 25 employees from a numerical list of employees.

Method 3: Randomly select 5 administrative assistants and ask them to select 5 employees from their departments.

Which of the above methods of sampling would give the most representative random sample of employees at the company? Use mathematics to justify your answer. Include in your justification why you chose that method and why you did not choose each of the other two methods.

POSTTEST

34 **The graph below shows a linear model of the relationship between the Celsius and Fahrenheit temperature scales.**

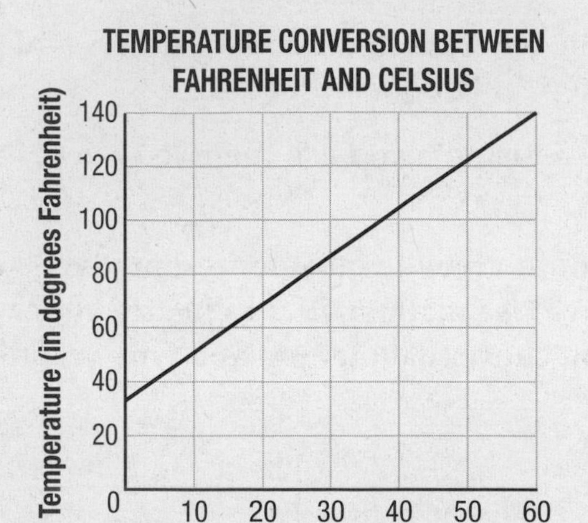

What is the slope, in degrees Celsius per degree Fahrenheit, of this linear model?

F $\frac{1}{32}$

G $\frac{5}{9}$

H $\frac{9}{5}$

J 32

35 **Dominique can use one of two pumps to empty a tank of water. Pump 1 needs to warm up before it can start pumping. Pump 2 can start emptying the tank right away, but it empties at a slower rate than Pump 1.**

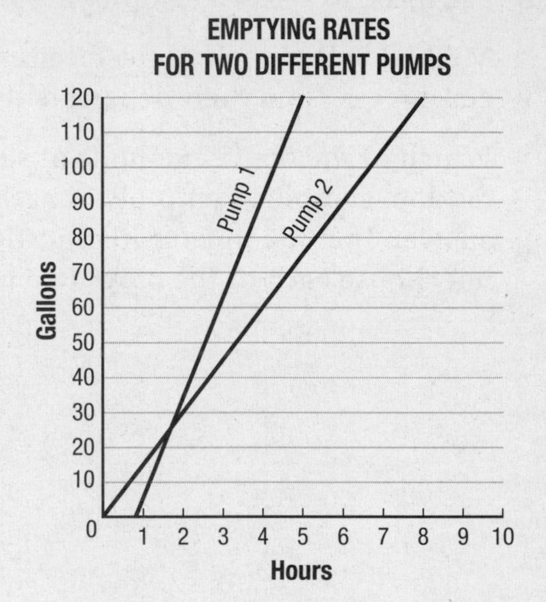

According to the graph, which of these statements is true?

A Pump 1 will empty a 10-gallon tank faster.

B Pump 2 is faster at emptying a 20-gallon tank.

C Pump 1 takes longer to empty a 40-gallon tank.

D The two pumps take the same amount of time to empty 30 gallons.

Use the Response Grids to complete Numbers 36 through 40.

36 The scatter plot below shows Penny's average weekly allowance for the years 1999 to 2007.

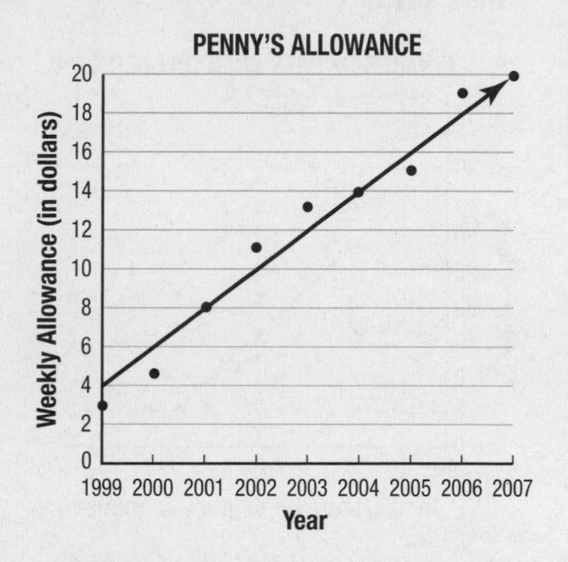

What is the slope of the line of best fit in dollars per year?

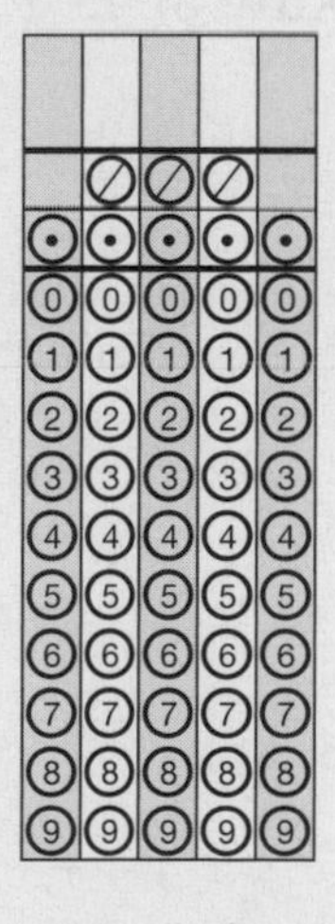

37 Colleen made the following tips on orders at her waitress job: \$1.75, \$2.50, \$3.00, \$4.00, \$3.75, \$2.50, and \$3.50. What is the mode tip that she made in dollars?

GO ON

POSTTEST

38 John recorded the number of students in his class whose birthdays fall in each month of the year. He made the following table to record his data.

	J	F	M	A	M	J	J	A	S	O	N	D
Number of Students	3	2	0	1	2	4	5	0	2	2	2	1

What is the mean number of students born in a single month?

39 Ivan sells hats at a corner store. He notices that the number of hats sold relates to the temperature. The graph below models the relationship between daily high temperature and the number of hats sold.

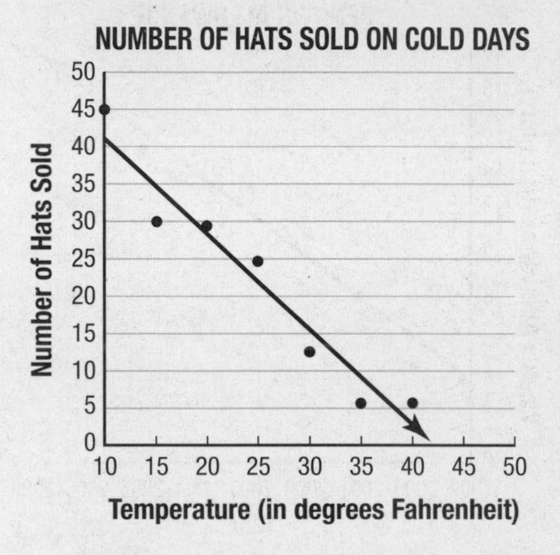

According to the line of best fit, how many hats would Ivan sell on a day with a temperature of 45°F?

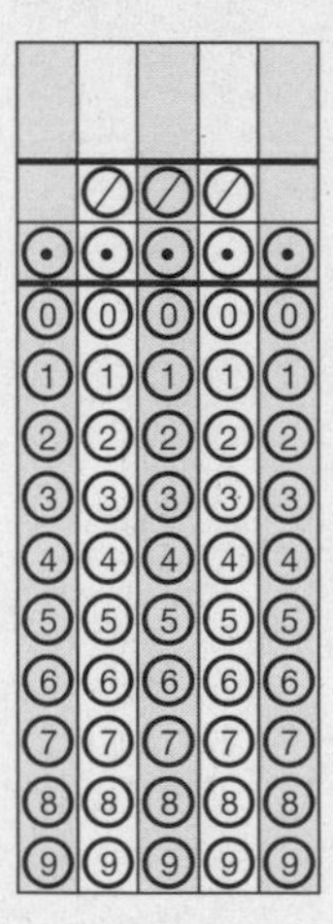

GO ON

Remove Posttest Here

POSTTEST

40 Mr. Jones writes the numbers 1 through 8 on 8 pieces of paper and places them in a hat. If Mr. Jones randomly chooses one piece of paper out of the hat, what is the probability that the number chosen is a 3 or a 5?

41 Jackie bought packs of printer paper for her office with a coupon that took 25% off the regular price of a pack. If the regular price of a pack of printer paper is x and she buys 50 packs, which of these expressions represents the total amount of money she saved using the coupon?

A $0.25x$

B $50(0.25x)$

C $0.25(x - 50x)$

D $50(x - 0.25x)$

GO ON

POSTTEST

Remove Posttest Here

42 ECR **Mrs. Fernandez divides the class into two groups to study for a test. She records the students' test scores in the following table.**

Group 1	Group 2
95	75
65	65
70	80
80	95
100	95
85	85
80	80
70	75

- **What are the range, interquartile range, and quartiles for each of these data sets?**

- **Draw box-and-whisker plots for these data sets.**

- **Which group has the greatest variability in the middle 50% of scores? Use mathematics to justify your answer.**

POSTTEST

43 A train ride from Philadelphia to Boston is x hours long. Along the way, the train stops in New Haven and Providence. The segment from Philadelphia to New Haven is $(x - 3)$ hours. The segment from Providence to Boston is $(x - 5)$ hours. Which expression represents the number of hours it takes the train to travel from New Haven to Providence?

A $(x - 3) - (x - 5)$

B $x - (x - 3) - (x - 5)$

C $\frac{(x - 3) + (x - 5)}{3}$

D $\frac{x + (x - 3) + (x - 5)}{3}$

44
BCR Two employees surveyed their coworkers about whether to start a carpool to and from work. One employee surveyed the first 50 employees who walked into the building that morning and recorded his results as Survey A. The other employee chose 50 employees by having a computer randomly choose names from a list of all employees. She recorded her results as Survey B. The results of both surveys are shown in the tables below.

SURVEY A RESULTS

Opinion	Number of Employees
Voted For the Carpool Program	12
Voted Against the Carpool Program	19
No Opinion	19

SURVEY B RESULTS

Opinion	Number of Employees
Voted For the Carpool Program	23
Voted Against the Carpool Program	15
No Opinion	12

- **Use principles of simple random sampling to justify why the employees should have more confidence in the results of Survey B.**

- **According to the data collected from Survey B, of the 300 total employees in the company, how many employees should be expected to vote for the carpool program? Use mathematics to explain how you determined your answer. Use words, symbols, or both in your explanation.**

POSTTEST

45
ECR **The matrix below shows the number of students enrolled in foreign language classes in four different grades at Valley High School.**

NUMBER OF STUDENTS ENROLLED IN FOREIGN LANGUAGE CLASSES

	9th Grade	10th Grade	11th Grade	12th Grade
French	75	65	25	15
Spanish	100	90	40	30
German	40	35	15	15

- **What is the total number of students enrolled in French classes?**

- **What is the total number of 10th-grade students enrolled in foreign language classes?**

- **Each year, 20% of foreign language students are offered a chance to go on a trip abroad. Make a matrix representing the number of students in each language at each grade level who are offered a chance to go abroad.**

- **What is the total number of students offered a chance to go abroad?**

46 Kelly records how many phone calls she gets each day for 20 days. She marks how many phone calls she gets in a day on the following line plot. What is the median number of phone calls?

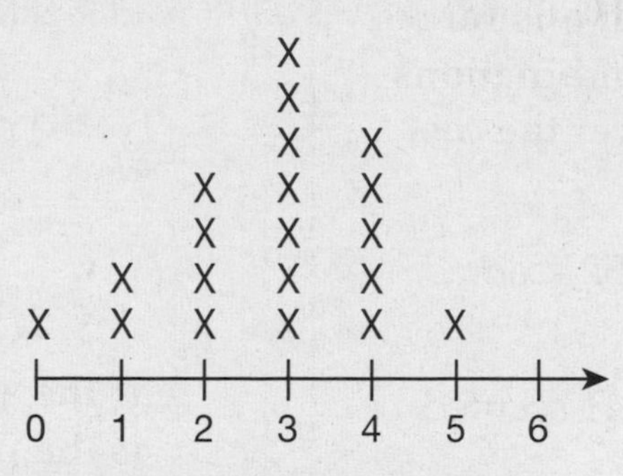

F 2

G 3

H 5

J 6

47 A souvenir stand sells umbrellas, balloons, and T-shirts in three different colors: red, yellow, and blue. The matrices below show the number of each type of souvenir sold during two different months.

JUNE

	R	Y	B
umbrellas	55	35	42
balloons	195	165	215
T-shirts	31	21	45

JULY

	R	Y	B
umbrellas	35	18	25
balloons	205	185	198
T-shirts	36	28	51

Which of these matrices represents the change in the number of each item sold from June to July?

A

	R	Y	B
umbrellas	−20	−17	−17
balloons	10	20	−17
T-shirts	5	7	6

B

	R	Y	B
umbrellas	−35	−18	−25
balloons	−205	−185	−198
T-shirts	−36	−28	−51

C

	R	Y	B
umbrellas	90	53	67
balloons	400	350	413
T-shirts	67	49	96

D

	R	Y	B
umbrellas	−20	−17	−17
balloons	195	165	215
T-shirts	31	21	45

POSTTEST

48 **Rosemary wants to rent a booth at the flea market. It costs $350 to rent the booth. She sells bars of soap for $2 each and scented bath oils for $6 each. Which of these combinations would be enough to cover the cost of renting the booth?**

F 16 bars of soap and 52 scented bath oils

G 54 bars of soap and 41 scented bath oils

H 33 bars of soap and 46 scented bath oils

J 62 bars of soap and 36 scented bath oils

49 **Look at the pattern below.**

$2x + 1, 4x + 8, 6x + 27, 8x + 64, \ldots$

If the pattern continues, what will be the seventh term?

A $7x + 49$

B $7x + 343$

C $10x + 125$

D $14x + 343$

50 **The spinner below is divided into 8 equal sections.**

If the arrow lands on a shape, what is the probability that it will land on a cross?

F $\frac{1}{8}$

G $\frac{1}{3}$

H $\frac{3}{8}$

J $\frac{1}{2}$

STOP

Formula Reference Sheet

Shape	Formulas for Area (A) and Circumference (C)
Triangle	$A = \frac{1}{2}bh = \frac{1}{2} \times$ base $\times$ height
Rectangle	$A = lw =$ length $\times$ width
Trapezoid	$A = \frac{1}{2}(b_1 + b_2)h = \frac{1}{2} \times$ sum of bases $\times$ height
Parallelogram	$A = bh =$ base $\times$ height
Circle	$A = \pi r^2 = \pi \times$ square of radius $C = 2\pi r = 2 \times \pi \times$ radius $C = \pi d = \pi \times$ diameter

Figure	Formulas for Volume (V) and Surface Area (SA)
Rectangular Prism	$V = lwh =$ length $\times$ width $\times$ height $SA = 2lw + 2hw + 2lh$ $= 2($length $\times$ width$) + 2($height $\times$ width$) + 2($length $\times$ height$)$
General Prisms	$V = Bh =$ area of base $\times$ height $SA =$ sum of the areas of the faces
Right Circular Cylinder	$V = Bh =$ area of base $\times$ height $SA = 2B + Ch = (2 \times$ area of base$) + ($circumference $\times$ height$)$
Square Pyramid	$V = \frac{1}{3}Bh = \frac{1}{3} \times$ area of base $\times$ height $SA = B + \frac{1}{2}P\ell$ $=$ area of base $+ (\frac{1}{2} \times$ perimeter of base $\times$ slant height$)$
Right Circular Cone	$V = \frac{1}{3}Bh = \frac{1}{3} \times$ area of base $\times$ height $SA = B + \frac{1}{2}C\ell$ $=$ area of base $+ (\frac{1}{2} \times$ circumference $\times$ slant height$)$
Sphere	$V = \frac{4}{3}\pi r^3 = \frac{4}{3} \times \pi \times$ cube of radius $SA = 4\pi r^2 = 4 \times \pi \times$ square of radius

Equations of a Line

Standard Form:

$Ax + By = C$

where A and B are not both zero

Slope-Intercept Form:

$y = mx + b$ or $y = b + mx$

where m = slope and b = y-intercept

Point-Slope Form:

$y - y_1 = m(x - x_1)$

where m = slope, (x_1, y_1) = point on line

Coordinate Geometry Formulas

Let (x_1, y_1) and (x_2, y_2) be two points in the plane.

slope $= \frac{y_2 - y_1}{x_2 - x_1}$ where $x_2 \neq x_1$

midpoint $= \left(\frac{x_1 + x_2}{2}, \frac{y_1 + y_2}{2}\right)$

distance $= \sqrt{(x_2 - x_1)^2 + (y_2 - y_1)^2}$

Distance Traveled

$d = rt$

distance = rate × time

Polygon Angle Formulas

Sum of degree measures of the interior angles of a polygon:

$180(n - 2)$

Degree measure of an interior angle of a regular polygon:

$\frac{180(n - 2)}{n}$

where n is the number of sides of the polygon

Simple Interest

$I = prt$

interest = principal × interest rate × time

Formulas for Right Triangles

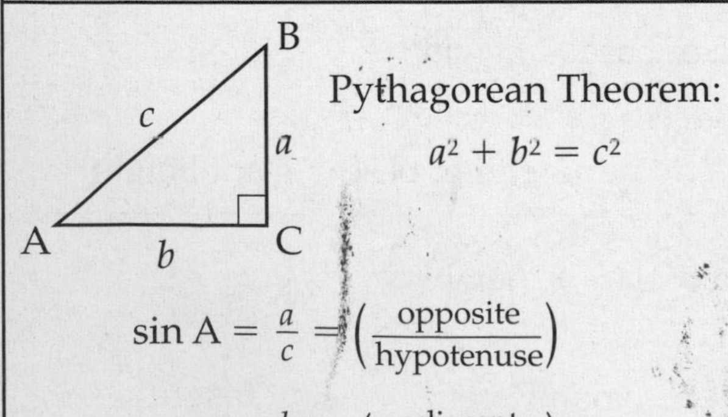

Pythagorean Theorem:

$a^2 + b^2 = c^2$

$\sin A = \frac{a}{c} = \left(\frac{\text{opposite}}{\text{hypotenuse}}\right)$

$\cos A = \frac{b}{c} = \left(\frac{\text{adjacent}}{\text{hypotenuse}}\right)$

$\tan A = \frac{a}{b} = \left(\frac{\text{opposite}}{\text{adjacent}}\right)$

Special Triangles

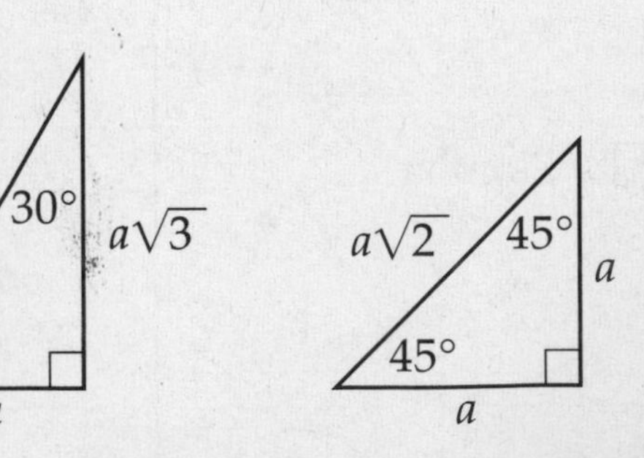